PRAISE FOR
DEPOSITION OBSTRUCTION

Mark provides solid, practical, and ethical ways to stop obstructions in deposition, but he does so much more. This book is a primer on all aspects of taking proper depositions under the rules. Every litigator should have a copy.

>Mark Lanier, recipient of the American Association for Justice Lifetime Achievement Award

The birth of a classic—a manifesto of freedom from ever again being shoved around in a deposition. *Deposition Obstruction* enhances whatever deposition books and methods you already use, because it allows you to use them without obstruction. Mark's thoroughly documented, clearly thought-out guide provides on-point, word-for-word instruction and in-practice examples. It's a lucid primer as well as a comprehensive advanced resource that you need regardless of your experience or skill. Next time I see the defense successfully obstruct, I'll know that someone has not yet read *Deposition Obstruction*. And I'll tell them so. I'm grateful to Mark for this prodigious contribution.

>David Ball, author of *David Ball on Damages 3*

With *Deposition Obstruction*, Mark has provided litigators, and the judges overseeing them, with a hornbook for dealing with behavior that flies in the face of the Rules of Civil Procedure and the case law construing them. Loaded with illuminating examples, tried-and-true techniques, and a treasure trove of supporting authority, this is a must-read, how-to manual for any litigator seeking to break through the barriers of improper objections, eliminate unnecessary verbal skirmishing, and focus on getting the truth.

Dave Jorstad, past president of the
Minnesota Association for Justice

Mark has done it again. The master of depositions has written the definitive work on everything you may ever need to know about taking and defending depositions. I have been practicing for over 25 years, and I learned new things. The book is clear, concise, and practical.

Joseph Fried, founder of the Academy of
Truck Accident Attorneys

Whether you are an experienced litigator or are dealing with your very first deposition "bully," Mark provides a toolbox of options for standing up to obstructionist opponents, intimidation, and unrelenting objections. With step-by-step instructions that are easy to implement and thoroughly researched, this book will give you the upper hand. Stop playing checkers—and start playing chess—in the pretrial discovery game.

Zoe Littlepage, member of the Inner Circle of
Advocates, Top 100 Trial Lawyers

Depositions are trial! As goes the deposition, so goes the value of the settlement, the solid verdict rather than defeat in the courtroom, and the result for your client. *Deposition Obstruction* is every lawyer's road map to navigate through the minefields of opposing-lawyer-created obstacles. This book will be for trial lawyers what the navigation system is to pilots—you can't go forward without it. Mark's book is loaded with assessments of both substantive and procedural law and rules. It is a comprehensive, how-to manual on dealing with interfering obstructionist lawyers in setting, preparing for, and taking depositions.

> John F. Romano, former president of the
> Academy of Florida Trial Lawyers

Mark is a great resource on how to take depositions of difficult adversaries. Now he adds to the arsenal this fine compendium of all the dirty tricks that are used to block the search for truth in depositions—and how to defeat them. Whether it be coaching objections or sneaky woodshedding during bathroom breaks, these and more obstructive techniques are brought into the light of day and beaten back with calm logic and profuse case law. This is an important book for anyone who takes depositions.

> Patrick Malone, author of *The Fearless Cross-Examiner*

Mark has explored the universe of deposition conduct in this book, and it includes hundreds of related case cites. For me, the most valuable chapter is Chapter 5, "Prohibited Objections," and I recommend that anyone read or at least skim the content before taking a deposition. Better yet, pull the cases cited and read them. It will make you a better lawyer. No one but Mark would take the effort to make this so easy for so many.

> Phillip Miller, author of *Focus Groups: Hitting the Bull's-Eye* and *Advanced Deposition Strategy and Practice*

Mark is one of the country's foremost experts on depositions and the rules governing deposition conduct. This work summarizes research Mark has done when confronted with real-life situations over his 39-year career as a nationally recognized trial lawyer. As usual, he unselfishly shares his work and knowledge with the rest of us.

> Tad Thomas, Treasurer of the American Association for Justice, 2018-19

Deposition Obstruction is an outstanding and comprehensive desk book for every litigator taking or defending depositions. It is on my "must have" reference shelf, next to the Harry Philo *Lawyers Desk Reference* and Mark's *30(b)(6)* book. The techniques and examples in the book are insightful, practical, and experience based. I highly recommend this treatise. Mark has done it again!

Jim Bartimus, fellow of the American College of Trial Lawyers

Deposition Obstruction is a book you will want within reach, no matter your experience level. Mark gives you practical examples and tips on how to take better depositions to obtain the truth and protect your record for the court and trial. I am a better lawyer and advocate after reading this book.

> Jennifer Lipinski, named Top 40 Under 40 by the National Trial Lawyers

I had the pleasure of teaching at an AAJ Education Deposition College, alongside Mark. I was surprised at the number of new and evolving issues that both attorney participants and fellow instructors continue to face during depositions. That's why this book is so valuable and timely, in order to help us all take more effective depositions and represent our clients better!

> Navan Ward, Secretary of the American Association for Justice, 2018-2019

Eye-opening and empowering—a declaration of independence for lawyers seeking to find and prove the truth in their cases. The dark age of commonplace deposition bullying, obstruction, and concealment of the truth is over. Mark's enlightened readers are now equipped to get what they came for in their depositions, despite the defense's repeated attempts to obstruct them. There are now two kinds of lawyers—those who are frustrated by defense tactics and those who have read this book.

> J.D. Hays, recipient of the Arkansas Trial Lawyers Association's Young Trial Lawyer of the Year (2013)

I try to help my clients—one at a time. But Mark's research in this book is helping tens of thousands of lawyers help their clients—one client at a time. I cannot overstate how thankful I am for Mark's wisdom, leadership, and strategic thinking in this field.

Render Freeman, faculty member of the
Gerry Spence Trial Lawyers College

On occasion, we may occupy a mansion called trial, but the house we live in day to day is the deposition house. And if you can't safely control your own home, you won't stand a chance when you get to the mansion. In this eloquently simple work, Mark shows us how to keep house.

Carl Bettinger, author of *Twelve Heroes, One Voice*

Mark's *Deposition Obstruction* is the seminal book on handling the "Rambo litigator" who disrupts and obstructs depositions. It will help both new and seasoned attorneys find the truth in their cases without obstruction. The inclusion of state and federal rules and statutes makes this book valuable to attorneys practicing in all states. I unequivocally endorse this book—it is a must-have for anyone taking depositions as part of their practice.

N. John Bey, named Top 40 Under 40 by
the National Trial Lawyers

Reading about great closing arguments and other trial techniques is certainly fun and can be helpful in prosecuting an injury case. However, the advice on depositions in these pages is far more beneficial in almost every case a trial lawyer handles. Another "must have" for your bookshelf.

> Ken Levinson, co-author of *Litigating Major Automobile Injury and Death Cases*

DEPOSITION OBSTRUCTION

BREAKING THROUGH

Mark Kosieradzki

American Association for Justice
AAJ Press
777 6th Street, NW, Suite 200
Washington, DC 20001

Copyright © 2019 Mark R. Kosieradzki
All Rights Reserved. Published 2019.
Printed in the United States of America.
Print ISBN: 978-1-54395-492-0
eBook ISBN: 978-1-54395-493-7

No part of this book may be reproduced in any form whatsoever or by any means, including electronic or mechanical methods, without the express written permission of Mark R. Kosieradzki, except in the case of brief quotations embodied in critical reviews.

Please direct inquiries to:
AAJ Publications
777 6th Street, NW Suite 200
Washington, DC 20001
(800) 424-2725
www.justice.org/publications

Jacket design by Kelly Smith

To my mother, Danuta, a freedom fighter in the Polish Underground who resisted the German occupation of Warsaw, and to my father, Henryk, a Polish soldier in the battle against Stalin. Your examples of courage have been an inspiration to all who had the privilege of knowing you.

Sto lat!

TABLE OF CONTENTS

Introduction   1

Chapter 1: Purpose and Scope of Depositions   5
Discovery   7
Depositions   8
Scope of Deposition Inquiry   9
Summary   11

Chapter 2: Deposition Logistics   13
Sequence of Depositions in Context of Discovery   15
Location of Depositions   16
    Location for 30(b)(1) Depositions—Individual Parties   17
    Location for 30(b)(6) Depositions—Organizations   18
    Location for a Nonparty Deposition   20
    Remote Depositions   21
Length of Depositions   21
    Length of 30(b)(6) Depositions—Organizations   22
Method of Recording Depositions   22
Summary   24

Chapter 3: Deposition Ethics — 27

Preamble to the Model Rules of Professional Conduct: Zealous Advocacy Must Be Within the Bounds of the Rules — 29

Model Rule of Professional Conduct 3.4: Obstruction Is Prohibited — 31

Model Rule of Professional Conduct 8.4: Abusive and Uncivil Behavior Is Unethical — 32

Example: Uncivil and Abusive Behavior Toward a Witness — 33

Example: Threatening Behavior Toward a Witness — 34

Summary — 36

Chapter 4: Proper Objections — 37

Procedural Objections to the Manner of Taking the Deposition — 40

Oath or Affirmation — 41

Parties' Conduct — 41

Objections to Deposition Questions — 42

Objections to Correctable Evidentiary and Foundational Errors — 43

Objections to the Form of the Question — 45

Are Leading Questions Appropriate? — 46

Technique: Proper Use of Leading Questions — 46

Technique: Curing Compound Questions — 47

Technique: Curing Excessive Narration — 48

How to Object Properly — 49

Objections Must Be Concise, Nonargumentative, and Nonsuggestive — 50

How to Object to Correctable Errors of Substance and Form: Two Schools of Jurisprudence — 50

Approach 1: "Objection to Form" Only — 51

  Approach 2: "Objections to Form or Foundation" Require a Concise Explanation   52

 Summary   54

Chapter 5: Prohibited Objections   57
Objections Asserting That the Substance of the Testimony Would Be Inadmissible at Trial   59

  Relevance Objections   60

  Beyond the Scope Objections   61

  Hearsay Objections   61

 Witness Coaching During a Deposition Is Universally Prohibited   62

  Example: Prohibited Witness Coaching—Passing Notes   63

  Speaking Objections   64

  Example: Improper Speaking Objection   65

  "If You Know" Interjections Are Prohibited Speaking Objections   66

  Technique: Make a Record of Speaking Objections   66

  Objecting to Vagueness Is a Prohibited Speaking Objection   67

  Example: Improper Objection to Vagueness   68

  Objecting Due to a Lawyer's "Lack of Understanding" Is Prohibited   68

  Technique: Preempt Objections to a Witness Not Understanding the Question   69

  Reinterpreting or Rephrasing the Examiner's Questions Is Prohibited   69

  "Asked and Answered" Interjections Are Improper   70

  Excessive Objections Are Prohibited   70

  Example: "Rambo Litigation"   72

 Summary   73

Chapter 6: Instructions Not to Answer   75
Only Three Permissible Reasons for an Instruction Not to Answer   77
   Proper Instruction Not to Answer: Privilege   78
   Example: Improper Claim of Attorney-Client Privilege   79
   Example: Attorney-Client Privilege Third-Party Waiver   81
   Technique: Make a Record of a Dubious Privilege Claim to Assess Later   82
   Proper Instruction Not to Answer: Court-Ordered Limitation   83
   Proper Instruction Not to Answer: Unilateral Suspension of Deposition   84
   Technique: Suspend a Deposition Due to Harassment   85
Improper Instructions Not to Answer   86
   Example: Calling It Harassment Does Not Make It Harassment   86
   Example: Instruction Not to Answer, Claiming Irrelevance   88
   Example: Instruction Not to Answer, Claiming Repetition   89
   Example: Failure to Instruct a Deponent to Answer   90
   Technique: Make a Record of Instructions Not to Answer   91
Summary   92

Chapter 7: 30(B)(6) Scope of Testimony   93
Limiting the Scope Is Not Allowed   96
   Example: Instructions Not to Answer Due to Scope of 30(b)(6)   98
Defending a 30(b)(6) Deposition   99
   Technique: Defending 30(b)(6) Depositions   99
Summary   100

Chapter 8: Attorney-Client Conferences — 101

Deposition Conduct Is the Same as Trial — 103

    Privilege Conferences Always Are Permissible — 104

    Example: Privilege Conference — 105

Conferencing During Recesses: Two Schools of Authority — 105

    Hall *Standard: All Attorney-Client Conferences Prohibited* — 106

    Stratosphere *Standard: Attorney-Client Conferences Permissible During Unrequested Breaks* — 107

    Variations of Hall *and* Stratosphere — 108

Changes in Testimony Following an Attorney-Client Conference — 109

    Immediately Following the Recess in Stratosphere *Jurisdictions* — 110

    Technique: Build a Record of Discussions During Breaks — 110

    Moving to Reopen the Deposition — 111

    Existing Jurisprudence: Testimony Changed After an Attorney-Client Conference — 111

    Analogous Rule: Errata Sheet Changes — 112

Summary — 113

Chapter 9: Sanctions — 115

Deposition Obstruction Is Sanctionable — 117

Remedies for Deposition Obstruction — 119

    "Meet and Confer" Requirement — 120

    Motion to Compel — 121

    Motion for Admonishment & Order for Deposition Protocol — 123

    Payment of Expenses and Attorney Fees — 123

Failure to Comply With a Court Order — 125

A Party's Failure to Attend Its Own Deposition — 126

Courts Have Broad Discretion to Control Discovery
by Imposing Sanctions   127

Summary   129

Appendix A: Federal Rules of Civil Procedure 1, 26, 30, 32 & 37   133
Rule 1. Scope and Purpose   133

Appendix B: Comparing Relevant Portions of Rules 30 & 32   161

Index   311

Index of Cases   318

ACKNOWLEDGMENTS

Throughout my career, I have worked with terrific trial lawyers and judges. These people have enriched my life, not only as a lawyer but also, more important, as a person.

I have also "engaged" with lawyers who, as Judge Edwin Torres described, are "deposition bullies masquerading as members of the bar."[1] I have learned from those lawyers as well. I learned who I didn't want to be. I learned what I didn't want to be. The deposition bullies challenged me to learn how to keep my emotions in check. They forced me to study the jurisprudence of deposition behavior. Because of them, I learned that knowing the Rules of Civil Procedure actually works. I learned we can professionally stop their obstructive games. Practicing law became much more fun.

For the last 25 years I have had the privilege of teaching at the Advanced Depositions College held by the American Association for Justice® (AAJ®). The Advanced Depositions College is more than a deposition education program. It is a think tank. Through that program, I have met countless faculty and participant lawyers who are passionate about mastering their craft. Everyone involved shared their experiences, their research, and their ideas. It is my intention to share what we have learned together in this book.

---

[1] *New World Network LTD v. M/V Norwegian Sea*, 2007 WL 1068124 at *4 (S.D. Fla. Apr. 6, 2007).

A final thanks to Sam Gibson, a law student who worked tirelessly on this project. His countless hours of research created a nationwide compendium of cases that enabled us to create this tool to arm every lawyer with the "rules of engagement." Well done, Skywalker.

—MRK

PUBLISHER'S NOTE

This book has been written as a tool to assist practicing attorneys. It does not offer legal advice. It does not take the place of advice from an attorney.

The information, ideas, and opinions found in this book should be used as tools to assist attorneys using their own research, expertise, and judgment. When making decisions, readers should also consult the applicable case law, rules, regulations, rules of procedure, and statutes, particularly those issued after the publication date of this book. Using all research available, readers must make independent decisions about whether and how to apply the information, ideas, and opinions applicable for particular cases.

Quotations from cases, pleadings, discovery, and other sources are included for illustrative purposes only and may not be suitable for use in litigation in any particular case.

All names that appear in illustrative examples have been fictionalized, and any resemblance between the fictional names and real people are strictly coincidental and unintentional. Real names are used only when found in reported cases that are cited throughout the book. The publisher disclaims any liability or responsibility for loss or damages resulting from the use of this book or the information, ideas, or opinions contained in this book.

CITATIONS AND SECONDARY MATERIALS

When annotations found in this book reference judicial opinions that cite and rely on secondary materials to support the decision or points being made, this book attempts to mirror the citation format that the court used for the secondary material at the time of the decision.

The current citation of the secondary source, including the name of the text, the authors, the secondary numbers, and names of the sections may have changed since the time the court quoted or relied on the material.

If you plan on citing the sources used in this text, it is important to confirm that the case law is still current and in the citation format required by your jurisdiction.

Remember, as with any legal concept, the law may have changed.

INTRODUCTION

As a young lawyer, much too long ago, I was thrown into depositions by my boss and was expected to fend for myself. It was terrifying. Law school left me wholly unprepared for the unsupervised, rough-and-tumble world of civil litigation. I had no idea what was permissible or expected—I just knew that my adversaries sensed inexperience and took advantage of it.

Without a judge or jury in the room to defend me, I was a kid facing bullies behind the schoolhouse. I quickly learned to stand up for myself, but the distasteful nonsense continued. Bravado seemed to be expected of anyone calling themselves "litigators."

In 1993, the case of *Hall v. Clifton Precision* came across my fax machine.[1] A federal judge in the Eastern District of Pennsylvania said, "Enough is enough." Judge Robert Gawthrop established rules for deposition conduct. This one case changed everything for me, his reasoning empowering me with the rules of engagement. He gave me a framework to represent my clients' interests in depositions zealously and professionally. The fights continued to be hard fought, but now they were structured fights.

---

1 *Hall v. Clifton Precision*, 150 F.R.D. 525 (E.D. Pa. 1993). This case is the seminal federal civil authority on deposition misconduct. It has been cited in judicial opinions 135 times, and its framework for proper deposition conduct is universally embraced. As such, *Hall* is referenced frequently throughout this book. The only disputed portion of Judge Gawthrop's opinion is his blanket prohibition of off-the-record attorney-client conferences during the deposition. Some courts have chosen not to adopt this strict prohibition, although many have embraced it. The propriety of attorney-client conferences and the breakdown by federal jurisdiction are discussed further in Chapter 8 of this book.

I never met Judge Gawthrop, but he made a difference in my life. I hope this book will make a difference in the lives of lawyers who face the same bullying that I did years ago. I hope that the tools found in this book will give those lawyers the strength to stand tall in the face of obstruction. I hope that these tools will help them discover the truth on behalf of their clients.

This book focuses on Federal Rules of Civil Procedure 1, 26, 30, 32, and 37, which are the rules that directly control depositions. The relevant portions of those rules are highlighted in Appendix A. Rule 1 establishes the purpose of the Rules of Civil Procedure. Specifically, Rule 1 provides that all rules "should be construed, administered, and employed by the court and the parties to secure the just, speedy, and inexpensive determination of every action and proceeding."[2] Rule 26 establishes the scope of discovery, the court's power to expand and limit discovery, the extent of work product and privilege protections, procedures for deposing experts and filing protective orders, and the timing and sequence of discovery.[3] Rule 30 authorizes depositions and describes the procedures for taking those depositions.[4] Rule 32 describes the use of depositions in court proceedings.[5] Finally, Rule 37 establishes the

---

[2] Fed. R. Civ. P. 1. (As amended Dec. 29, 1948, eff. Oct. 20, 1949; Feb. 28, 1966, eff. July 1, 1966; Apr. 22, 1993, eff. Dec. 1, 1993; Apr. 30, 2007, eff. Dec. 1, 2007; Apr. 29, 2015, eff. Dec. 1, 2015.)

[3] Fed. R. Civ. P. 26. (As amended Dec. 27, 1946, eff. Mar. 19, 1948; Jan. 21, 1963, eff. July 1, 1963; Feb. 28, 1966, eff. July 1, 1966; Mar. 30, 1970, eff. July 1, 1970; Apr. 29, 1980, eff. Aug. 1, 1980; Apr. 28, 1983, eff. Aug. 1, 1983; Mar. 2, 1987, eff. Aug. 1, 1987; Apr. 22, 1993, eff. Dec. 1, 1993; Apr. 17, 2000, eff. Dec. 1, 2000; Apr. 12, 2006, eff. Dec. 1, 2006; Apr. 30, 2007, eff. Dec. 1, 2007; Apr. 28, 2010, eff. Dec. 1, 2010; Apr. 29, 2015, eff. Dec. 1, 2015.)

[4] Fed. R. Civ. P. 30. (As amended Jan. 21, 1963, eff. July 1, 1963; Mar. 30, 1970, eff. July 1, 1970; Mar. 1, 1971, eff. July 1, 1971; Nov. 20, 1972, eff. July 1, 1975; Apr. 29, 1980, eff. Aug. 1, 1980; Mar. 2, 1987, eff. Aug. 1, 1987; Apr. 22, 1993, eff. Dec. 1, 1993; Apr. 17, 2000, eff. Dec. 1, 2000; Apr. 30, 2007, eff. Dec. 1, 2007; Apr. 29, 2015, eff. Dec. 1, 2015.)

[5] Fed. R. Civ. P. 32. (As amended Mar. 30, 1970, eff. July 1, 1970; Nov. 20, 1972, eff. July 1, 1975; Apr. 29, 1980, eff. Aug. 1, 1980; Mar. 2, 1987, eff. Aug. 1, 1987; Apr. 22, 1993, eff. Dec. 1, 1993; Apr. 30, 2007, eff. Dec. 1, 2007; Mar. 26, 2009, eff. Dec. 1, 2009.)

sanctions available to the court in response to abusive discovery practices, which include depositions.[6]

A well-established body of jurisprudence governs conduct and objections at depositions. Following the rules is essential to the fair development of facts that cases are to be adjudicated on. Adhering to the laws of deposition discovery is critical to civility, professionalism, and reinforcing a positive view of the legal profession and its critical role in society. Litigators are responsible for following the Rules of Civil Procedure and the Rules of Professional Conduct. If members of the bar violate these rules, the factual basis supporting those violations must be presented to the court. In turn, it is the court's responsibility to take appropriate steps to deter future violations.

All state courts have established rules for depositions. Many of those state rules are substantially similar, if not functionally identical, to the Federal Rules. When the state rule is based on its federal counterpart, those states usually look to federal authority for guidance in interpreting their state rule. Appendix B provides a quick reference to individual states' deposition rules and the states' case law discussing the use of federal precedent when interpreting their respective rules.

This book is intended to provide members of the bench and bar a reference guide to the laws and jurisprudence governing the taking of depositions. Attorneys who understand the "rules of engagement" will have a road map for maintaining standards of civility and professionalism in their deposition practice.

---

6   Fed. R. Civ. P. 37. (As amended Dec. 29, 1948, eff. Oct. 20, 1949; Mar. 30, 1970, eff. July 1, 1970; Apr. 29, 1980, eff. Aug. 1, 1980; Pub. L. 96–481, § 205(a), Oct. 21, 1980, 94 Stat. 2330, eff. Oct. 1, 1981; Mar. 2, 1987, eff. Aug. 1, 1987; Apr. 22, 1993, eff. Dec. 1, 1993; Apr. 17, 2000, eff. Dec. 1, 2000; Apr. 12, 2006, eff. Dec. 1, 2006; Apr. 30, 2007, eff. Dec. 1, 2007; Apr. 16, 2013, eff. Dec. 1, 2013; Apr. 29, 2015, eff. Dec. 1, 2015.)

CHAPTER 1
PURPOSE AND SCOPE OF DEPOSITIONS

"I'm for truth, no matter who tells it."

—Malcolm X[1]

---

[1] Malcolm X & Alex Haley, The Autobiography of Malcolm X, ch. 19 (1st ed. 1965).

Introduction

The purpose of the U.S. civil justice system is to enable people to resolve their disputes in a peaceful manner. Dispute resolution should not be based on the "sporting theory of justice."[2] Rather, disputes should be resolved by applying legal principles to an established set of facts. Therefore, all parties' ability to have a full and mutual understanding of all the relevant facts in a dispute is essential to resolving it fairly. The Federal Rules of Civil Procedure were created as a framework to provide fair access to all relevant information. The U.S. Supreme Court has made it abundantly clear that discovery procedures are intended to ensure the disclosure of relevant information well before trial, "thus reducing the possibility of surprise."[3]

Discovery

Discovery is the process through which parties to a lawsuit obtain relevant information from the opposing party and from people or entities that are not part of the lawsuit. Federal Rules of Civil Procedure 26 to 37 govern the scope and mechanisms for the discovery of information in all federal lawsuits. Rule 26(b)(1) details the scope of discovery in general:

> ***Scope in General.*** Unless otherwise limited by court order, the scope of discovery is as follows: *Parties may obtain discovery regarding any nonprivileged matter that is relevant to any party's claim or defense and proportional to the needs of the case*, considering the importance of the issues at stake in the action, the amount in controversy, the parties' relative access to relevant information, the parties' resources, the importance of the discovery in resolving the issues, and whether the burden or expense of the proposed discovery outweighs its likely

---

2   Roscoe Pound, Dean of Univ. of Neb. Coll. of Law, The Causes of Popular Dissatisfaction with the Administration of Justice, American Bar Association Annual Convention (1906), *in* 29 *A.B.A. Rep.*, pt. I, 395-417, 1906 (where Dean Roscoe Pound criticized the "sporting theory of justice," as an approach designed to prevail in a lawsuit by outmaneuvering an adversary rather than seeking resolution based on truth and justice).

3   *Hickman v. Taylor*, 329 U.S. 495, 507 (1947).

benefit. Information within this scope of discovery need not be admissible in evidence to be discoverable.[4]

Establishing the importance of discovery, the Supreme Court stated in *Hickman v. Taylor*, "Mutual knowledge of all the relevant facts gathered by both parties is essential to proper litigation."[5] By allowing adverse parties access to the same nonprivileged information, the discovery process creates an equal playing field in civil suits and ensures that the truth is the primary factor in determining the outcome of lawsuits.

Depositions

The formal questioning of witnesses under oath, before trial, is known as deposition testimony. Rule 30 authorizes depositions by oral examination:

> **(a) When a Deposition May Be Taken.**
>
> **(1) *Without Leave.*** A party may, by oral questions, depose any person, including a party, without leave of court except as provided in Rule 30(a)(2). The deponent's attendance may be compelled by subpoena under Rule 45.[6]

The rule details the procedures and requirements for administering depositions, which will be discussed throughout this book.

Questioning witnesses is the best way to identify which facts are disputed, which facts are agreed on, and the validity of any dispute. The court in *Hall v. Clifton Precision* clearly explained the critical function of deposition testimony:

> One of the purposes of the discovery rules in general, and the deposition rules in particular, is to elicit the facts of a case before trial. . . . Depositions serve another purpose as well: the memorialization, the freezing, of a witness's testimony at an early stage of the proceedings, before that witness's recollection of the events at issue either has faded or has been altered by intervening events, other discovery, or the helpful suggestions of lawyers. The underlying purpose of a deposition is to

---

[4] Fed. R. Civ. P. 26(b)(1) (emphasis added).

[5] *Hickman*, 329 U.S. at 507.

[6] Fed. R. Civ. P. 30(a)(1).

find out what a witness saw, heard, or did—what the witness thinks. A deposition is meant to be a question-and-answer conversation between the deposing lawyer and the witness.[7]

Judge Robert Gawthrop also described the vast influence of depositions in today's lawsuits:

> Depositions are the factual battleground where the vast majority of litigation actually takes place. It may safely be said that Rule 30 has spawned a veritable cottage industry. The significance of depositions has grown geometrically over the years to the point where their pervasiveness now dwarfs both the time spent and the facts learned at the actual trial—assuming there is a trial, which there usually is not. The pretrial tail now wags the trial dog. Thus, it is particularly important that this discovery device not be abused.[8]

The resolution of any dispute, whether by trial or settlement, is based on the information that will be presented to the fact-finder. Cases are resolved on the basis of "facts" developed during discovery, particularly at oral depositions. "If the truth finding function of discovery has been obstructed by improper conduct of the attorneys, then the settlement will not reflect a just result based upon the truth."[9]

Scope of Deposition Inquiry

The scope of permissible inquiry at a deposition is broader than what can be presented during an evidentiary proceeding.[10]

> [D]iscovery may be used to elicit information that will lead to relevant evidence; each question and answer need not be one that could be one that would itself be proper at trial.[11]

---

7   *Hall v. Clifton Precision*, 150 F.R.D. 525, 528 (E.D. Pa. 1993).

8   *Hall*, 150 F.R.D. at 531.

9   *Damaj v. Farmers Ins. Co., Inc.*, 164 F.R.D. 559, 560 (N.D. Okla. 1995).

10 *Gall v. St. Elizabeth Med. Ctr.*, 130 F.R.D. 85, 87 (S.D. Ohio 1990).

11 *Redwood v. Dobson*, 476 F.3d 462, 469 (7th Cir. 2007).

While the Federal Rules of Evidence prohibit introducing certain types of evidence, the rules govern the admissibility of evidence at trial, *not* during the discovery stage.[12]

> Rule 26(b) of the Federal Rules of Civil Procedure is widely recognized as a discovery rule which is liberal in scope and interpretation, extending to those matters which are relevant and reasonably calculated to lead to the discovery of admissible evidence.[13]

This book shares both the statutory and precedential authority that governs lawyers' ability to marshal information to advance or defend their clients' cases. Broadly speaking, all deposition conduct is constrained by the requirement that attorneys conduct themselves in the same manner as they would at trial. Rule 30(c)(1) states:

> ***Examination and Cross-Examination.*** The examination and cross-examination of a deponent proceed as they would at trial under the Federal Rules of Evidence, except Rules 103 and 615.[14]

The court in *Damaj v. Farmers Ins. Co., Inc.*, eloquently explained why adherence to the rules governing trial conduct is necessary during discovery to ensure just outcomes:

> Since the fact (truth) finding process in civil litigation is almost exclusively conducted in the discovery phase of litigation, it follows logically that the efficacy of the discovery process as the central truth finding mechanism would be enhanced by employing, to the extent possible, the same rules of procedure during discovery as employed at trial.[15]

---

12 See *Herchenroeder v. Johns Hopkins Univ. Applied Physics Lab.*, 171 F.R.D. 179, 181 (D. Md. 1997).

13 *Hofer v. Mack Trucks, Inc.*, 981 F.2d 377, 380 (8th Cir. 1992) (citing *Kramer v. Boeing Co.*, 126 F.R.D. 690, 692 (D. Minn. 1989) (and cases cited therein)).

14 Fed. R. Civ. P. 30(c)(1).

15 *Damaj*, 164 F.R.D. at 560 (N.D. Okla. 1995).

As the "factual battleground" of modern litigation, depositions are central to the pursuit of truth. Understanding the rules and the interpretive jurisprudence is vital to the administration of civil justice.

Summary

- Rules 26 to 37 govern discovery.
- Rule 26 authorizes the discovery of any nonprivileged matter that is relevant to any party's claim or defense and is proportional to the needs of the case.
- Rule 30 authorizes pretrial testimony under oath of both parties and nonparties.
- Attorneys must conduct themselves at depositions in the same manner as they would at trial.

CHAPTER 2
DEPOSITION LOGISTICS

"The line between disorder and order lies in logistics."

—SunTzu

Introduction

This chapter addresses the logistical requirements of depositions, mandated by the Federal Rules of Civil Procedure. Understanding the jurisprudence of deposition logistics can eliminate unnecessary debates about collateral issues such as sequence, location, duration, and method of recording testimony.

Sequence of Depositions in Context of Discovery

Fed. R. Civ. P. 26(d) governs the timing and sequence of discovery in civil litigation. The relevant portion reads:

(1) Timing. A party may not seek discovery from any source before the parties have conferred as required by Rule 26(f). . . .[1]

Rule 26(f) details the requirements for a discovery planning conference between adverse parties, which must be held before beginning any form of discovery.[2] A Rule 26(f) discovery planning conference is the only prerequisite to scheduling and taking depositions.[3]

Rule 26(d)(3) explicitly authorizes each party to make its own decisions about the sequence of discovery:

(3) *Sequence.* Unless the parties stipulate or the court orders otherwise for the parties' and witnesses' convenience and in the interests of justice:

(A) methods of discovery may be used in any sequence; and

(B) discovery by one party does not require any other party to delay its discovery.[4]

The Advisory Committee Notes on the 1970 amendments reiterate that Rules 26(d)(3)(A-B) were intended to "eliminate any fixed priority in

---

1 Fed. R. Civ. P. 26(d)(1).
2 Fed. R. Civ. P. 26(f).
3 Fed. R. Civ. P. 26(d)(1).
4 Fed. R. Civ. P. 26(d)(3).

the sequence of discovery."[5] Adverse parties can conduct discovery simultaneously. Neither party is required to wait to begin its discovery until the other has completed it.[6] Therefore, an attorney representing a party or witness who has been served with a valid notice of deposition may not demand preconditions linked to the client's attendance, unless the court grants a protective order.[7]

If either side files a motion to determine their adversary's sequence of depositions, the burden is on the moving party to establish good cause and prove it is in the interest of justice to alter the sequence.[8] Tactical advantage is not good cause. It does not promote justice if the court chooses sides and upholds one party's request for a tactical advantage over the other.[9] As such, courts usually do not grant protective orders altering the sequence of depositions.[10]

Location of Depositions

Rule 30 controls the administration of oral depositions. Every deposition notice must include the "time and place of the deposition."[11] However, the rule does not require any specific location for depositions.[12] The court in *Turner v. Prudential Insurance Co. of America* explained:

> Certain general principles apply in selecting the place to conduct a deposition. *A party may unilaterally choose the place for deposing an opposing party,* subject to the granting of a

---

5 Fed. R. Civ. P. 26(d)(3)(A-B), 1970 committee notes subd. d.

6 *Cont'l Ill. Nat. Bank & Trust Co. of Chi. v. Caton*, 130 F.R.D. 145, 148 (D. Kan. 1990).

7 *Hill v. Forward Air Sols., Inc.*, 2011 WL 1130868 at *2 (W.D.N.C. 2011) (quoting *Keller v. Edwards*, 206 F.R.D. 412, 416 (D. Md. 2002)).

8 *Stein v. Tri-City Healthcare Dist.*, 2014 WL 458021 at *2 (S.D. Cal. Feb. 4, 2014).

9 *Stein*, 2014 WL 458021 at *2.

10 *Stein*, 2014 WL 458021 at *1.

11 Fed. R. Civ. P. 30(b)(1).

12 *In re Outsidewall Tire Litig.*, 267 F.R.D. 466, 470 (E.D. Va. 2010); *see* Fed. R. Civ. P. 30(a)(1) (detailing when a party may depose an individual without leave of court); Fed. R. Civ. P. 30(b)(6) (detailing the rules for deposing organizations).

protective order by the Court pursuant to [Rule 26(c)(1)], . . . designating a different place.[13]

If the responding party disagrees with the location, that party may move for a Rule 26(c)(1) protective order to change the deposition's location.[14] The burden is on the moving party to demonstrate good cause for the court to grant the protective order and alter the location.[15] In *Phillips v. General Motors Corp.*, the court explained how good cause is demonstrated:

> For good cause to exist, the party seeking protection bears the burden of showing specific prejudice or harm will result if no protective order is granted. . . . "[B]road allegations of harm, unsubstantiated by specific examples or articulated reasoning, do not satisfy the Rule 26(c) test."[16]

Location for 30(b)(1) Depositions—Individual Parties

If a party disputes the deposition location, it is within the court's discovery oversight powers to consider the fairness to the parties in deciding the location.[17] Because the plaintiff normally chooses the forum district, courts usually require the plaintiff to appear for a deposition located in the forum district.[18] A defendant, however, does not choose the forum, so courts are less likely to require them to travel to a deposition set in the forum district.[19] Generally, it is presumed that a nonresident defendant's

---

13   *Turner v. Prudential Ins. Co. of Am.*, 119 F.R.D. 381, 383 (M.D.N.C. 1988) (citing 8 C. Wright & A. Miller, Federal Practice and Procedure § 2112 at 403 (1970)) (emphasis added).

14   Fed. R. Civ. P. 26(c)(1).

15   *Cadent Ltd. v. 3M Unitek Corp.*, 232 F.R.D. 625, 629 (C.D. Cal. 2005) (quoting *Phillips v. Gen. Motors Corp.*, 307 F.3d 1206, 1210-11 (9th Cir. 2002)).

16   *Phillips*, 307 F.3d at 1210-11 (citing *Beckman Indus., Inc. v. Int'l Ins. Co.*, 966 F.2d 470, 476 (9th Cir. 1992)).

17   *Leist v. Union Oil Co. of Cal.*, 82 F.R.D. 203, 204 (E.D. Wis. 1979).

18   *Turner*, 119 F.R.D. at 383.

19   *Turner*, 119 F.R.D. at 383.

deposition will be held where they reside or work, because the defendant is not party to the lawsuit by choice.[20]

Location for 30(b)(6) Depositions—Organizations

The deposition of a Rule 30(b)(6) designee for an organization that is party to a lawsuit is usually taken at the organization's principal place of business.[21] If the organization's principal place of business is disputed, the disputing party must prove the principal place of business is different from the location designated in the notice.[22] In such instances, courts use the "total activity" test to determine an organization's principal place of business. The test considers multiple factors, including the location of the organization's nerve center, administrative offices, production facilities, and employees, and then it balances these factors based on the facts of the case.[23]

Although there is a general presumption that the 30(b)(6) deposition of an organization should take place at its principal place of business, courts also have the discretion to recognize that other factors might justify a change in location.[24] When considering whether to relocate the 30(b)(6) deposition of an organization from its principal place of business, courts have considered these factors:[25]

---

20   Bank of N.Y. v. Meridian BIAO Bank Tanzania Ltd., 171 F.R.D. 135, 155 (S.D.N.Y. 1997); see Farquhar v. Shelden, 116 F.R.D. 70, 72 (E.D. Mich. 1987); Mill-Run Tours, Inc. v. Khashoggi, 124 F.R.D. 547, 550 (S.D.N.Y. 1989).

21   Turner, 119 F.R.D. at 383 (citing Wright & Miller, Federal Practice and Procedure at 403); see Farquhar v. Shelden, 116 F.R.D. 70 (E.D. Mich. 1987).

22   Starlight Int'l, Inc. v. Herlihy, 186 F.R.D. 626, 644 (D. Kan. 1999).

23   Starlight Int'l, 186 F.R.D. at 644; see White v. Halstead Indus., 750 F. Supp. 395, 398 (E.D. Ark. 1990).

24   E.I. DuPont de Nemours & Co. v. Kolon Indus., Inc., 268 F.R.D. 45, 54 (E.D. Va. 2010); see Cadent Ltd. v. 3M Unitek Corp., 232 F.R.D. 625, 629 (C.D. Cal. 2005); Turner, 119 F.R.D. at 383; Rapoca Energy Co., L.P. v. AMCI Export Corp., 199 F.R.D. 191, 193 (W.D. Va. 2001).

25   Mark Kosieradzki, 30(b)(6): Deposing Corporations, Organizations & the Government 62–63 (2015).

- the location of counsel for the parties in the forum district[26]
- the number of corporate representatives a party is seeking to depose[27]
- the likelihood of significant discovery disputes arising, which the forum court would need to resolve[28]
- the amount of travel to the forum jurisdiction the witnesses engage in for business purposes[29]
- the equities with regard to the nature of the claim and the parties' relationship[30]
- the danger associated with traveling to the location of the testimony[31]
- the location of documents the parties will need[32]
- the relative financial positions of the parties[33]

Ultimately, it is within the court's broad discretion to consider all relevant facts and equities for determining both the appropriate place for examination and its conditions, such as who pays for travel expenses.[34]

---

26   *E.I. DuPont de Nemours & Co.*, 268 F.R.D. at 54; *Cadent Ltd.*, 232 F.R.D. at 630.

27   *E.I. DuPont de Nemours & Co.*, 268 F.R.D. at 54.

28   *E.I. DuPont de Nemours & Co.*, 268 F.R.D. at 54.

29   *E.I. DuPont de Nemours & Co.*, 268 F.R.D. at 54; *see In re Outsidewall Tire Litig.*, 267 F.R.D. at 472; *Afram Export Corp. v. Metallurgiki Halyps, S.A.*, 772 F.2d 1358, 1365–66 (7th Cir. 1985).

30   *E.I. DuPont de Nemours & Co.*, 268 F.R.D. at 54; *Cadent Ltd.*, 232 F.R.D. at 629 (citing *Armsey v. Medshares Mgmt. Servs.*, 184 F.R.D. 569, 571 (W.D. Va.1998); *Resolution Trust Corp. v. Worldwide Ins. Mgmt. Corp.*, 147 F.R.D. 125, 127 (N.D. Tex. 1992)).

31   *Cadent Ltd.*, 232 F.R.D. at 630 (citing *United States v. $160,066.98 from Bank of Am.*, 202 F.R.D. 624, 627-28 (S.D. Cal. 2001)).

32   *Mill-Run Tours, Inc. v. Khashoggi*, 124 F.R.D. 547, 551 (S.D.N.Y. 1989); *Turner*, 119 F.R.D. at 382–83 (M.D.N.C. 1988).

33   *Cadent Ltd.*, 232 F.R.D. at 629 (citing *Baker v. Standard Indus., Inc.*, 55 F.R.D. 178, 179 (D.P.R. 1972); Wright, Miller & Marcus, *Federal Practice and Procedure: Civil 2d* § 2112 at 84–85 (1994 rev.)); *Tomingas v. Douglas Aircraft Co.*, 45 F.R.D. 94, 96–97 (S.D.N.Y. 1968).

34   *Branyan v. Koninklijke Luchtvaart Maatschappij*, 13 F.R.D. 425, 429 (S.D.N.Y. 1953).

Each case is determined "on its own facts and the equities of the particular situation."[35]

Location for a Nonparty Deposition

If a deponent is a nonparty who is required to testify, attendance can be compelled with a subpoena under Fed. R. Civ. P. 45(c)(1), which lays out specific requirements for the location of such a deposition:

> **(1)** *For a Trial, Hearing, or Deposition.* A subpoena may command a person to attend a trial, hearing, or deposition only as follows:
>
> **(A)** within 100 miles of where the person resides, is employed, or regularly transacts business in person; or
>
> **(B)** within the state where the person resides, is employed, or regularly transacts business in person, if the person
>
> > **(i)** is a party or a party's officer; or
> >
> > **(ii)** is commanded to attend a trial and would not incur substantial expense.[36]

In federal cases, individual nonparty witnesses must have their depositions taken "within 100 miles of where the person resides, is employed, or regularly transacts business in person."[37] If the nonparty witness is a 30(b)(6) entity, the court usually calculates the Rule 45(c)(1)(A) 100-mile territorial requirement based on the location of the organization's headquarters.[38] If the nonparty organization's designee resides outside of that area, the 45(c)(1) location requirements are based on the location of the designee, not the organization.[39]

---

35 *Turner*, 119 F.R.D. at 383 (citing *Leist v. Union Oil Co. of Cal.*, 82 F.R.D. 203 (E.D. Wis. 1979)).

36 Fed. R. Civ. P. 45(c)(1).

37 Fed. R. Civ. P. 45(c)(1)(A).

38 *See VirtualAgility, Inc. v. Salesforce.com, Inc.*, 2014 WL 459719 at *3 (E.D. Tex. Jan. 31, 2014).

39 *Cates v. LTV Aerospace Corp.*, 480 F.2d 620, 623 (5th Cir. 1973).

Remote Depositions

Rule 30(b)(4) allows for a deposition to be taken remotely, either by stipulation from the parties or by a court order. The rule states:

> ***By Remote Means.*** The parties may stipulate—or the court may on motion order—that a deposition be taken by telephone or other remote means. . . . [T]he deposition takes place where the deponent answers the questions.[40]

In today's litigation, depositions often are taken via telephone or digital video conferencing. In these instances, regardless of where the lawyers are located, the deposition is considered to take place in the location where the deponent is physically answering the questions.[41]

Length of Depositions

Rule 30(d)(1) sets the presumptive durational limit of a deposition at a single day of seven hours. According to the Advisory Committee Notes to the 2000 amendment, "[t]his limitation contemplates that there will be reasonable breaks during the day for lunch and other reasons, and that the only time to be counted is the time occupied by the actual deposition."[42] In *Wilson v. Kautex, A Textron Co.*, the court ruled that only the actual time examining the deponent is counted when calculating the limit; lunch and other breaks do not count.[43]

The presumptive durational limit can be changed by a stipulation between the parties.[44] The presumptive limit of 10 depositions per side provided in Rule 30(a)(2)(A)(i) can also be changed by stipulation.[45] If the parties cannot agree, a party may submit a motion for extra time to depose a

---

40   Fed. R. Civ. P. 30(b)(4).
41   Fed. R. Civ. P. 30(b)(4).
42   Fed. R. Civ. P. 30(d)(1), 2000 committee notes subd. d.
43   *Wilson v. Kautex, A Textron Co.*, 2008 WL 189568 at *3 (N.D. Ind. 2008).
44   Fed. R. Civ. P. 30(d)(1).
45   Fed. R. Civ. P. 30(a)(2)(A).

witness.[46] Rule 30(d)(1) requires the courts to "allow additional time consistent with Rule 26(b)(1) and (2) if needed to fairly examine the deponent or if the deponent, another person, or any other circumstance impedes or delays the examination."[47] The Advisory Committee Notes to Rule 26 cautioned that courts "must be careful not to deprive a party of discovery that is reasonably necessary to afford a fair opportunity to develop and prepare the case."[48]

Length of 30(b)(6) Depositions—Organizations

When responding to a Rule 30(b)(6) deposition notice, the organization can designate as many witnesses as it believes are necessary to comply with the matters of examination in the notice.[49] However, each designee is allotted the full seven hours established by Rule 30(d)(1) when calculating the time limit of a Rule 30(b)(6) deposition.[50] For example, if the organization designates three people to respond to the notice, each designee has a separate seven-hour limit, for a total of 21 hours. The combination of all of the designees counts as a single deposition against the presumptive limit of 10.[51]

Method of Recording Depositions

Rule 30(b)(3)(A) requires the requesting party to state the method of recording the testimony in the deposition notice:

> *Method Stated in the Notice.* The party who notices the deposition must state in the notice the method for recording the testimony. Unless the court orders otherwise, testimony may be recorded by audio, audiovisual, or stenographic means. The noticing party bears the recording costs. Any party may arrange to transcribe a deposition.[52]

---

46 *Canal Barge Co. v. Commonwealth Edison Co.*, 2001 WL 817853 at *4 (N.D. Ill. 2001) (allowing deposition of a 30(b)(6) designee to last for three seven-hour days to question about 56 different barges).

47 Fed. R. Civ. P. 30(d)(1).

48 Fed. R. Civ. P. 26, advisory committee notes to 1983 amendments.

49 Fed. R. Civ. P. 30(b)(6).

50 Fed. R. Civ. P. 30(d)(1), 2000 committee notes subd. d; *see* Fed. R. Civ. P. 30(a)(2)(A)(i).

51 Fed. R. Civ. P. 30(d)(1), 2000 committee notes subd. d; *see* Fed. R. Civ. P. 30(a)(2)(A)(i).

52 Fed. R. Civ. P. 30(b)(3)(A).

The requesting party is explicitly authorized to record the testimony through audio, audiovisual, *or* stenographic means, with the requesting party bearing the associated recording costs.[53] If any other party wishes to record the testimony through any other means, Rule 30(b)(3)(B) allows them to do so, provided they bear the costs of the additional recording:

> *Additional Method.* With prior notice to the deponent and other parties, any party may designate another method for recording the testimony in addition to that specified in the original notice. That party bears the expense of the additional record or transcript unless the court orders otherwise.[54]

In *Pioneer Drive, LLC v. Nissan Diesel America, Inc.*, the court ruled that a deposition being recorded by an official stenographer did not have to have the video of the deposition recorded by an independent professional.[55] The court determined that "[t]he Federal Rules of Civil Procedure allow, at the very least, counsel to videotape a deposition in concert with a stenographer recording it."[56] The court observed:

> [The] Defendant's concerns over accuracy and objectivity were misplaced from the start. There was an authorized officer to stenographically record the examination present at the deposition. This provided both an assurance of an accurate record of the deposition, as well as a benchmark upon which the video record could be challenged if that was necessary.[57]

---

53 Fed. R. Civ. P. 30(b)(3)(A).

54 Fed. R. Civ. P. 30(b)(3)(B).

55 *Pioneer Drive, LLC v. Nissan Diesel Am., Inc.*, 262 F.R.D. 552, 555–56 (D. Mont. 2009).

56 *Pioneer Drive,* F.R.D. at 555.

57 *Pioneer Drive,* 262 F.R.D. at 556.

Recognizing the importance of videotaped testimonies at trial, most federal decisions on the issue have allowed counsel to include audiovisual recordings with stenographic recordings in depositions.[58]

Summary

- **Sequence of discovery:**

  - Parties in discovery may sequence depositions as they choose.

  - The adverse party can move for a protective order to change the sequence of depositions but must demonstrate good cause to do so.

- **Deposition location:**

  - The requesting party may unilaterally choose the deposition location for an opposing party.

  - The responding party can move for a protective order to change the deposition location but must demonstrate good cause to do so.

  - There is a rebuttable presumption that a defendant's 30(b)(6) deposition should take place at its principal place of business.

---

58 See *Pioneer Drive*, 262 F.R.D. at 555; *Marlboro Prods. Corp. v. North Am. Philips Corp.*, 55 F.R.D. 487, 489–90 (S.D.N.Y. 1972); *Carpenter v. Forest Meadows Owners Ass'n*, 2011 WL 3207778 at *8 (E.D. Cal July 27, 2011) (denying motion to prohibit use of a video recorded deposition where the plaintiff's attorney, who was operating the video equipment, failed to repeat the instructions required by Fed. R. Civ. P. 30(b)(5)(B) because "the written deposition transcript [recorded by an independent stenographer] ensures there has been no falsification of the recordings."); *Anderson v. Dobson*, 627 F. Supp. 2d 619, 624–25 (W.D.N.C. 2007) (holding that recording a deposition by a party's attorney is not a per se violation of the rules, and denying a motion to strike the video deposition absent "any indication of irregularities in the video recording process"); *Duncan v. Husted*, 2011 WL 1540550 at *1–2 (S.D. Ohio Apr. 7, 2015) (permitting the plaintiff to operate recording equipment to record a deposition provided that an independent notary performs the other duties required by Rules 28 and 30); *Am. Gen. Life Ins. Co. v. Billard*, 2010 WL 4367052 at *6 (N.D. Iowa Oct. 28, 2010) (party's attorney "is under no obligation to hire a professional videographer" so long as the attorney adheres to the requirements of Fed. R. Civ. P. 30(b)(5)); *Maranville v. Utah Valley Univ.*, 2012 WL 1493888 at *2 (D. Utah Apr. 27, 2012); *Roberts v. Homelite Div. of Textron, Inc.*, 109 F.R.D. 664, 667 (N.D. Ind. 1986); *Ott v. Stipe Law Firm*, 169 F.R.D. 380, 381 (E.D. Okla. 1996).

- A nonparty individual deposition must occur within 100 miles of the witness's home or work.
- A nonparty 30(b)(6) deposition must occur within 100 miles of the designated witness's home or principal place of business.
- Remote depositions are allowed, by either stipulation or a court order.
- Remote depositions are considered to take place where the deponent physically answers the questions.

- **Timing depositions:**
  - Depositions are limited to one day of seven hours unless a stipulation or court order extends the time.
  - Only the time spent actually examining the witness counts toward the durational limit.
  - When multiple witnesses are designated to appear for Rule 30(b)(6), each witness will be allotted a full seven hours.

- **Recording depositions:**
  - Deposition testimony must be recorded through audio, audiovisual, or stenographic means by an authorized official.
  - As long as there is an official transcript of the testimony, other recorded forms of the testimony may be used at trial.

CHAPTER 3
DEPOSITION ETHICS

"Be good."

—E.T.[1]

---

1   E.T. the Extra-Terrestrial (Universal Pictures 1982).

Introduction

Some members of the bar mistakenly believe their role in defending depositions is to control what their opponent asks, to impede access to discoverable information, and to tactically disrupt the deposition process. The belief that the ethical duty to "zealously advocate" on the client's behalf requires obstructionist conduct is misplaced.

Attorney conduct at depositions is governed by the Model Rules of Professional Conduct, as well as the Federal Rules of Civil Procedure. Adherence to the Rules of Professional Conduct ensures attorneys comply with the highest ethical standards of legal practice. Each state has its own rules of professional conduct, most of which closely imitate the ABA Model Rules.

When lawyers advocate on clients' behalf, the Rules of Professional Conduct must be read as a whole. Those rules, as well as corresponding jurisprudence, make it eminently clear that litigation obstruction is prohibited and unethical. This chapter will discuss the Rules of Professional Conduct as they apply to depositions.

Preamble to the Model Rules of Professional Conduct: Zealous Advocacy Must Be Within the Bounds of the Rules

The Preamble to the Model Rules of Professional Conduct states:

> As [an] advocate, a lawyer zealously asserts the client's position *under the rules of the adversary system.*[2]

The chapters that follow will explain the laws governing attorney conduct at depositions. Lawyers who violate the mandatory rules governing depositions in the name of zealous advocacy are not "zealously advocating." Rather, they are violating the Rules of Professional Conduct.

---

2 Model Rules of Prof'l Conduct Pmbl. 2 (2007) (emphasis added).

U.S. District Court Judge Mark Bennett observed the often-distorted interpretation of "zealous advocacy" by many of today's attorneys:

> Whatever the reason, obstructionist discovery conduct is born of a *warped view of zealous advocacy*, often formed by insecurities and fear of the truth. This conduct fuels the astronomically costly litigation industry at the expense of "the just, speedy, and inexpensive determination of every action and proceeding."[3]

Zealousness cannot be used as an excuse for violating the Rules of Civil Procedure:

> The idea that zealousness can be an excuse for unethical and unprofessional behavior is a pernicious disease that threatens to eat away at the integrity and nobility of the court as an institution. Zealousness is commendable, but it is not and cannot ever be an acceptable excuse for unprofessional and unethical conduct.[4]

Chief Judge Frank Easterbrook, in *Redwood v. Dobson*, highlighted the critical importance of the Rules of Civil Procedure governing depositions:

> It is precisely when animosity runs high that playing by the rules is vital. Rules of legal procedure are designed to defuse, or at least channel into set forms, the heated feelings that accompany much litigation. Because depositions take place in law offices rather than courtrooms, adherence to professional standards is vital, for the judge has no direct means of control.[5]

Seemingly endless jurisprudence condemns deposition obstruction. There is no gray area regarding obstruction. It is impermissible and, therefore, unethical.

---

[3] *Sec. Nat'l Bank of Sioux City, Iowa v. Abbott Labs.*, 299 F.R.D. 595, 597 (N.D. Iowa 2014) (emphasis added), *rev'd,* 800 F.3d 936 (8th Cir. 2015); *see also* Mark Kosieradzki & Kara Rahimi, *Keep Discovery Civil*, 44 Trial (June 2008).

[4] *In re Moncier*, 550 F. Supp. 2d 768, 806 (E.D. Tenn. 2008).

[5] *Redwood v. Dobson*, 476 F.3d 462, 469-70 (7th Cir. 2007).

Model Rule of Professional Conduct 3.4: Obstruction Is Prohibited

Rule 3.4 requires that lawyers conduct themselves with "fairness to opposing party and counsel."[6] Subsection (a) expressly states:

A lawyer shall not:

(a) unlawfully obstruct another party's access to evidence or unlawfully alter, destroy or conceal a document or other material having potential evidentiary value.[7]

Lawfulness is not governed by the criminal code. Instead, lawfulness is the adherence to rules and laws that govern our judicial system. Failure to comply with the Rules of Civil Procedure is an unlawful obstruction of access to material having potential evidentiary value.[8] The comment on Rule 3.4 makes it clear that the rule was specifically designed to prohibit obstructive tactics:

The procedure of the adversary system contemplates that the evidence in a case is to be marshalled competitively by the contending parties. Fair competition in the adversary system is secured by prohibitions against destruction or concealment of evidence, improperly influencing witnesses, *obstructive tactics in discovery procedure*, and the like.[9]

In *Redwood*, Chief Judge Easterbrook made it clear that when attorneys engage in obstructive deposition tactics, the conduct constitutes ethical violations as well as sanctionable violations of the Rules of Civil Procedure.[10]

---

6 Model Rules of Prof'l Conduct r. 3.4 (2007).

7 Model Rules of Prof'l Conduct r. 3.4(a) (2007) (emphasis added).

8 Mark Kosieradzki, 30(b)(6): Deposing Corporations, Organizations & the Government 303 (Trial Guides 2015).

9 Model Rules of Prof'l Conduct r. 3.4 cmt. 1 (2007) (emphasis added).

10 *Redwood*, 476 F.3d at 469.

Model Rule of Professional Conduct 8.4: Abusive and Uncivil Behavior Is Unethical

Chapter 8 of the Model Rules focuses on lawyers' ethical duty to "maintain the integrity" of the profession.[11] Rule 8.4(d) states:

> It is professional misconduct for a lawyer to:
>
> (d) engage in conduct that is prejudicial to the administration of justice.[12]

The annotations to Rule 8.4(d) make it clear that "abusive or uncivil behavior toward opposing counsel as well as parties and witnesses" is conduct prejudicial to the administration of justice.[13] In *Zottola v. Anesthesia Consultants of Savannah*, the court admonished the deposing attorney's obstructive and uncivil antics as conduct unbecoming of a member of the bar:

> Yelling at deposition witnesses, harassing and embarrassing them with questions about highly sensitive matters irrelevant to the litigation, and rudely tossing a phone at opposing counsel in anger are all offensive behaviors that fall well outside the bounds of professional conduct. Such incivilities not only constitute conduct unbecoming a member of the bar but violate specific rules that govern the practice of law before this Court.[14]

---

11   Model Rules of Prof'l Conduct r. 8 (2007).

12   Model Rules of Prof'l Conduct r. 8.4(d) (2007).

13   Annotated Model Rules of Prof'l Conduct r. 8.4(d) (Behavior Toward Opposing Parties, Their Counsel, or Witnesses) (2015); *see also Horton v. Maersk Line, Ltd.*, 294 F.R.D. 690, 698 (S.D. Ga. 2013) (describing obstructive deposition conduct as "manipulatively abusive" and "caustically unprofessional"); *Clay v. Consol Penn. Coal Co., L.L.C.*, 2013 WL 5408064 at *2, 6 (N.D. Wa. Sept. 24, 2013) (publicly reprimanding deposing attorney for "outrageous conduct" during the deposition that was "clearly improper and reprehensible"); *Rojas v. X Motorsport, Inc.*, 275 F. Supp. 3d 898, 908 (N.D. Ill 2017) (censuring deposing attorney for deposition misconduct unbecoming of a member of the bar); *Ross v. Kansas City Power & Light Co.*, 197 F.R.D. 646, 664 (W.D. Mo. 2000) (declaring that deposing attorney's misconduct had "brought dishonor upon . . . attorneys and the profession as a whole").

14   *Zottola v. Anesthesia Consultants of Savannah, P.C.*, 2012 WL 6824150 at *6 (S.D. Ga. June 7, 2012).

Example: Uncivil and Abusive Behavior Toward a Witness

Deposing counsel repeatedly belittles and attempts to intimidate the deponent, who has no counsel present, throughout the deposition.

Q Don't get snide with me. Just answer my questions or you are going to be in severe difficulty, especially if you make me angry at you. I'm not going to try to get angry with you. Just answer my questions.

Q You are coming across as an absolutely ridiculous person. But that's okay, you will learn the hard way.

Q You are not smart enough to question my questions. You are not smart enough to even answer my questions. But do the best you can.

Q Do you understand English? I speak real clear English.

Q You are just not smart enough to know what a restraining order is.

Q So you think it is your scintillating personality that caused him to want to play chess with you?

In re Golden, 496 S.E.2d 619, 620 (S.C. 1999).

Both the court and the disciplinary panel admonished the offending attorney. In its opinion, the court issued a public reprimand for his deposition misconduct:

> Here, we do not have a momentary loss of cool, but rather, a repeated pattern of misconduct over the course of an entire deposition. . . . The [disciplinary] Panel, which had an opportunity to hear first-hand the testimony of the witnesses, summed up Attorney's actions in the following way:
>
> [Attorney's] conduct . . . exemplifies the worst stereotype of an arrogant, rude, and overbearing attorney. It goes far beyond the tactical aggressiveness to a level of gratuitous insult, intimidation, and degradation of the witness. It is behavior that brings the legal profession into disrepute.
>
> We agree.[15]

---

15 *In re Golden*, 496 S.E.2d 619, 623 (S.C. 1999).

Example: Threatening Behavior Toward a Witness

A lawyer is sued in a defamation action. The lawyer, acting pro se, examines the plaintiff in a deposition. The deposition becomes contentious. Both the witness and examining lawyer use vulgarities. Ultimately, the examining lawyer displays a gun he has holstered on his hip.

Q Because apparently somebody thinks they're entitled to damages, and, in reality, they're not entitled to anything, because somebody is the dipshit younger brother—

Defending lawyer: All right.

A Did you just call me a dipshit?

Q Yes. Dipshit. Yes.

A This is over.

Defending lawyer: This depo is over.

Q Good for you. Have fun.

Defending lawyer: Mark, Mark, Mark.

A You called me a dipshit, mother——.

Q Yeah. You're a dipshit, f——.

Defending lawyer: Hey, hey.

Q F— you.

Defending lawyer: Hey, hey.

A Get my keys. Did you see that?

Defending lawyer: Mark, Mark.

Q Are you ready for it?

Defending lawyer: Mark.

Q Are you ready for it?

A I'm ready all day long.

·····

Defending lawyer: What are you doing now? If you pull the gun, I'm going to call the police.

Q Get out of here. Get out of here right now.

Defending lawyer [to reporter]: Are you recording this?

Q Get out of here.

A   You pulled a gun on me, Pengilly.

Defending lawyer: Mark—hey, hey, hey, I don't want to get shot.

A   He pulled a gun on me.

Defending lawyer: Hey.

A   Get out of here. Get out of my office.

Defending lawyer: He's grabbing a gun with his right hand in his back pocket.

A   Put that down in the f—— notes.

Defending lawyer: You got it?

A   He's got a gun in his back pocket. The mother—— comes to a deposition with a gun.

Defending lawyer: Let's go.[16]

The Nevada Supreme Court described the conduct of the lawyer asking questions:

> When questioning the deponent, Pengilly used vulgarities, called the deponent derogatory names, aggressively interrupted the deponent and opposing counsel, answered questions for the deponent, and repeatedly made inappropriate statements on the record. Pengilly went on to ask the deponent if he was "ready for it" while positioning his hand near his hip. The deponent briefly left the room, but when he returned Pengilly displayed a firearm he had holstered on his hip to the deponent and opposing counsel.[17]

The Nevada Supreme Court concluded that this conduct was a violation of Rule 8.4(d), which prohibits an attorney from engaging in conduct that is prejudicial to the administration of justice. The offending attorney was suspended from practicing law for six months and one day, and he was fined $2,500 plus costs.[18]

---

16   Debra Cassens Weiss, *Lawyer Denies Brandishing His Gun During a Deposition; Court Reporter Kept Typing in Tense Situation,* ABA Journal (Oct. 6, 2016).

17   *In the Matter of Discipline of James W. Pengilly, Esq.*, Bar No. 6085, at 1, Supreme Court of Nevada, No. 74316 (NV. S. Ct. Sept. 7, 2018).

18   *In the Matter of Discipline of James W. Pengilly, Esq.*, Bar No. 6085, Supreme Court of Nevada, No. 74316 (NV. S. Ct. Sept. 7, 2018).

Summary

- Zealous advocacy does not permit circumventing the Rules of Civil Procedure.
- Rule 3.4 forbids attorneys from unlawfully obstructing another party's access to evidence.
- Rule 8.4(d) forbids abusive behavior toward opposing counsel.
- Rule 8.4(d) forbids abusive behavior toward a witness.
- Violation of the Model Rules of Professional Conduct is unethical.

CHAPTER 4
PROPER OBJECTIONS

"Always do right; this will gratify some people, and astonish the rest."

—Mark Twain[1]

---

1 Mark Twain, Note to the Young People's Society, Greenpoint Presbyterian Church, February 16, 1901.

Introduction

Fed. R. Civ. P. 32 allows for objections to the admissibility of certain deposition testimony at trial:

Objections to Admissibility. Subject to Rules 28(b) and 32(d)(3), an objection may be made at a hearing or trial to the admission of any deposition testimony that would be inadmissible if the witness were present and testifying.[2]

This chapter and the following chapter identify which trial objections must be raised at a deposition, and which objections are preserved for trial and therefore improper during a deposition.

"The rules distinguish objections to the manner of taking the deposition from objections as to the substance of the testimony. . . ."[3] Fed. R. Civ. P. 32(d)(3) preserves all objections for trial unless the basis for the objection is one that might have been corrected if raised at the deposition.[4] If an objection "relates to the manner of taking the deposition, the form of a question or answer, the oath or affirmation, a party's conduct, or other matters that might have been corrected at that time," the defending attorney must raise it promptly during the deposition, or it will be waived for trial.[5] Conversely, evidentiary objections to substance, such as relevance, competence, and materiality, are not waived by failure to object during the deposition, so they should not be raised during a deposition.[6]

Limiting deposition objections to issues that are immediately correctable helps ensure the fair presentation of evidence at trial. If meritless or unnecessary objections are used to disrupt the flow of inquiry, those objections violate both the Rules of Civil Procedure and the Rules

---

2 Fed. R. Civ. P. 32(b).

3 *Cabello v. Fernandez-Larios*, 402 F.3d 1148, 1160 (11th Cir. 2005).

4 Fed. R. Civ. P. 32(d)(3).

5 Fed. R. Civ. P. 32(d)(3)(B)(i).

6 Fed. R. Civ. P. 32(d)(3)(A); *see Cincinnati Ins. Co v. Serrano*, 2012 WL 28071 at *4 (D. Kan. Jan. 5, 2012).

of Professional Conduct.[7] This chapter explains the legal parameters of proper deposition objections.

Procedural Objections to the Manner of Taking the Deposition

Rule 32(d)(3)(B)(i) provides the criteria for objections that must be raised contemporaneously at the deposition to preserve those objections for trial:

> *Objection to an Error or Irregularity.* An objection to an error or irregularity at an oral examination is waived if:
>
> (i) it relates to the manner of taking the deposition, the form of a question or answer, the oath or affirmation, a party's conduct, or other matters that might have been corrected at that time.[8]

If objections to correctable errors *are not* raised promptly at the deposition, those objections are considered waived. The U.S. Court of Appeals for the Sixth Circuit, in *Bahamas Agricultural Industries Ltd. v. Riley Stoker Corp.*, explained the rationale for requiring that correctable errors be objected to at the deposition:

> If the objection could have been obviated or removed if made at the time of the taking of the deposition, but was not made, then that objection is waived. The focus of the Rule is on the necessity of making the objection at a point in the proceedings where it will be of some value in curing the alleged error in the deposition. When a party waits until trial to object to testimony in the deposition, the only manner in which to cure the deposition is to bar the objectionable portions from the trial. It is important that objections be made during the process of taking the deposition, so that the deposition retains some use at the time of trial; otherwise counsel would be encouraged to wait until trial before making any objections, with the hope

---

7   Fed. R. Civ. P. 30(d)(2); Model Rules of Prof'l Conduct r. 3.4(a); Model Rules of Prof'l Conduct r. 8.4(d).

8   Fed. R. Civ. P. 32(d)(3)(B)(i).

that the testimony, although relevant, would be excluded altogether because of the manner in which it was elicited.[9]

Oath or Affirmation

Objections to the manner of taking the deposition and the oath or affirmation apply narrowly to technical and procedural issues, and they occur infrequently.[10] For example, if nobody is legally authorized to administer the oath under the jurisdiction's rules, an objection to the oath must be raised at the deposition's outset.[11]

Parties' Conduct

Objections to a party's conduct encompass misconduct among attorneys and witnesses, including both physical and verbal abuse, but are unrelated to the substance of the deponent's testimony itself.[12] By stating an objection to the examining attorney's conduct, the defending attorney gives the examiner an opportunity to correct the misconduct.

If abusive and properly objectionable conduct persists, the appropriate procedure is to suspend the deposition under Fed. R. Civ. P. 30(d)(3)(A), to move for a protective order.[13] Rule 30(d)(3)(A) states:

> At any time during a deposition, the deponent or a party may move to terminate or limit it on the ground that it is being

---

9 *Bah. Agric. Indus. Ltd. v. Riley Stoker Corp.*, 526 F.2d 1174, 1181 (6th Cir. 1975); *see Kirschner v. Broadhead*, 671 F.2d 1034, 1037-38 (7th Cir. 1982) (adopting the same reasoning from *Bah. Agric. Indus. Ltd.*).

10 *See Cabello v. Fernandez-Larios*, 402 F.3d 1148, 1160 (11th Cir. 2005); *Feeley v. City of Billings, Mont.*, 2013 WL 65410 at *3 (D. Mont. Jan. 3, 2013).

11 *Cabello*, 402 F.3d at 1160 (defending counsel constructively waived the right at trial to object to a defect in the oath by refusing to accept plaintiffs' offer to procure an authorized notary for the remaining depositions: "The rules distinguish objections to the manner of taking the deposition from objections as to the substance of the testimony (such as relevancy or competency) because allowing counsel to wait until trial to object might encourage sandbagging.").

12 *See GMAC Bank v. HTFC Corp.*, 248 F.R.D. 182, 186-193 (E.D. Pa. 2008); *Zottola v. Anesthesia Consultants of Savannah, P.C.*, 2012 WL 6824150 at *6 (S.D. Ga. June 7, 2012).

13 *See* Chapter 6 of this book for more information on suspending the deposition due to harassment.

conducted in bad faith or in a manner that unreasonably annoys, embarrasses, or oppresses the deponent or party.[14]

When the lawyer asking questions faces continued disruptions, he or she has the authority to suspend the deposition to file a motion for protective order.[15] The lawyer also may choose to continue with the deposition and seek sanctions following its conclusion.

Objections to Deposition Questions

Objections to questions during depositions fall within three general categories:

1. Objections asserting that the substance of the testimony would be inadmissible at trial

Objections claiming that the substance of the testimony would be inadmissible can be decided only by the court. Therefore, those objections are preserved for trial and are improper during the deposition. (See Chapter 5 for further discussion.)

2. Objections to immediately correctable evidentiary issues (also known as "objections to foundation")

If the lawyer can cure an evidentiary problem, such as the failure to establish the foundational requirement that the witness has personal knowledge, such an objection *must* be made during the deposition.

3. Objections to how a question is phrased (also known as "objections to form")

Objections to correctable form errors must be made at the time of the deposition. This chapter discusses what makes the structure of a question objectionable, as well as the appropriate way to raise such objections.

---

14   Fed. R. Civ. P. 30(d)(3)(A).

15   Fed. R. Civ. P. 30(d)(3)(A).

Objections to Correctable Evidentiary and Foundational Errors

Rule 32(d)(3)(A) requires lawyers to raise objections to evidentiary issues if the ground for the objection can be corrected at the deposition.

> *Objection to Competence, Relevance, or Materiality.* An objection to a deponent's competence—or to the competence, relevance, or materiality of testimony—is not waived by a failure to make the objection before or during the deposition, *unless the ground for it might have been corrected at that time.*[16]

The inclusion of "competence" in the rule's language causes confusion, because competence objections are explicitly preserved for trial, yet the rule also requires raising objections to immediately correctable evidentiary defects in the questions. The distinction between Federal Rules of Evidence 601 and 602 helps resolve this confusion. Rule 601 requires a witness to have the mental capacity to testify.[17] Rule 602 requires that a witness have personal knowledge of the facts for the testimony to be admissible—commonly known as foundation.[18]

Under Rule 601, every witness is presumed to have the mental capacity to testify at trial.[19] However, if a given witness does not, state common law is used to determine whether that witness is competent to testify. Rule 601 states:

> [I]n a civil case, state law governs the witness's competency regarding a claim or defense for which state law supplies the rule of decision.[20]

The Advisory Committee Notes to the rules clarify the practical application of Rule 601:

---

16 Fed. R. Civ. P. 32(d)(3)(A) (emphasis added).
17 Fed. R. Evid. 601.
18 Fed. R. Evid. 602.
19 Fed. R. Evid. 601.
20 Fed. R. Evid. 601.

A witness wholly without capacity is difficult to imagine. The question is one particularly suited to the jury as one of weight and credibility, subject to judicial authority to review the sufficiency of the evidence.[21]

Under Rule 32(d)(3)(A), objections to a witness's competence due to a lack of capacity are preserved and therefore unnecessary during the deposition.

Although a witness's mental capacity is a competence objection preserved for trial, the witness's basis to testify regarding personal knowledge is different. Whether the court has sufficient information to rule that the witness has or lacks this basis is an evidentiary issue that could be corrected or established during the deposition. This is known as evidentiary "foundation." Fed. R. Evid. 602 requires witnesses to testify at trial only to matters of personal knowledge. Rule 602 states:

> A witness may testify to a matter only if evidence is introduced sufficient to support a finding that the witness has personal knowledge of the matter. Evidence to prove personal knowledge may consist of the witness's own testimony. This rule does not apply to a witness's expert testimony under Rule 703.[22]

For the deposition to be admissible at trial, the foundational requirements that the witness had the opportunity to observe and actually did observe the fact or occurrence must be established.[23] The Advisory Committee Notes explain the requirements to establish the testimony's foundation:

> "[T]he rule requiring that a witness who testifies to a fact which can be perceived by the senses must have had an opportunity to observe, and must have actually observed the fact" is a "most pervasive manifestation" of the common law insistence upon "the most reliable sources of information."

---

21 Fed. R. Evid. 601, advisory committee's note on proposed rules (citing 2 Wigmore, Evidence §§ 501, 509 (3d ed. 1940).

22 Fed. R. Evid. 602.

23 Fed. R. Evid. 602, advisory committee's note on proposed rules.

McCormick § 10, p. 19. These foundation requirements may, of course, be furnished by the testimony of the witness himself; hence personal knowledge is not an absolute but may consist of what the witness thinks he knows from personal perception. 2 Wigmore § 650.[24]

If the deposition testimony does not establish that the witness has personal knowledge of the matter in question, then the defending attorney must make a Rule 602 objection to the witness's competence to preserve it for trial.[25] The examining attorney can then ask the foundational questions necessary to establish that the witness has personal knowledge of the facts being discussed. Objections to speculation or opinion without qualification fall under correctable Rule 602 objections to competence, which are collectively known as foundation objections. These objections are waived for trial if not raised at the deposition.

Objections to the Form of the Question

Objections to foundational errors differ from objections to form: Objections to foundation relate to the failure to establish that the witness has personal knowledge, while form objections relate to the structure of a question.

Rule 32(d)(3)(B)(i) requires defending lawyers to raise objections to the form of a question at the deposition so the examining lawyer can correct the error. The rule states:

> *Objection to an Error or Irregularity.* An objection to an error or irregularity at an oral examination is waived if:
>
> (i) it relates to the manner of taking the deposition, *the form of a question or answer*, the oath or affirmation, a party's conduct, or other matters that might have been corrected at that time.[26]

---

24 Fed. R. Evid. 602, advisory committee's note on proposed rules.

25 *Jordan v. Medley*, 711 F.2d 211, 218 (D.C. Cir. 1983); *Nutterville v McLam*, 367 P.2d 576, 578-79 (Idaho 1961).

26 Fed. R. Civ. P. 32(d)(3)(B)(i) (emphasis added).

An error in the form of a question involves the improper structure of the question itself. Common examples include questions that are leading, compound, overbroad, or argumentative, or that call for excessive narration.[27] Objections to the question's form enable the examining lawyer to recraft the question and cure the objection before trial.

Are Leading Questions Appropriate?

Whether a leading question is permissible at a deposition depends on the deponent's legal relationship to the examiner. Fed. R. Evid. 611(c) states:

> **Leading Questions.** Leading questions should not be used on direct examination except as necessary to develop the witness's testimony. Ordinarily, the court should allow leading questions:
>
> **(1)** on cross-examination; and
>
> **(2)** when a party calls a hostile witness, an adverse party, or a witness identified with an adverse party.[28]

Applying Fed. R. Evid. 611(c) to depositions, leading questions must be objected to when the examining lawyer is questioning his or her own client or a fact witness that he or she has selected. The only exception is when a witness is unable to communicate effectively.[29] In these situations, leading questions may be allowed to develop the testimony. If the witness is an adverse party, identified with an adverse party, or deemed a hostile witness, leading questions are permissible.

Technique: Proper Use of Leading Questions

You, the plaintiff's attorney, are deposing the defendant driver in an auto accident lawsuit:

Q Isn't it true that you saw the red car when you entered the intersection?

---

27 *Kirschner*, 671 F.2d at 1037-38; *Oberlin v. Marlin Am. Corp.*, 596 F.2d 1322, 1328 (7th Cir. 1979); *Elyria-Lorain Broad. Co. v. Lorain Journal Co.*, 298 F.2d 356, 360 (6th Cir. 1961).

28 Fed. R. Evid. 611(c).

29 3 Wigmore §§ 774-778 (examples include children, people with diminished mental capacity, and witnesses whose memory has temporarily lapsed).

Objection, leading.

Q Are you suggesting that I can't lead an adverse party?

No.

Q Isn't it true that you saw the red car when you entered the intersection?

A Yes.

You have now established on the record that the objection was spurious. Leading questions are allowed when the deponent is an adverse party, and any additional objections to leading questions during your questioning are improper.

Technique: Curing Compound Questions

You, the plaintiff's attorney, are deposing a witness in a wrongful death lawsuit:

Q Why did you wait so long to call the police, and when you finally did call them, what exactly did you say?

Objection, form.

At this point, there are two scenarios based on your understanding of the objection.

Scenario 1: You realize you asked a compound question and correct the problem by rephrasing:

Q Why did you wait so long to call the police?

A I was so shocked—I didn't know what to do.

Q What did you say to the dispatcher when you finally did call?

Scenario 2: The error in the form isn't immediately evident, so you ask for clarification:

Q Counsel, please briefly clarify the ground for your form objection.

Compound question.

Q Why did you wait so long to call the police?

A I was so shocked—I didn't know what to do.

Q What did you say to the dispatcher when you finally did call?

Technique: Curing Excessive Narration

You, the plaintiff's lawyer in an auto accident lawsuit, want to establish that the defendant driver did not maintain proper awareness, which caused the collision:

Q Tell us what happened when you entered the intersection.

Objection, form.

Q What is the problem with the form?

Calls for excessive narration.

At this point, the technique is to continue with the broad question to learn the universe of information known to the witness. Then, restate and summarize the answer using one question for each fact to ensure a clear record.[30]

Q Go ahead and answer, please.

A I was driving down 8th. When I got to the intersection, I stopped for the stop sign and looked left and right. I didn't see any cars coming, so I turned left. I knew it was clear because it was a flat highway. I've been on it a million times. I was good. It was a beautiful day and I was maintaining a proper lookout, because I always do. That's what I was taught in school, and I always do it because I am always a safe driver. That's the way my daddy taught me. Anyway, I turned left and turned on my radio. And I'm rolling along listening to the Stones. Probably almost a minute. They are the best. Anyway, I am cruising and out of nowhere I see this car stopped on the road with some fool behind it. What the hell. . . . Anyway, there isn't anything I can do. BAM! It's a wreck—damn, I can't believe that guy was between me and his car. It was a crash.

Q Let me make sure I understand what you just said. To begin, you pull up to the stop sign?

A Yes.

Q You know the intersection?

A Yep, been on it hundreds of times.

Q The road is flat?

A Yes.

---

30 Phillip H. Miller & Paul J. Scoptur, Advanced Depositions Strategy & Practice 67–77 (Trial Guides 2013).

Q It is straight?
A That's what I said, isn't it? Yes.
Q You have a clear view to the horizon?
A Yes.
Q And you have a clear view of the highway?
A Yep.
Q So you turn left?
A Yes.
Q You accelerate?
A Yes. That's how you drive a car, last time I checked.
Q You turn on the car radio?
A Yes, I did. I always play the radio in the car.
Q The Stones are playing?
A Yes sir. Saw 'em in '93. They're my favorite band.
Q All of a sudden you see a disabled car in the road?
A Yeah. It came out of nowhere.
Q You see a man behind it?
A Well, yeah.
Q You crash into the car?
A Yes.
Q You crush the man between your cars?
A Uh, yeah. I guess I hit him.

You have now cured the objection to excessive narration by summarizing and confirming the crucial sequence of facts with the deponent.[31]

How to Object Properly

When raising any objections at the deposition stage, lawyers must tread carefully. There is a precarious balance between preserving an objection and coaching the witness.

---

31   Miller & Scoptur, 67–77.

Objections Must Be Concise, Nonargumentative, and Nonsuggestive

Federal Rule of Civil Procedure 30(c)(2) details the procedure for proper objections at an oral deposition:

> **Objections.** An objection at the time of the examination—whether to evidence, to a party's conduct, to the officer's qualifications, to the manner of taking the deposition, or to any other aspect of the deposition—must be noted on the record, but the examination still proceeds; the testimony is taken subject to any objection. *An objection must be stated concisely in a nonargumentative and nonsuggestive manner.* A person may instruct a deponent not to answer only when necessary to preserve a privilege, to enforce a limitation ordered by the court, or to present a motion under Rule 30(d)(3).[32]

The court in *In re Stratosphere* explained this rule's broad and binding scope:

> This Court can find no better or more succinct definition or description of what is and what is not a valid deposition objection than that found in [Rule 30(c)(2)].[33]

As such, an objection's appropriateness always must be evaluated based on the requirement that all objections be concise, nonargumentative, and nonsuggestive.[34]

How to Object to Correctable Errors of Substance and Form: Two Schools of Jurisprudence

Inherent tension lies between the requirements of Rule 30(c)(2) and Rules 32(d)(3)(A-B). Rule 30(c)(2) requires all objections to "be stated concisely in a nonargumentative and nonsuggestive manner."[35] This is the lens

---

32 Fed. R. Civ. P. 30(c)(2) (emphasis added).

33 *In re Stratosphere Corp. Sec. Litig.*, 182 F.R.D. 614, 617 (D. Nev. 1998) (referencing Fed. R. Civ. P. Rule 30(d)(1) (amended 1993), which was equivalent to current Rule 30(c)(2) and read: "Any objection to evidence during a deposition shall be stated concisely and in a non-argumentative and non-suggestive manner.").

34 Fed. R. Civ. P. 30(c)(2).

35 Fed. R. Civ. P. 30(c)(2).

through which courts evaluate the propriety of all deposition objections. However, Rules 32(d)(3)(A-B) also require attorneys to raise objections to form, substance, and other matters that "might have been corrected at that time," to preserve them for trial.

If the Rule 32(d)(3) objection suggests how the deponent should answer the question, the rules conflict. The method of stating the objection is critical to reconciling this tension between the rules. Courts have created two approaches to properly raising objections at depositions—with contradicting requirements.

Approach 1: "Objection to Form" Only

Many courts have recognized the potential that any explanation of the ground for the objection, no matter how concise, suggests a preferred answer to the deponent. In response, these courts have banned any explanation of the ground for an objection *unless the examining attorney requests it*. Jurisdictions seeking to strictly limit the possibility of any suggestive objections by defending counsel have instituted the requirements the court established in *Damaj v. Farmers Insurance Co. Inc.*:[36]

> Counsel's statements when making objections should be succinct and verbally economical, stating the basis of the objection and nothing more. If the form of the question is objectionable, counsel should say nothing other than "object to the form of the question." Should deposing counsel desire clarification of the precise basis of the objection, that inquiry shall be made outside the presence of the witness.[37]

---

36   *See Damaj v. Farmers Ins. Co., Inc.*, 164 F.R.D. 559, 561 (N.D. Okla. 1995); *Auscape Int'l v. Nat'l Geographic Soc'y*, 2002 WL 31014829 at *1 (S.D.N.Y. Sept. 6, 2002); *Turner v. Glock, Inc.*, 2004 WL 5511620 at *1 (E.D. Tex. Mar. 29, 2004); *In re St. Jude Med. Inc.*, 2002 WL 1050311 at *5 (D. Minn. May 24, 2002); *Meyer Corp. US v. Alfay Designs, Inc.*, 2012 WL 3536987 at *4 (E.D.N.Y. Aug. 13, 2012); *Valencia v. City of Santa Fe*, 2013 WL 12180535 at *2 (D.N.M. Jan. 11, 2013); *Quantachrome Corp. v. Micromeritics Instrument Corp.*, 189 F.R.D. 697, 701 n.4 (S.D. Fla. 1999); *Applied Telematics, Inc. v. Sprint Corp.*, 1995 WL 79237 at *1 (E.D. Pa. Feb. 22, 1995).

37   *Damaj*, 164 F.R.D. at 561; *see Fort Worth Emps.' Ret. Fund v. J.P. Morgan Chase & Co.*, 2013 WL 6439069 at *4 (S.D.N.Y Dec. 9, 2013).

The court in *Damaj* recognized the valid concern that a perceptive witness could use any explanation of an objection's ground, regardless of its brevity, as a cue to parrot his or her attorney's objection in his or her response. This scenario occurred in *Meyer Corp. U.S. v. Alfay Designs, Inc.*, when the deponent responded "I don't know" almost every time the defending attorney made a concise objection to the question being speculative.[38] In *Applied Telematics, Inc. v. Sprint Corp.*, the court required that objections be limited to the word "form":

> Such suggestive [speaking] objections should be prohibited, limiting responses by counsel to the statement "objection to form." . . . "Objection to form" should be sufficient explanation to notify the interrogator of the ground for the objection, and thereby allow revision of the question.[39]

Following this reasoning, Judge John Tunheim, in his pretrial order in *In re St. Jude Medical, Inc.*, required that "[o]bjecting counsel shall say simply the word 'objection', and no more, to preserve all objections as to form."[40]

These same requirements extend to the correctable evidentiary objections required by Rules 32(d)(3)(A-B). "Similarly [to form objections], objections as to foundation should be simply stated as such: 'Objection, foundation.'"[41]

Approach 2: "Objections to Form or Foundation" Require a Concise Explanation

Other courts have expressed frustration with repeated deposition disruptions due to often unfounded objections to form, which ultimately require

---

[38] See *Meyer Corp.*, 2012 WL 3536987 at *4 ("There should not be any comment that a question is speculative. Elaboration is permitted only where examining counsel requests the basis of the objection.").

[39] *Applied Telematics*, 1995 WL 79237 at *1.

[40] *In re St. Jude Med., Inc.*, 2002 WL 1050311 at *5 (D. Minn. May 24, 2002).

[41] *Meyer Corp.*, 2012 WL 3536987 at *4.

extensive judicial rulings.[42] The court in *Vargas v. Florida Crystals Corp.* criticized a procedure in which a lawyer could repeatedly state "objection, form" at a deposition without specifying the specific nature of the defect, which would then allow the objecting lawyer to "conjure up" numerous reasons why the form was improper in a subsequent motion.[43] Further, unspecified form objections place undue responsibility on the court to decide deposition disputes after the fact:

> When called upon to rule on an unspecified "form" objection, a judge either must be clairvoyant or must guess as to the objection's basis. Neither option is particularly realistic or satisfying.[44]

These courts require counsel to specify the defect in the objection *without suggesting how a question should be answered*.[45] If a lawyer fails to specify the basis for the objection, these courts consider those objections to be waived.[46]

This approach creates a Herculean task for attorneys defending depositions. Any explanatory word embedded in the objection is inherently suggestive to a perceptive witness. Once the cue is given, a Pavlovian response from the witness often follows.

---

42   See *Henderson v. B & B Precast & Pipe, LLC*, 2014 WL 4063673 at *1 (M.D. Ga. Aug. 14, 2014); *Sec. Nat. Bank of Sioux City, Iowa v. Abbott Labs.*, 299 F.R.D. 595, 601-602 (N.D. Iowa 2014), *rev'd on other grounds sub nom. Sec. Nat. Bank of Sioux City, IA v. Day*, 800 F.3d 936 (8th Cir. 2015); *Fletcher v. Honeywell Int'l, Inc.*, 2017 WL 775852 at *1 (S.D. Ohio Feb. 28, 2017).

43   *Vargas v. Fla. Crystals Corp.*, 2017 WL 1861775 at *6 (S.D. Fla. May 5, 2017).

44   *Sec. Nat'l Bank of Sioux City, Iowa*, 299 F.R.D. at 603; *see Ethox Chem., LLC v. Coca-Cola Co.*, 2016 WL 7053351 at *7 n.5 (D.S.C Feb. 29, 2016) ("It would be impossible for the court to judge the validity of the unspecified form objections as the undersigned would have to guess as to each objection's basis.").

45   See *Vargas*, 2017 WL 1861775 at *6; *Fletcher*, 2017 WL 775852 at *1; *Sec. Nat'l Bank of Sioux City, Iowa*, 299 F.R.D. at 602-03; *Henderson*, 2014 WL 4063673 at * 1; *Ethox Chem.*, 2016 WL 7053351 at *7; *Abu Dhabi Commercial Bank v. Morgan Stanley & Co. Inc.*, 2011 WL 4526141 at *8 (S.D.N.Y. Sept. 21, 2011).

46   See *Vargas*, 2017 WL 1861775 at *6; *Fletcher*, 2017 WL 775852 at *1; *Sec. Nat'l Bank of Sioux City, Iowa*, 299 F.R.D. at 602-03 (ruling that form objections without providing the ground for the objection would be sanctioned, but the court did not rule whether they would be waived); *Henderson*, 2014 WL 4063673 at *1.

Unscrupulous attorneys could coach their clients before the deposition to respond to certain recognizable objections with specific answers, such as "I don't know" and "What do you mean?" U.S. District Judge James Rosenbaum addressed the inherent dangers of witness coaching and improperly communicating with the jury by way of suggestive objections. In the trial of *Boswell v. County of Sherburne*, Judge Rosenbaum required all objections to be limited to the word "objection" and the corresponding evidentiary rule number.[47] For example, a lawyer objecting to hearsay had to state "objection, 801," rather than "objection, hearsay." By requiring the lawyers to know the Rules of Evidence by number, Judge Rosenbaum mitigated the danger of improperly sending signals to the witness and jury. Judge Rosenbaum's approach is an effective solution that balances the need to preserve a record with the need to avoid suggesting an answer to the witness.

Summary

- **Correctable objections are waived for trial if not raised at the deposition:**

    - Objections to the manner of taking the deposition must be raised.

    - Objections to the oath or affirmation of the officer must be raised.

    - Objections to a party's misconduct must be raised.

    - Objections to immediately correctable evidentiary issues (Fed. R. Evid. 602, foundation) must be raised.

    - Objections to the form of the question must be raised.

- **Deposition objections must be concise, nonargumentative, and nonsuggestive.**

---

47   In 1989, Mark Kosieradzki tried a civil rights case, *Boswell v. Cty. of Sherburne*, Civ. No. 4-86-156, before Judge Rosenbaum. In that trial, Judge Rosenbaum ordered that all objections be restricted to stating the word "objection" and the evidence rule (by number only) alleged to have been violated.

- **There are two schools of jurisprudence on how to properly object to form:**
  - Approach 1: State only "objection as to form."
  - Approach 2: Objections to form require a concise explanation.

CHAPTER 5
PROHIBITED OBJECTIONS

*"If they can get you asking the wrong questions,
they don't have to worry about answers."*

—Thomas Pynchon[1]

---

1 Thomas Pynchon, Gravity's Rainbow 255 (1973).

Introduction

The previous chapter discussed objections that must be made at the time of the deposition. This chapter describes the objections that should not be made at the deposition and should be saved for trial instead.

Objections Asserting That the Substance of the Testimony Would Be Inadmissible at Trial

Fed. R. Civ. P. 32(d)(3) preserves for trial all objections to the admissibility of the testimony's substance, except objections that could notify the examiner of an evidentiary defect. These objections must be raised if the defect is immediately curable.

Rule 32(d)(3)(A) expressly lists competence, relevance, and materiality of a witness or testimony as objections that are preserved for trial.

> *Objection to Competence, Relevance, or Materiality.* An objection to a deponent's competence—or to the competence, relevance, or materiality of testimony—is not waived by a failure to make the objection before or during the deposition, unless the ground for it might have been corrected at that time.[2]

Regardless of how the question is asked, admissibility will be determined by the judge at trial. There is no way to rephrase an examiner's question to cure these purported evidentiary defects.

The Advisory Committee, in the notes to the 1993 amendments, explained why objections should be limited to correctable errors:

> Depositions frequently have been unduly prolonged, if not unfairly frustrated, by lengthy objections and colloquy, often suggesting how the deponent should respond. While objections may, under the revised rule, be made during a deposition,

---

2   Fed. R. Civ. P. 32(d)(3)(A).

they ordinarily should be limited to those that under Rule 32(d)(3) might be waived if not made at that time.[3]

The purpose of allowing objections to be raised later is to permit the preliminary examination to proceed without constant interruptions.[4] Interference with the deposition's orderly flow and the meaningful elicitation of testimony by excessive objections is prohibited.[5] *Therefore, objections that are not required to be asserted at the deposition are inappropriate if raised then.*[6]

Relevance Objections

Relevance objections are impermissible at depositions—they are preserved by Rule 32(d)(3)(A)'s express language. Objections to relevance run counter to the deposition's overall purpose and spirit and should be reserved for trial.[7] The court in *In re Stratosphere Corp. Securities Litigation* explained why relevance objections are unnecessary at depositions:

> It is difficult to conceive of the likelihood that a question which calls for irrelevant information can be "cured" by restating the question, unless the question is changed to ask for relevant (*i.e.,* different) information. Accordingly, it would be rare that an irrelevant question could be cured. Thus, the objecting party may wait until trial (or just prior to trial) to make the objection when, and if, the deposition testimony is offered into evidence.[8]

Because the relevance of a question or line of inquiry will be determined by the judge at the pretrial or trial, a relevance objection need not

---

[3] Fed. R. Civ. P. 30, 1993 advisory committee's note subd. d.

[4] Herr & Haydock, Civil Rules Annotated § 30.22, at 107 (3d ed. 1998).

[5] *See In re Stratosphere Corp. Sec. Litig.*, 182 F.R.D. 614, 616-19 (D. Nev. 1998) (citing *Am. Directory Serv. Agency, Inc. v. Beam*, 131 F.R.D. 15, 18-19 (D.D.C. 1990)); *see also* Fed. R. Civ. P. 30(d)(2).

[6] Herr & Haydock at 107.

[7] *See Hall v. Clifton Precision, a Div. of Litton Sys., Inc.*, 150 F.R.D. 525, 528 (E.D. Pa. 1993) ("One of the purposes of the discovery rules in general, and the deposition rules in particular, is to elicit the facts of a case before trial.").

[8] *In re Stratosphere Corp. Sec. Litig.*, 182 F.R.D. at 618.

be raised at the deposition. It is not a curable evidentiary issue and is therefore improper during the deposition.

Beyond the Scope Objections

Objections to questions being "beyond the scope" of permissible discovery are functionally the same as objections to relevance, even though they are not explicitly mentioned in Rule 32(d)(3)(A). In *Cincinnati Insurance Co. v. Serrano*, the court explained that scope objections do not pertain to questions of evidentiary admissibility. Rather, like relevance, "beyond the scope" focuses on Rule 26(b), which is not a permissible objection at a deposition:

> [A]n objection that the question, . . . exceeds the scope of discovery under Rule 26(b) . . . does not come within the rule or exceptions to Rule 32, which is concerned with the admissibility of deposition responses as evidence. . . . [T]he principle suggests that such objections are inappropriate. The scope of discovery under Rule 26 is broad, and such an objection will rarely prevail.[9]

If defending counsel legitimately believes that the examiner is asking questions so far beyond the proper scope of discovery that the deposition is being conducted "in bad faith or in a manner that unreasonably annoys, embarrasses, or oppresses the deponent," the proper recourse is to suspend the questioning and file a Rule 30(d)(3)(A) motion to limit the deposition.[10]

Hearsay Objections

Hearsay is an evidentiary objection that is preserved for trial, although it is not expressly enumerated in Rule 32(d)(3)(A). Whether a question calls for hearsay is strictly a substantive evidentiary matter that cannot be resolved by rephrasing a question. In *Johnson v. Nationwide Mutual Insurance Co.*, the U.S. Court of Appeals for the Fourth Circuit stated:

---

9   *Cincinnati Ins. Co. v. Serrano*, 2012 WL 28071 at *5 (D. Kan. Jan. 5, 2012).

10   Fed. R. Civ. P. 30(d)(3)(A); *see* Chapter 6 of this book for more information on Rule 30(d)(3)(A) motions.

Since the [hearsay] objection was to the admissibility of the evidence, the ground of the objection could not have been obviated or removed at the time of the taking of the depositions.[11]

Courts have cited *Johnson* repeatedly, with universal agreement that hearsay objections are preserved for trial.[12] Objections to hearsay are improper during the deposition.

Witness Coaching During a Deposition Is Universally Prohibited

"[T]he law clearly prohibits a lawyer from coaching a witness during a deposition."[13] In *Hall v. Clifton Precision*, Judge Robert Gawthrop precisely summarized why witness coaching is antithetical to the purpose of depositions:

> The underlying purpose of a deposition is to find out what a witness saw, heard, or did—what the witness thinks. A deposition is meant to be a question-and-answer conversation between the deposing lawyer and the witness. There is no proper need for the witness's own lawyer to act as an intermediary, interpreting questions, deciding which questions the witness should answer, and helping the witness to formulate answers. The witness comes to the deposition to testify, not to indulge in a parody of Charlie McCarthy, with lawyers coaching or bending the witness's words to mold a legally convenient record. It is the witness—not the lawyer—who is the witness.[14]

---

11 *Johnson v. Nationwide Mut. Ins. Co.*, 276 F.2d 574, 579 (4th Cir. 1960).

12 *See* 7 James William Moore, Moore's Federal Practice § 3242 (2012); *Farr Man Coffee, Inc. v. Chester*, 1993 WL 248799 at *20 (S.D.N.Y. June 28, 1993); *Henderson v. Turner*, 2012 WL 3109481 at *1 (M.D. La. July 31, 2012); *NGM Ins. Co. v. Walker Const. & Dev., LLC*, 2012 WL 6553272 at *2 (E.D. Tenn. Dec. 13, 2012) (entertaining hearsay objections that were not raised at the deposition); *Sequoia Prop. & Equip. Ltd. P'ship v. US*, 2002 WL 507537 at *2 (E.D. Cal. Feb. 5, 2002) (objections on the ground of hearsay are not valid during a deposition based on the breadth of discovery).

13 *The Sec. Nat'l Bank of Sioux City, Iowa v. Abbott Labs.*, 299 F.R.D. 595, 604 (N.D. Iowa 2014); *see also Hall*, 150 F.R.D. at 530.

14 *Hall*, 150 F.R.D. at 528.

Prohibited witness coaching includes coaching under the guise of meritorious objections as well as blatant instructions. Despite the Federal Rules' prohibition on witness coaching, some lawyers prompt witnesses to give particular, desired answers to the examiner's questions in numerous subtle and not-so-subtle ways.

Example: Prohibited Witness Coaching—Passing Notes

Some lawyers have used brazen methods to impermissibly coach their clients mid-deposition.

Written Notes:

In *Vnuk v. Berwick Hospital Co.*, the defending attorney communicated with the deponent throughout the deposition. He whispered to his client during pending questions and showed his client a notepad that had directions written on it. The court ruled the defending attorney's communication with his client mid-deposition to be "wholly inappropriate, unprofessional, and . . . sanctionable."

Vnuk v. Berwick Hosp. Co., 2016 WL 907714 at *4 (M.D. Pa. Mar. 2, 2016).

Text Messages:

In *Ngai v. Old Navy*, the witness was testifying remotely through a video stream, and his hands were not visible on screen. The defending attorney sent text messages to the deponent during active questioning in the deposition. His conduct was discovered only when he accidentally sent a text to examining counsel instead of the deponent, which read, "[you][are] doing fine." The defending attorney claimed the text message was intended for his son, which was untrue. The court ruled that the messages sent between the attorney and the deponent during the deposition were not protected under attorney-client privilege, and that the attorney's conduct directly violated Rule 30. The court ordered the preservation and disclosure of all the text messages to opposing counsel.

Ngai v. Old Navy, 2009 WL 2391282 at *1, 4 (D.N.J. July 31, 2009).

Speaking Objections

Speaking objections occur when the defending counsel uses objections and interruptions to suggest answers to the deponent.[15] Using comments contained in the objection, the lawyer directs the witness's attention to what the "correct answer should be."[16] When witnesses are coached through objections, they often parrot the lawyer's comment in the answer.[17] Rule 30(c)(2) prohibits this form of witness coaching.[18] The court in *Hall v. Clifton Precision* explained the logic behind the prohibition, as well as its importance:

> The Federal Rules of Evidence contain no provision allowing lawyers to interrupt the trial testimony of a witness to make a statement. Such behavior should likewise be prohibited at depositions, since it tends to obstruct the taking of the witness's testimony. It should go without saying that *lawyers are strictly prohibited from making any comments, either on or off the record, which might suggest or limit a witness's answer to an unobjectionable question.*
>
> In short, depositions are to be limited to what they were and are intended to be: question-and-answer sessions between a lawyer and a witness aimed at uncovering the facts in a lawsuit. When a deposition becomes something other than that

---

15   *Applied Telematics, Inc. v. Sprint Corp.*, 1995 WL 79237 at *1 (E.D. Pa. Feb. 22, 1995).

16   *Applied Telematics*, 1995 WL 79237 at *1 (citing the Federal Bar Council Comm. on Second Circuit Courts, A Report on the Conduct of Depositions, 131 F.R.D. 613, 617 (1990) (quoted by Virginia E. Hench, "Mandatory Disclosure and Equal Access to Justice: The 1993 Federal Discovery Rules Amendments and the Just, Speedy and Inexpensive Determination of Every Action," *Temp. L. Rev.* 67 (1994): 179, 218 n.182).

17   *McDonough v. Keniston*, 188 F.R.D. 22, 24 (D.N.H. Nov. 1998); *see also Cordova v. United States*, 2006 WL 4109659 at *3 (D.N.M. July 30, 2006) (awarding sanctions based on a lawyer's deposition coaching because "it became impossible to know if [a witness's] answers emanated from her own line of reasoning or whether she adopted [the] lawyer's reasoning from listening to his objections").

18   *See Specht v. Google, Inc.*, 268 F.R.D. 596, 598 (N.D. Ill. 2010) (citing *Jadwin v. Abraham*, 2008 WL 4057921 at *6-7 (E.D. Cal. Aug. 22, 2008); *Heriaud v. Ryder Transp. Servs.*, 2005 WL 2230199 at *2-9 (N.D. Ill. Sept. 8, 2005); *AG Equip. Co. v. AIG Life Ins. Co.*, 2008 WL 5205192 at *2-4 (N.D. Okla. Dec. 10, 2008); *Deville v. Givaudan Fragrances Corp.*, 2010 WL 2232718 at *6-8 (D.N.J. June 1, 2010)); *see also Applied Telematics*, 1995 WL 79237; *McDonough*, 188 F.R.D. at 24 ("Speaking objections and coaching objections are simply not permitted in depositions in federal cases.").

because of the strategic interruptions, suggestions, statements, and arguments of counsel, it not only becomes unnecessarily long, but it ceases to serve the purpose of the Federal Rules of Civil Procedure: to find . . . the truth.[19]

Objections to correctable errors must be made with caution to ensure that the comment does not coach or suggest an answer to the witness.[20] If the objection suggests how to answer the question, it directly violates the controlling "nonsuggestive" requirement in Rule 30(c)(2).

Example: Improper Speaking Objection

Defending counsel launched into a lengthy statement about the broadness of the examiner's question:

Q   . . . why don't you do your best to tell me what you say he did wrong?

I think that's a very broad, broad question. I think it's too broad to be answered. It calls for legal characterizations. He had no connection, he had no contact directly with Chuck Douglas except for one hearing. . . .

McDonough v. Keniston, 188. F.R.D 22, 24 (D.N.H. 1998).

The deponent then adopted his lawyer's language by complaining that the questions were too broad.[21] The court declared that the lawyer's conduct was an impermissible speaking objection and issued sanctions, ruling that "[s]peaking objections and coaching objections are simply not permitted in depositions in federal cases."[22]

---

19   *Hall*, 150 F.R.D. at 530-31 (emphasis added).

20   *Cullen v. Nissan N. Am., Inc.*, 2010 WL 11579750 at *5 (M.D. Tenn. Feb. 2, 2010) ("Providing the basis for the objection without coaching or suggesting an answer to the deponent requires some finesse.").

21   *McDonough*, 188. F.R.D. at 25.

22   *McDonough*, 188. F.R.D. at 24.

"If You Know" Interjections Are Prohibited Speaking Objections

The tactic of concluding objections by telling the witness, "you can answer if you know" is prohibited coaching. As the court in *Cincinnati Insurance Co. v. Serrano* explained, "if you know" interjections are never appropriate:

> Instructions to a witness that they may answer a question "if they know" or "if they understand the question" are *raw, unmitigated coaching and are never appropriate.* This conduct, if it persists after the deposing attorney requests that it stop, is misconduct and sanctionable.[23]

The court in *Security National Bank of Sioux City, Iowa v. Abbott Laboratories* explained the underlying purpose of the "if you know" prohibition:

> When a lawyer tells a witness to answer "if you know," it not-so-subtly suggests that the witness may not know the answer, inviting the witness to dodge or qualify an otherwise clear question.[24]

"If you know" speaking objections are a subtle form of coaching the deponent not to answer, which Rule 30(c)(2) expressly prohibits.[25] After receiving this instruction, witnesses often claim to be unable to answer the question. This "if you know" technique is sanctionable misconduct.[26] Defending counsel is never allowed to coach the witness being examined.

Technique: Make a Record of Speaking Objections

If the defending lawyer states speaking objections, make a record of them. For example:

Q Are these ten ingredients in every bottle of lotion that you sell?

If you know. Don't guess.

---

23 *Serrano*, 2012 WL 28071 at *5 (emphasis added).

24 *Sec. Nat'l Bank of Sioux City, Iowa*, 299 F.R.D. at 607.

25 Fed. R. Civ. P. 30(c)(2) (only three instances when an instruction not to answer is proper: to preserve a privilege, to enforce a court-ordered discovery limitation, or to file a motion under Rule 30(d)(3)); *see* Chapter 6 of this book for analysis of instructions not to answer.

26 *Serrano*, 2012 WL 28071 at *5.

Q   Please don't make suggestive comments in the presence of the witness.

Q   Are these ten ingredients in every bottle of lotion that you sell?

A   Could you rephrase the question? I don't personally observe the production of every bottle we sell, so I can't say for sure.

"If you know" clearly is a speaking objection, because the defending lawyer is implicitly suggesting the deponent should ask the examiner for clarification instead of answering the question, which is functionally the same as a direct instruction not to answer.[27] By asking the defending lawyer to refrain from making suggestive comments in front of the witness, you establish a clear record of the defending lawyer's misconduct and have initiated the "meet and confer" process that Rule 37 requires for the subsequent motion.[28]

Objecting to Vagueness Is a Prohibited Speaking Objection

An objection to a question being "vague" constitutes a speaking objection:

> An objection that a question is "vague" is . . . a speaking objection disguised as a form objection. It essentially expresses a concern that the witness may not understand the question.[29]

An attorney's concern that the witness may not understand the question is not relevant:

> Only the witness knows whether she understands a question, and the witness has a duty to request clarification if needed. This duty is traditionally explained to the witness by the questioner before the deposition. If defending counsel feels that an answer evidences a failure to understand a question, this may

---

[27] Proper and improper instructions not to answer are analyzed in Chapter 6 of this book and are governed by Fed. R. Civ. P. 30(c)(2).

[28] Fed. R. Civ. P. 37(a)(1): "On notice to other parties and all affected persons, a party may move for an order compelling disclosure or discovery. The motion must include a certification that the movant has in good faith conferred or attempted to confer with the person or party failing to make disclosure or discovery in an effort to obtain it without court action." *See* Chapter 9 of this book for more information on Rule 37 sanctions.

[29] *Serrano*, 2012 WL 28071 at *5.

be remedied [during their own examination of the witness following the completion of the other attorney's questioning].[30]

Example: Improper Objection to Vagueness

This products liability action alleged that baby formula became contaminated with bacteria during the manufacturing process. In a simple line of questions involving access to the manufacturing equipment, the defending lawyer interjected a pedantic speaking objection about the form of the question being too vague.

Q Are there certain levels that one can get, that have catwalks or some similar apparatus so I can get to the dryer?

A The dryer is totally enclosed. You cannot get into the dryer from any of the levels.

Q Can I get on the outside of the dryer?

Object to the form of the question; outside of the dryer? Everything is—I mean, outside of the dryer is a huge expanse of space; anything that's not inside the dryer is outside the dryer, so I object to it as vague and ambiguous. Object to the form of the question.

Sec. Nat'l Bank of Sioux City, Iowa v. Abbot Labs., 299 F.R.D. 595, 601 (N.D. Iowa 2014).

Objecting Due to a Lawyer's "Lack of Understanding" Is Prohibited

A claim that a lawyer does not understand the examiner's question is never a proper reason to object.[31] Whether the defending lawyer understands the examiner's question is irrelevant, because the lawyer is not the one being deposed. As such, a lawyer's alleged lack of understanding is unequivocally an impermissible speaking objection. In *Hall*, the court explained:

---

30 *Serrano*, 2012 WL 28071 at *5.

31 *Applied Telematics,* 1995 WL 79237 at *2 (citing *Hall*, 150 F.R.D. 525, 530 n.10).

If the witness needs clarification, the witness may ask the deposing lawyer for clarification. A lawyer's purported lack of understanding is not a proper reason to interrupt a deposition.[32]

Technique: Preempt Objections to a Witness Not Understanding the Question

Only the witness knows whether he or she understands a question. The court in *Hall* said it is the witness's responsibility to request clarification if needed.[33]

You should establish a record at the outset of the deposition that the witness understands the obligation to request clarification. Rather than giving the witness a laundry list of deposition rules, having the witness commit that *he or she will ask* for clarification when necessary preempts this type of objection.

Q   Will you tell me if you don't understand my question?

Q   Will you tell me if you find my question to be confusing?

Q   Will you tell me if I have assumed an incorrect fact in a question?

Q   Will you tell me if you don't know the answer to my question?

Q   Will you need to be reminded to follow these rules?

If the witness testifies that he or she understands the need to notify you if he or she does not understand a question, or if the question contains an incorrectly assumed fact, you will have a record establishing that the witness understood and accepted this obligation.

Reinterpreting or Rephrasing the Examiner's Questions Is Prohibited

Reinterpreting and rephrasing questions are prohibited witness coaching. This practice gives the witness additional information to consider in formulating an answer, and it suggests how the defending lawyer would like the answer to be framed. When a lawyer acts as an intermediary, the

---

32   *Hall*, 150 F.R.D. at 530 n.10.

33   *Hall*, 150 F.R.D. at 530 n.10.

deposition is no longer a question-and-answer session between the examiner and the witness.[34]

> [C]ounsel are not permitted to state on the record their interpretations of questions since those interpretations are irrelevant and often suggestive of a particularly desired answer.[35]

"Asked and Answered" Interjections Are Improper

Lawyers defending a deposition often interject that a question has been "asked and answered." This is a coaching technique lawyers use when the examining attorney rephrases an earlier question. "Asked and answered" is simply a speaking objection that signals to the witness how to answer the question. An examiner approaching an important concept from different angles does not constitute objectionable conduct. Rather, effective cross-examination tests the validity of a witness's statement by challenging it from different perspectives. This ensures that the statement is authentic, instead of a memorized sound bite scripted by the defending lawyer.

Excessive Objections Are Prohibited

The Advisory Committee Notes to Rule 30 explain that "[t]he making of an excessive number of unnecessary objections may itself constitute sanctionable conduct."[36] If excessive objections during a deposition disrupt the information-seeking process, this conduct may be sanctionable under Rule 30(d)(2), regardless of the individual objections' validity. Rule 30(d)(2) states:

> **Sanction.** The court may impose an appropriate sanction—including the reasonable expenses and attorney's fees incurred by any party—on a person who *impedes, delays, or frustrates the fair examination of the deponent.*[37]

---

34   *Hall*, 150 F.R.D. at 528; *see Alexander v. F.B.I.*, 186 F.R.D. 21, 52–53 (D.D.C. 1998).

35   *Hall*, 150 F.R.D. at 530 n.10.

36   Fed. R. Civ. P. 30(d), 1993 committee's note subd. d; *see also Morales v. Zondo, Inc.*, 204 F.R.D. 50, 54–57 (S.D.N.Y. 2001) (example of sanctionable interference with a deposition through pervasive objections).

37   Fed. R. Civ. P. 30(d)(2) (emphasis added).

Strategically disrupting the deposition with objections impedes the examination. This technique is called "Rambo litigation."[38] Rambo tactics directly contradict the "just, speedy, and inexpensive determination of every action" that Fed. R. Civ. P. 1 requires.[39] In *American Directory Service Agency, Inc. v. Beam*, the court prohibited Rambo tactics:

> [C]ounsel should avoid the prohibited practice of engaging in so-called Rambo tactics where counsel attacks or objects to every question posed, thus interfering with, or even preventing, the elicitation of any meaningful testimony and disrupting the orderly flow of the deposition.[40]

In *BNSF Railway. Co. v. San Joaquin Valley Railroad Co.*, the court sanctioned defending counsel for disrupting the deposition with unnecessary objections:

> The Court concludes that of the hundreds of objections lodged by Mr. Hicks, many were without legal basis or were unnecessary because less obstructive methods for preserving a challenge were clearly available. The Court was particularly concerned with the frequency of the interruptions and the defensiveness of Mr. Hicks. The Court finds that Mr. Hicks engaged in repeated, unnecessary objections that slowed the progress of the examination, impeded the flow of information from the witness, and unnecessarily prolonged the proceedings. Mr. Hicks's conduct impeded, delayed, and frustrated the fair examination of the deponent.[41]

When taken collectively, excessive objections for the sole purpose of impeding the deponent's fair examination are improper.

---

38 *Applied Telematics*, 1995 WL 79237 at *3; *see also Hall*, 150 F.R.D. at 530 (quoting Fed. R. Civ. P. Proposed Amendments, H.R.Doc. No. 74, at 261-63); *Craig v. St. Anthony's Med. Ctr.*, 2010 WL 2802492 at *1 (8th Cir. 2010); Judicial Conference, Federal Circuit, 146 F.R.D. 205, 216–32 (1992) (discussing the causes of and solutions to this problem).

39 *Applied Telematics*, 1995 WL 79237 at *3; Fed. R. Civ. P. 1.

40 *Am. Directory Serv. Agency, Inc. v. Beam*, 131 F.R.D. 15, 18-19 (D.D.C. 1990); *see also In re Stratosphere Corp. Sec. Litig.*, 182 F.R.D. at 619; *BNSF Ry. Co. v. San Joaquin Valley R. Co.*, 2009 WL 3872043 at *2 (E.D. Cal. Nov. 17, 2009); *Odone v. Croda Int'l PLC*, 170 F.R.D. 66, 68 n.3 (D.D.C. 1997).

41 *BNSF Ry. Co.*, 2009 WL 3872043 at *2.

Example: "Rambo Litigation"

At the beginning of the deposition, the examining attorney asked the deponent if he understood that he was testifying as a designated fact witness, immediately prompting this exchange:

Q [Do you understand why you're here and that you've been designated as a fact witness in this case?]

A No, I wouldn't—

Object—stop. You've got to let—you've got to let me object. Object to the form of that question as calling for material that would constitute work product. It's argumentative.

A I'm going to refuse to answer that based on attorney-client privilege and work product doctrine.

Q But do you understand why you're here today as a witness, sir?

Yeah. Because he's been subpoenaed. That's why he's here. You issued a subpoena, and we accepted service of the subpoena. That's why he's here.

Q [Defense counsel], do you have an objection, rather than just speaking and testifying for the witness?

Well, these questions are ridiculous. Why is he here? He's here pursuant to [sic] legal process. That's why he's here, because you guys issued a subpoena, and we accepted service. That's why we're here.

Q And we've asked if he understands—

He's not here—sorry?

Q Mr. Fleming—

That's the answer. Okay. Answer the question. Why are you here, Mr. Murphy?

A Pursuant to a subpoena.

Specht v. Google, Inc., 268 F.R.D. 596, 598-99 (N.D. Ill. 2010).

The court aptly summarized defending counsel's misconduct:

This [exchange] set the pattern for the deposition. [Examiner] would ask a simple question, and [defending counsel], through extensive, argumentative speaking objections, would take the procedure off on some wild excursion, meanwhile coaching the witness on how to answer.[42]

Summary

- **Noncorrectable objections are preserved for trial and should not be raised at the deposition:**

  - Objections to relevance are improper.

  - Objections to a question being "beyond the scope" are improper.

  - Objections to hearsay are improper.

  - Objections to a witness's mental competence are improper.

- **Witness coaching and speaking objections are prohibited at the deposition:**

  - "If you know" interjections are prohibited.

  - Objections to vagueness are prohibited.

  - Objections due to an attorney's "lack of understanding" are prohibited.

  - Reinterpreting or rephrasing the examiner's question is prohibited.

  - Interjections that a question has been "asked and answered" are prohibited.

  - Excessive objections, known as "Rambo litigation," are prohibited.

---

42 *Specht*, 268 F.R.D. at 599.

CHAPTER 6
INSTRUCTIONS NOT TO ANSWER

"Every obstruction of the course of justice,—is a door opened to betray society. . . ."

—Laurence Sterne[1]

---

[1] Laurence Sterne, The Life and Opinions of Tristram Shandy, Gentleman (1759).

Introduction

The integrity of the civil litigation process depends on an adversary's ability to uncover falsehoods.[2] Cross-examination is the foundation of the litigation process. It is the tool that exposes the purposeful nondisclosure of relevant information. Any attempt to limit an attorney's ability to uncover the truth is antithetical to our system of justice.[3] Some lawyers mistakenly believe they can decide what opposing counsel can ask in a deposition. This chapter describes the narrow circumstances in which an instruction not to answer is permissible and explains why all other instances are improper, sanctionable misconduct.

Only Three Permissible Reasons for an Instruction Not to Answer

A lawyer defending a deposition does not have the authority to decide which questions the witness should or should not answer.[4] The Federal Rules of Civil Procedure establish clear limits on when lawyers can instruct their clients not to answer questions during a deposition. Only three permissible reasons exist for a valid instruction not to answer a deposition question:

1. to preserve a privilege;

2. to enforce a limitation ordered by the court; or

3. to present a motion to terminate or limit the deposition under Rule 30(d)(3).[5]

---

2   See *Cox v. Burke*, 706 So. 2d 43, 47 (Fla. Dist. Ct. App. 1998).

3   See Model Rules of Prof'l Conduct r. 3.4(a); Model Rules of Prof'l Conduct r. 8.4(d).

4   See *Hall v. Clifton Precision, a Div. of Litton Sys., Inc.*, 150 F.R.D. 525, 528 (E.D. Pa. 1993).

5   Fed. R. Civ. P. 30(c)(2); see Fed. R. Civ. P. 30(d)(3)(A) ("At any time during a deposition, the deponent or a party may move to terminate or limit it on the ground that it is being conducted in bad faith or in a manner that unreasonably annoys, embarrasses, or oppresses the deponent or party.")

Instructing a witness not to answer a question for any other reason is sanctionable.[6] Any other objection, valid or otherwise, is not an excuse to stop a deponent from answering a question. Unless the objection falls within one of the three prescribed categories, the testimony is taken subject to any objection, and the examination proceeds.[7]

Proper Instruction Not to Answer: Privilege

The fundamental concepts of privilege are embraced universally throughout the federal court system. Privilege arose from the common law and was ultimately adopted in Federal Rule of Evidence 501, which states:

> Rule 501. Privilege in General
>
> The common law—as interpreted by United States courts in the light of reason and experience—governs a claim of privilege unless any of the following provides otherwise:
>
> - the United States Constitution;
>
> - a federal statute; or
>
> - rules prescribed by the Supreme Court.
>
> But in a civil case, state law governs privilege regarding a claim or defense for which state law supplies the rule of decision.[8]

The law of privilege allows a person to withhold evidence in a reasonably defined set of circumstances, as developed in the common law. Four elements are usually needed to claim a valid privilege:

> 1. The communications must originate in a *confidence* that they will not be disclosed.

---

6 *Ralston Purina Co. v. McFarland*, 550 F.2d 967, 973 (4th Cir. 1977); *Detoy v. City & Cty. of S.F.*, 196 F.R.D. 362, 365–66 (N.D. Cal. 2000); *Boyd v. Univ. of Md. Med. Sys.*, 173 F.R.D. 143, 144–47 (D. Md. 1997); *Int'l Union of Elec., Radio & Mach. Workers AFL-CIO v. Westinghouse Elec. Corp.*, 91 F.R.D. 277, 279–80 (D.D.C. 1981); *Preyer v. U.S. Lines, Inc.*, 64 F.R.D. 430, 431 (E.D. Pa. 1973).

7 Fed. R. Civ. P. 30(c)(2).

8 Fed. R. Evid. 501.

2. This element of *confidentiality must be essential* to the full and satisfactory maintenance of the relation between the parties.

3. The *relation* must be one which in the opinion of the community ought to be *sedulously fostered*.

4. The *injury* that would inure to the relation by the disclosure of the communications must be *greater than the benefit* thereby gained for the correct disposal of the litigation.[9]

Not all questions of privilege raise these four elements, but most do. The most frequent occurrence of an appropriate instruction not to answer based on privilege is when an attorney asserts attorney-client privilege. Fed. R. Evid. 502(g)(1) codified the common law governing attorney-client privilege: "'[A]ttorney-client privilege' means the protection that applicable law provides for confidential attorney-client communications. . . ."[10] The attorney-client privilege allows clients to refuse to disclose confidential communications with a lawyer. However, as the U.S. Supreme Court explained in *Upjohn Co. v. United States*:

> [T]he protection of the privilege extends only to *communications* and not to facts. A fact is one thing and a communication concerning that fact is an entirely different thing. The client cannot be compelled to answer the question, "What did you say or write to the attorney?" but may not refuse to disclose any relevant fact within his knowledge merely because he incorporated a statement of such fact into his communication to his attorney.[11]

Example: Improper Claim of Attorney-Client Privilege

Defending counsel instructed the client not to answer questions regarding a 19-minute mid-deposition recess, called by the defending counsel, to view and discuss with

---

9   8 Wigmore, Evidence § 2285.

10 Fed. R. Evid. 502(g)(1).

11 *Upjohn Co. v. United States*, 449 U.S. 383, 395–96 (1981).

the client a previously unseen video that was the subject of the deposing counsel's upcoming line of questions.

Q Have you finished your deposition prep?

Don't respond to that. It's not appropriate.

Q . . . During the break did you watch the video? Did you watch any videos?

A I did.

Q How many?

A Three.

Q Have you seen those videos before?

A Never.

Q Did you discuss the videos with your counsel? You can answer yes or no.

Don't answer.

Q You can answer yes or no.

Don't answer.

Q That's a proper question. We can mark it and decide what to do.

Gavrity v. City of N.Y., 2014 WL 4678027 at *3 (E.D.N.Y. Sept. 19, 2014).

Fed. R. Civ. P. 26(b)(5)(A)(ii) requires the party claiming a privilege to "describe the nature of the documents, communications, or tangible things not produced or disclosed—and do so in a manner that, without revealing information itself privileged or protected, will enable other parties to assess the claim."[12] In *Gavrity*, the court found no evidence on the record of the factual basis for the privilege. "[T]he fact of a conversation with counsel is not privileged."[13] Therefore, the information sought was not privileged, because the question did not inquire into the substance of their communication. The court required the defendant to respond about the existence of a conversation with his counsel.[14]

---

12 Fed. R. Civ. P. 26(b)(5)(A)(ii) (emphasis added).

13 *Gavrity v. City of N.Y.*, 2014 WL 4678027 at *3 (E.D.N.Y. Sept. 19, 2014).

14 *Gavrity*, 2014 WL 4678027 at *5.

Also, any attorney-client privilege may be waived if a third party was present during the privileged communications.[15]

Example: Attorney-Client Privilege Third-Party Waiver

Q What did you do then?

A We got together and talked about what happened.

Q What was said?

Objection. Attorney-client privilege. Don't answer that question.

Q When did this conversation occur?

A Saturday after the event.

Q Who was present during that conversation?

A My attorney, Ms. Adams, my wife and my neighbor, Tommy Champlain.

Q What was the subject matter of discussion?

A What my wife and Mr. Champlain saw.

Q Did you tell anyone about that conversation?

A Yeah, we talked about it at Lucky's Pub that night.

Q Who was present for that conversation?

A I can't really remember. Just the usuals hanging out at the bar.

Q Please tell us what was said that Saturday after the event in the meeting with you, Ms. Adams, your wife, and Mr. Champlain.

Objection. Attorney-client privilege. Don't answer that question.

At this point, a clear record has been established that attorney-client privilege was waived because other people were present during the conversation, and its content was discussed with others. If the attorney persists in instructing the deponent not to answer, the court has a record on which to base its ruling.

---

15 *United States v. Jones*, 696 F.2d 1069 (4th Cir. 1982).

When claiming a privilege in response to a deposition question, creating a proper record of the privilege is essential.[16] Fed. R. Civ. P. 26(b)(5)(A)(ii) requires the party claiming the privilege to note on the record the "nature of the ... communications, ... and do so in a manner that, without revealing information itself privileged or protected, *will enable other parties to assess the claim.*"[17] In the case of *In re St. Jude Medical, Inc.*, the court detailed what is required to establish a clear record of the privilege:

> When a privilege is claimed, the witness shall nevertheless answer questions relevant to the existence, extent or waiver of the privilege, such as the date of a communication, who made the statement, to whom and in whose presence the statement was made, other persons to whom the contents of the statement was made, any other person to whom the contents of the statement has been disclosed, and the general subject matter of the communication.[18]

Technique: Make a Record of a Dubious Privilege Claim to Assess Later

Q What do you understand were the reasons Sally Smith was terminated?

Objection. Attorney-client privilege.

At this point, Rule 26(b)(5)(A)(ii) requires the deponent to answer factual questions on the record about the allegedly privileged communication. *In re St. Jude* provided the framework of factual questions to pursue in establishing a clear privilege record.

Q Without going into the details, have you learned the reasons why she was terminated?

Q When did you learn it?

Q From whom did you learn it?

---

16 If the privilege is asserted immediately after the deponent and his or her counsel requested a break to confer during a pending question, the conferring attorney must place on the record the existence of the conference, its subject matter, and the decision reached concerning the exercise of the deponent's privilege. *Hall*, 150 F.R.D. at 530.

17 Fed. R. Civ. P. 26(b)(5)(A)(ii) (emphasis added).

18 *In re St. Jude Med., Inc.*, 2002 WL 1050311 at *5 (D. Minn. May 24, 2002).

Q Who was present?

Q Have you shared the reasons she was terminated with anyone else?

Q Who?

Q When?

With a clear record, a reviewing court has a factual basis to determine whether the party claiming the privilege has met its burden.

Proper Instruction Not to Answer: Court-Ordered Limitation

A lawyer may validly instruct his or her client not to answer a deposition question on the basis of a court-ordered limitation.[19] Fed. R. Civ. P. 26(b)(2)(C) authorizes a trial court to limit the scope of discovery when appropriate:

> On motion or on its own, the court must limit the frequency or extent of discovery otherwise allowed by these rules or by local rule if it determines that:
>
> (i) the discovery sought is unreasonably cumulative or duplicative, or can be obtained from some other source that is more convenient, less burdensome, or less expensive;
>
> (ii) the party seeking discovery has had ample opportunity to obtain the information by discovery in the action; or
>
> (iii) the proposed discovery is outside the scope permitted by Rule 26(b)(1).[20]

The condition precedent to a Rule 30(c)(2) instruction not to answer based on a court order is the existence of a court order.

Rule 26(c)(1) is the vehicle for moving for a protective order.[21] On showing good cause, a party may request that the court issue an order to protect a party or person from annoyance, embarrassment, oppression, or

---

19 Fed. R. Civ. P. 30(c)(2).

20 Fed. R. Civ. P. 26(b)(2)(C).

21 Fed. R. Civ. P. 26(c)(1).

undue burden or expense.[22] The motion may request, among other things, an order "forbidding disclosure or discovery"[23] or an order "forbidding inquiry into certain matters, or limiting the scope of disclosure or discovery to certain matters."[24] However, if the court does not issue an order, an instruction not to answer based on an objection that the inquiry is for the purpose of annoyance, embarrassment, or oppression is inappropriate and sanctionable (but see the following section on suspending the deposition). It is well established that "it is not the prerogative of counsel, but of the court, to rule on objections."[25]

Proper Instruction Not to Answer: Unilateral Suspension of Deposition

When necessary, a lawyer may instruct a deponent not to answer and suspend the deposition to present a motion for a protective order under Fed. R. Civ. P. 30(d)(3)(A). The rule states:

> At any time during a deposition, the deponent or a party may move to terminate or limit it on the ground that it is being conducted in bad faith or in a manner that unreasonably annoys, embarrasses, or oppresses the deponent or party.[26]

If a lawyer instructs the client not to answer for the purpose of seeking a protective order, the lawyer must promptly move for that protective order. In *Redwood v. Dobson,* Chief Judge Frank Easterbrook made it clear that an instruction not to answer based on claims of harassment, without suspending the deposition to move for protective order, is both unethical and sanctionable:

> [I]nstructions not to respond that neither shielded a privilege nor supplied time to apply for a protective order—were

---

22 Fed. R. Civ. P. 26(c)(1).

23 Fed. R. Civ. P. 26(c)(1)(A).

24 Fed. R. Civ. P. 26(c)(1)(D).

25 *Plaisted v. Geisinger Med. Ctr.,* 210 F.R.D. 527, 533 (M.D. Penn. 2002).

26 Fed. R. Civ. P. 30(d)(3)(A).

unprofessional and violated the Federal Rules of Civil Procedure as well as the ethical rules that govern legal practice.[27]

The proper approach requires the defending counsel to suspend the deposition and then apply for a protective order. Instructing the witness not to answer because the defending lawyer thinks the questions are harassing is improper.[28]

Technique: Suspend a Deposition Due to Harassment

The deposing lawyer harasses the witness in a nursing home wrongful death lawsuit.

Q   Isn't it true that your life has been much easier after your mother's death?

A   No. I miss her so much.

Q   Yeah, but your life is easier now, isn't it?

A   No, it isn't. I don't think that's fair.

Q   Come on, you don't have to lie. There's nothing wrong with admitting that your life is much easier now that you don't have to deal with your sickly mother.

Objection. Harassing the witness. If you continue this line of questions, I will instruct my client not to respond and suspend the deposition until we can have the court rule on whether these questions are appropriate.

If the deposing attorney persists, causing you to suspend the deposition, you must promptly move for a Rule 30(d)(3)(A) protective order for the instruction not to answer to be proper.[29]

---

27   *Redwood v. Dobson*, 476 F.3d 462, 469 (7th Cir. 2007).

28   *Redwood*, 476 F.3d at 467-68.

29   Fed. R. Civ. P. 30(d)(3)(A).

Improper Instructions Not to Answer

By definition, any instruction not to answer that does not fall within one of the three acceptable circumstances Fed. R. Civ. P. 30(c)(2) articulates is improper and sanctionable. Rule 30(d)(2) states:

> The court may impose an appropriate sanction—including the reasonable expenses and attorney's fees incurred by any party—on a person who impedes, delays, or frustrates the fair examination of the deponent.[30]

The following are examples from real deposition transcripts of common improper instructions not to answer.

Example: Calling It Harassment Does Not Make It Harassment[31]

Defending counsel objected to a line of questions, claiming they were irrelevant, and called the inquiry "harassment."

Q Now, with respect to the order of Judge Bennett [in a prior case] that you take a course, let's say, in the constitution with emphasis on the 1st amendment, what did you do to comply with that order?

A I took an online class.

Q How much did that class cost?

A I'm not sure.

Q Who paid for it?

I object to this as nothing more than harassment. The issue of who paid for his course is not related in any way to the four remaining claims in this case. It's—

Q It's a civil rights claim.

Don't interrupt me. Nor is it likely to lead to the discovery of admissible evidence. For that reason, I'm instructing him not to answer. You are not going to harass him about this.

Q There is no harassment, sir. I am going to pose my question, and if you shout at me again, I'm going to terminate

---

30   Fed. R. Civ. P. 30(d)(2).

31   This quote is derivative of an old anecdote popularized by Abraham Lincoln during his presidency: "Calling a calf's tail a leg don't make it a leg." Garson O'Toole, *Suppose You Call A Sheep's Tail a Leg, How Many Legs Will the Sheep Have?*, Quote Investigator (Nov. 15, 2015).

this deposition and get it continued to a date where you can control yourself.

If you interrupt me, I'll shout.

Q How long have you known Dan DeKoter?

A Oh, since he first came to town. Early '80s.

Q Now, did Dan DeKoter raise funds for you to take your online course in the 1st amendment?

I object for the reasons I just stated, and instruct him not to answer that question.

Q I assume you will seek a protective order?

Your assumption is correct. Probably not going to get to it until we finish with tomorrow's work, but I will.

> Van Stelton v. Van Stelton, 2013 WL 5574566 at *12-13 (N.D. Iowa Oct. 9, 2013).

In *Van Stelton*, the court explained that calling an inquiry harassment doesn't necessarily make it harassment:

> [I]t is black-letter law that relevance is not an appropriate basis for an instruction not to answer (or for a refusal to answer). Couching the instruction or refusal in terms of "harassment" does not change the analysis when the cry of "harassment" is based solely on an argument that certain topics are not relevant.[32]

The court sanctioned the defending attorney for instructing the deponent not to answer instead of bringing a motion for protective order:

> Unfortunately, . . . [deponent] (through his counsel) decided to take manners into their own hands. Having failed to procure a court order imposing subject matter limits on [his] deposition[], they imposed their own limits. They repeatedly refused to answer questions they unilaterally deemed to be irrelevant. Making matters worse, they did not bother to comply with Rule 30(c)(2), or [the court's] prior order, by making a motion for protective order upon refusing to answer questions. This conduct was blatantly improper.[33]

---

32 *Van Stelton v. Van Stelton*, 2013 WL 5574566 at *17 (N.D. Iowa Oct. 9, 2013).

33 *Van Stelton*, 2013 WL 5574566 at *17.

Example: Instruction Not to Answer, Claiming Irrelevance

The defending lawyer instructed the witness not to answer, claiming the inquiry was irrelevant.

Q What's your—what was your mobile phone number during the time period that you investigated the Morantes case?

I'm going to object to that question. I think it's personal. It's private. It's irrelevant. He's here as an investigator of EEOC, and I don't think you're entitled to know his private phone number . . . I'm going to direct the witness not to answer that question.

Q [Y]ou're instructing the witness not to answer the question what his mobile phone number [was] while investigating—?

I am. That's private information. You are not entitled to that.

> EEOC v. Bok Fin. Corp., 2013 WL 12045019 at *2 (D.N.M. Apr. 19, 2013).

Once again, the court simply cited black-letter law in explaining the impropriety of the instructions not to answer:

> Essentially, [counsel] instructed [deponent] not to answer because the question, in her mind, was irrelevant. The problem is that *Dabney* specifically precluded an instruction not to answer under that circumstance. "It is inappropriate to instruct a witness not to answer a question on the basis of relevance." *Dabney*, 73 F.3d at 266.
>
> Rule 30 allows [deponent's counsel] to state her objection for purposes of the record, but the examination proceeds and [deponent] responds to the question, subject to the objection. Fed. R. Civ. P. 30(c)(2). Moreover, if [counsel] felt so aggrieved by the question, . . . the deposition could have been terminated and [counsel] could have sought a protective order under Rule 26(c). Fed. R. Civ. P. 30(d)(3)(A).[34]

---

34 *EEOC v. Bok Fin. Corp.*, 2013 WL 12045019 at *2 (D. N.M. Apr. 19, 2013).

The court reopened the deposition and ordered sanctions on EEOC's counsel that required payment of costs and attorney fees for the first deposition, the filing of the motion, the reopened deposition, and the court reporter's fees for the reopened deposition.[35]

Example: Instruction Not to Answer, Claiming Repetition

Defending counsel claimed the inquiry was repetitious and instructed the client not to answer.

Q Do you know whether or not there was a TAC meeting on October 23, 2014?

Objection. And I'm directing the witness not to answer that question. It has been asked and answered several times.

Q It's not an objection.

Well, it's harassment.

Q To ask if there was a TAC meeting is harassment?

You went through a very long series of questions in regard to TAC plans, TAC meetings, whether one occurred on this day. We're not going back down that road.

. . .

Q Do you know if there are any entries that are specifically required in your memo book, when you're doing a SNEU operation?

Objection. Asked and answered.

A I don't have that information of what's required.

Q But to your knowledge?

Objection. Asked and answered.

Q Asked and answered is not an appropriate objection.

Harassment.

. . .

---

35 *EEOC*, 2013 WL 12045019 at *19.

Like I said, it's harassment and if it continues, I'm going to direct him not to answer the question. So if you want to keep asking the same questions, that is going to be the result.

Cordero v. City of New York, 2017 WL 2116699 at *2–3 (E.D.N.Y. May 12, 2017).

The *Cordero* court rejected defending counsel's position and issued sanctions for obstruction. The court ruled:

[T]he vast majority of counsel's instructions not to answer appear to be based on assertions that the questions had been previously "asked and answered" or were not relevant; neither of these grounds is a proper basis for instructing a witness not to answer in a deposition.[36]

The court ordered the deponent's counsel to pay the costs of the first deposition and allowed for a second deposition if requested.[37]

Example: Failure to Instruct a Deponent to Answer

Following a series of relevance objections, the deponent independently refused to answer a question.

Q All right. What previous Interface companies were there?

A It's irrelevant to the claim.

Objection. Not relevant nor—

A What's it got to do with his overtime?

Q All right. Are you refusing to answer that question as well[?]

A I respectfully decline.

Q All right.

Counsel, would you like to explain why that's even remotely germane, whether it's relevant or reasonably calculated to lead. Would you like to explain that?

Q I'm not going to respond to that.

---

[36] *Cordero v. City of N.Y.*, 2017 WL 2116699 at *8 (E.D.N.Y. May 12, 2017).

[37] *Cordero*, 2017 WL 2116699 at *8.

Luangisa v. Interface Operations, 2011 WL 6029880 at *10 (D. Nev. Dec. 5, 2011).

In *Luangisa*, the court admonished the defending attorney for making speaking objections and not taking affirmative steps to ensure that the client complied with the deposition rules:

> [D]efense counsel made no effort to advise his client of his obligation to answer the questions which were asked. It is not enough for an attorney to refrain from instructing a client not to answer. In fulfilling his or her duties as an officer of the court an attorney must take some affirmative step to ensure the deponent complies with deposition rules. *See cf., GMAC Bank v. HTFC Corp.*, 252 F.R.D. 253, 258 (E.D. Pa. 2008) (the failure of an attorney to take remedial steps to curb client misconduct may be considered the functional equivalent of advising the misconduct). The failure of an attorney to curb client misconduct during a deposition can have the effect, as it did here, of empowering continued misconduct. *Id.*[38]

Technique: Make a Record of Instructions Not to Answer

If your opponent instructs a witness not to answer, it is important that you make a record of the basis for that instruction. There are only three permissible bases for instructing the witness not to answer a question.[39] They are to preserve a privilege, to enforce a limitation by the court, and to submit a motion for unilateral termination. If you want to bring a motion for sanctions against the obstructing attorney, you must establish a record as to why the attorney instructed the witness not to answer.

Objection. I'm instructing the witness not to answer.

Q What is the basis of that instruction, please?

It's beyond the scope of the notice.

Q Is there any other basis?

No.

---

38 *Luangisa v. Interface Operations*, 2011 WL 6029880 at *11 (D. Nev. Dec. 5, 2011).

39 Fed. R. Civ. P. 30(c)(2).

You now have the record to bring a motion to compel answers to this line of questioning and to request that the court sanction your adversary for violating federal discovery procedure.

Summary

- There are only three proper instances to instruct a deponent not to answer:

    1. to preserve a privilege

    2. to adhere to a court-ordered discovery limitation

    3. to suspend the deposition and move for a protective order

- All other justifications to instruct a deponent not to answer a question are improper and sanctionable.

- Failure to instruct a client to answer may be sanctionable.

CHAPTER 7
30(b)(6) SCOPE OF TESTIMONY

"Nevertheless, she persisted."

—Sen. Maj. Leader Mitch McConnell[1]

---

1 163 Cong. Rec. S855 (Feb. 7, 2017) (referring to Sen. Elizabeth Warren's insistence on reading a letter from Coretta Scott King on the Senate floor over Republican senators' repeated attempts to silence her).

Introduction

Fed. R. Civ. P. 30(b)(6) provides rules for specialized depositions directed to organizations.[2] Depositions conducted under Rule 30(b)(6) focus on information known to the organization as a whole, rather than to the single person being deposed. To properly invoke Rule 30(b)(6), the requesting party must describe with *reasonable particularity* the matters for intended examination.[3] The responding organization must, in turn, designate one or more people who are fully prepared to provide all information known, or reasonably available, to the organization regarding the described matters of examination.[4]

If the questions during the 30(b)(6) witness's testimony go beyond the scope of what the deposition notice described, some lawyers instruct their clients not to answer the questions. That instruction is improper. "Beyond the scope of the 30(b)(6) notice" is not one of the three Rule 30(c)(2) permissible reasons for instructing a witness not to answer.[5]

In *Batts v. County of Santa Clara*, the court emphasized that there is no gray area when it comes to instructions not to answer:

> [W]hatever lack of clarity may exist in the law with respect to the proper scope of a Rule 30(b)(6) deposition, no such lack of clarity exists with respect to the limited circumstances in which counsel may instruct a witness not to answer a question. Thus, regardless of County Counsel's arguably understandable confusion regarding the propriety of

---

2   For an in-depth analysis of the use of 30(b)(6) depositions, *see* Mark Kosieradzki, 30(b)(6): Deposing Corporations, Organizations & the Government (Trial Guides 2015).

3   Fed. R. Civ. P. 30(b)(6) reads: "In its notice or subpoena, a party may name as the deponent a public or private corporation, a partnership, an association, a governmental agency, or other entity and must describe with reasonable particularity the matters for examination. The named organization must then designate one or more officers, directors, or managing agents, or designate other persons who consent to testify on its behalf; and it may set out the matters on which each person designated will testify. A subpoena must advise a nonparty organization of its duty to make this designation. The persons designated must testify about information known or reasonably available to the organization. This paragraph (6) does not preclude a deposition by any other procedure allowed by these rules."

4   Fed. R. Civ. P. 30(b)(6).

5   Fed. R. Civ. P. 30(c)(2).

Plaintiff's counsel's questioning, County Counsel's instruction to the witness not to answer was clearly improper.[6]

Even if the defending lawyer believes the question is clearly beyond the scope of the 30(b)(6) notice, the deponent must answer and the deposition must continue, subject to objection that the notice's scope has been exceeded.[7]

Limiting the Scope Is Not Allowed

The seminal case involving the scope of Rule 30(b)(6) deposition testimony is *King v. Pratt & Whitney*.[8] The court ruled:

> Rule 30(b)(6) cannot be used to limit what is asked of a designated witness at a deposition. Rather, the Rule simply defines a corporation's obligations regarding whom they are obligated to produce for such a deposition and what that witness is obligated to be able to answer.[9]

The court then explained the underlying policy behind Rule 30(b)(6):

> The reason for adopting Rule 30(b)(6) was not to provide greater notice or protections to corporate deponents, but rather to have the right person present at the deposition. The Rule is not one of limitation but rather of specification within the broad parameters of the discovery rules.[10]

Therefore, the matters of examination in the deposition notice set forth the *minimum* that the witness must be prepared to testify about, not the maximum.[11] Because Rule 30(b)(6) does not provide any specific

---

6 *Batts v. County of Santa Clara*, 2010 WL 545847 *2 (N.D. Ca. Feb. 11, 2010).

7 *King v. Pratt & Whitney, a Div. of United Techs. Corp.*, 161 F.R.D. 475 (S.D. Fla. 1995), *aff'd sub nom. King v. Pratt & Whitney*, 213 F.3d 646 (11th Cir. 2000), *aff'd sub nom. King v. Pratt & Whitney*, 213 F.3d 647 (11th Cir. 2000).

8 *King*, 161 F.R.D. 475, *aff'd sub nom. King*, 213 F.3d 646, *aff'd sub nom. King*, 213 F.3d 647.

9 *King*, 161 F.R.D. at 476.

10 *King*, 161 F.R.D. at 476.

11 *Detoy v. City & Cty. of S.F.*, 196 F.R.D. 362, 366 (N.D. Cal. 2000), citing *King*, 161 F.R.D. 475.

limitation on what can be asked at a deposition, the general deposition standards set forth in Rule 26 are controlling.[12]

King rejected *Paparelli v. Prudential Insurance. Co. of America*, which was the first case to consider the scope of 30(b)(6) inquiry.[13] In *Paparelli*, the court ruled that the examining party should confine the examination of a 30(b)(6) corporate designated witness to matters stated with reasonable particularity in the deposition notice.[14] However, the court also ruled that, consistent with Rule 30(c), "[e]vidence objected to *shall be taken* subject to objections."[15] Both *King* and *Paparelli* prohibit instructions not to answer based on 30(b)(6) scope of inquiry. The *Paparelli* court stated, "Only the Court, not counsel, can order that a deposition be limited or that certain questions not be answered."[16]

The *Paparelli* aspirational standard—which directed the lawyer asking questions to limit the inquiry to the matters identified in the notice, while simultaneously allowing questions that go beyond that notice—didn't make sense. *King* established the standard that required a 30(b)(6) designee to testify as to all relevant matters, regardless of whether those matters were identified in the 30(b)(6) notice. *Paparelli* has not been adopted since *King*, which is now universally embraced as the standard.[17]

---

12   *Detoy,* 196 F.R.D. at 366, citing *King,* 161 F.R.D. 475.
13   *Paparelli v. Prudential Ins. Co. of Am.*, 108 F.R.D. 727 (D. Mass. 1985).
14   *Paparelli*, 108 F.R.D. 727.
15   *Paparelli*, 108 F.R.D. at 730.
16   *Paparelli*, 108 F.R.D. at 731.
17   *Rivas v. Greyhound Lines, Inc.*, 2015 WL 13710124 at *5 (W.D. Tex. 2015) ("The Court has been unable to find a case rejecting the reasoning in *King* and adopting *Paparelli*. . . .").

Example: Instructions Not to Answer Due to Scope of 30(b)(6)

In an insurance bad-faith case, the 30(b)(6) matters of examination in the notice were:

Matters of Examination

Claims Management Standards

1. Describe the claims handling policies, practices, and procedures.

2. Describe the claims resolution standards.

3. Describe any financial targets for claims departments and claims handling.

4. Describe policies and procedures for notifying insured of settlement opportunities.

5. Describe all standards for protecting the interests of the insurance company's insureds.

At the 30(b)(6) designee's deposition, along with questions that were clearly within the scope of the notice, the lawyer representing the plaintiff asked about databases used in the claims resolution process. A debate arose as to whether those questions were within the notice's scope.

Q When evaluating how to settle the claim, did anyone at [insurance company] consult any databases to determine what was an appropriate settlement range for the claim?

Objection. Instruction not to answer.

Q What is the basis for the instruction not to answer, please?

It's beyond the scope of the notice. She's not going to answer that.

Q Is there any other basis for the instruction not to answer?

No.

This approach creates a record of the sole basis of the instruction not to answer. Then the court can use this factual record to apply the *King* jurisprudence to compel testimony and order sanctions.

Defending a 30(b)(6) Deposition

If an attorney defending a Rule 30(b)(6) deposition objects to questions being outside the scope of the 30(b)(6) designation, the objection should simply state: "Beyond the scope." Subject to that objection, the witness still must answer the question to the best of his or her ability.[18] The trial court will ultimately determine whether the testimony was actually within the scope of the 30(b)(6) deposition notice. Because the organization has a duty to prepare the witness only for the matters specified, only questions that elicit testimony *within* the scope of the 30(b)(6) notice are binding on the organization.[19] If the court rules that the questions are beyond the scope of the 30(b)(6) notice, the answers to that line of inquiry will convert to individual 30(b)(1) testimony.[20] If the objection is overruled, the testimony will bind the organization.

Technique: Defending 30(b)(6) Depositions

Using the same insurance bad-faith case example above, if debate arises as to whether the deposing attorney exceeded the notice's scope, the appropriate method of preserving the record is to simply state "beyond the scope."

Q   When evaluating how to settle the claim, did anyone at [insurance company] consult any databases to determine what was an appropriate settlement range for the claim?

Objection. Beyond the scope of the 30(b)(6) notice.

A   Yes. John McCoughlin reviewed a database that compiled jury verdicts and settlements.

With the objection on the record, the trial court can later determine whether the response to the question is subject to the binding effect on the organization.[21]

---

18   *Detoy*, 196 F.R.D. at 367.

19   *King*, 161 F.R.D. at 476 (emphasis added), *aff'd sub nom. King*, 213 F.3d 646, *aff'd sub nom. King*, 213 F.3d 647.

20   *Dravo Corp. v. Liberty Mut. Ins. Co.*, 164 F.R.D. 70, 74 (D. Neb. 1995).

21   *See Rainey v. Am. Forest and Paper Ass'n, Inc.*, 26 F. Supp. 2d 82 (D.C. 1998).

Summary

- Rule 30(b)(6) questions are not limited to the scope of the deposition notice.

- Rule 30(b)(6) cannot be used to limit what is asked.

- The 30(b)(6) notice sets forth the *minimum* about which the witness must be prepared.

- Rule 26 controls the scope of the examination.

- Testimony outside the scope of the notice converts to individual testimony.

- Instructions not to answer based on the notice's scope are improper and sanctionable.

CHAPTER 8
ATTORNEY-CLIENT CONFERENCES

"It is too late once the ball has been snapped for the coach to send in a different play."

—The Hon. Harlington Wood Jr.[1]

---

1 *Eggleston v. Chi. Journeymen Plumber's Local Union 130, U.A.*, 657 F.2d 890, 902 (7th Cir. 1981).

Introduction

In efforts to zealously advocate on their clients' behalf, some lawyers mistakenly believe they have the right to confer with their clients to guide the testimony as it develops. Lawyers are obligated to prepare their clients for testimony, but they have neither the obligation nor the right to manipulate their clients' testimony during the inquiry.

The Federal Rules of Civil Procedure clearly prohibit witness coaching. However, differing schools of authority have developed regarding the extent to which witnesses can communicate with their lawyers during deposition breaks. This chapter explores when attorney-client conferences are prohibited, when they are permitted, what can be discussed during breaks, and the consequences of a post-conference testimony change.

Deposition Conduct Is the Same as Trial

Fed. R. Civ. P. 30(c)(1) requires depositions to "proceed as they would at trial under the Federal Rules of Evidence."[2] The U.S. Supreme Court has clearly defined the lawyer's role during a client's testimony:

> [W]hen a defendant becomes a witness, he has no constitutional right to consult with his lawyer while he is testifying. He has an absolute right to such consultation before he begins to testify, but neither he nor his lawyer has a right to have the testimony interrupted in order to give him the benefit of counsel's advice.[3]

It is fundamental that, at trial, a witness's lawyer does not sit beside the witness and tell him or her what to say or what not to say. In *Hall v. Clifton Precision*, the court emphasized that this standard of conduct applies to depositions as well:

> During a civil trial, a witness and his or her lawyer are not permitted to confer at their pleasure during the witness's

---

[2] Fed. R. Civ. P. 30(c)(1).

[3] *Perry v. Leeke*, 488 U.S. 272, 281 (U.S. 1989).

testimony. Once a witness has been prepared and has taken the stand, that witness is on his or her own. The same is true at a deposition. The fact that there is no judge in the room to prevent private conferences does not mean that such conferences should or may occur.[4]

The time for a lawyer and client to prepare for a deposition is before the deposition, not during it. In *Eggleston v. Chicago Journeymen Plumber's Local Union 130*, the Seventh Circuit condemned off-the-record conferences and explained: "It is too late once the ball has been snapped for the coach to send in a different play."[5]

Privilege Conferences Always Are Permissible

"[A] deponent and the deponent's attorney have no right to confer during a deposition in a civil proceeding, except for the purpose of determining whether a privilege shall be asserted."[6]

Fed. R. Civ. P. 30(c)(2) permits an attorney to instruct the client not to answer a question when necessary to preserve a privilege.[7] "Since the assertion of a privilege is a proper, and very important, objection during a deposition, it makes sense to allow the witness the opportunity to consult with counsel . . . before making a statement which might reveal privileged information."[8] Following an appropriate off-the-record privilege conference while a question is pending, the conferring attorney must place on the record the existence of the conference, its subject matter, and the decision reached concerning the exercise of the client's privilege.[9]

---

4 *Hall v. Clifton Precision, a Div. of Litton Sys., Inc.*, 150 F.R.D. 525, 528 (E.D. Pa. 1993).

5 *Eggleston*, 657 F.2d at 902.

6 *United States v. Philip Morris Inc.*, 212 F.R.D. 418, 420 (D.D.C. 2002); *see also Hall*, 150 F.R.D. at 529; *Morales v. Zondo, Inc.*, 204 F.R.D. 50, 54 (S.D.N.Y. 2001); Moore et al., *Moore's Federal Practice*, ¶ 30.42[2] (3d ed. 1997).

7 Fed. R. Civ. P. 30(c)(2).

8 *Hall*, 150 F.R.D. at 529-30.

9 *Hall*, 150 F.R.D. at 529-30; *In re St. Jude Med., Inc.*, 2002 WL 1050311 at *5 (D. Minn. May 24, 2002).

Example: Privilege Conference

Q   Are there any documents that describe the transactions?

A   Yes.

Q   What do they say?

Objection—we need to confer about a potential privilege issue.

[off-the-record discussion]

There was an e-mail string in January between Ms. Samson and myself [attorney] discussing the history of the transactions. No one else was in the string. Ms. Samson is asserting attorney-client privilege and will therefore not discuss the contents of that correspondence.

Conferencing During Recesses: Two Schools of Authority

There is no dispute that an attorney is absolutely prohibited from communicating with his or her client during the active questioning of a deposition, except to protect privilege. However, there is a split in authority as to whether an attorney may confer with his or her client during breaks. Courts have embraced two conflicting positions on whether attorneys and their clients may confer during recesses that are *not requested* by the defending attorney.

Hall *Standard: All Attorney-Client Conferences Prohibited*

In *Hall*, the court expressly held that "conferences between witness and lawyer are prohibited both during the deposition and during recesses."[10] This strict approach prohibits all attorney-client conferences throughout the deposition regarding the testimony's substance, except when the conference's purpose is to decide whether to assert a privilege. "Private conferences are barred during the deposition, and the fortuitous occurrence of a coffee break, lunch break, or evening recess is no reason to change the rules. Otherwise, the same problems would persist."[11]

If an attorney conducts a prohibited off-the-record conference in a *Hall* jurisdiction, "[those] conferences are not covered by the attorney-client privilege, at least as to what is said by the lawyer to the witness. Therefore, any such conferences are fair game for inquiry by the

---

10 *Hall*, 150 F.R.D. at 529; *see Chassen v. Fid. Nat'l Title Ins. Co.*, 2010 WL 5865977 at *1-2 (D.N.J. July 21, 2010); *Peronist v. United States*, 2017 WL 6906132 at *2 (W.D. Pa. Feb. 17, 2017); *Vnuk v. Berwick Hosp. Co.*, 2016 WL 907714 at *3-4 (M.D. Pa. Mar. 2, 2016); *Craig v. St. Anthony's Med. Ctr.*, 2009 WL 690210 at *3 (E.D. Mo. Mar. 12, 2009); *Bracey v. Delta Tech. Coll.*, 2016 WL 918939 at *1 (Mar. 9, 2016); *S. La. Ethanol, L.L.C. v. Fireman's Fund Ins. Co.*, 2013 WL 1196604 at *7 (E.D. La. Mar. 22, 2013); *United States v. Black*, 2010 WL 11520578 at *2 (E.D. Wash. Jan. 14, 2010); *United States v. Phillip Morris, Inc.*, 212 F.R.D. at 420 (D.D.C. 2002); *LM Ins. Corp. v. ACEO, Inc.*, 275 F.R.D. 490, 491 (N.D. Ill. 2011); *In re Amezaga*, 195 B.R. 221, 228 (Bankr. D.P.R. 1996); *Fisher v. Goord*, 184 F.R.D. 45, 48 (W.D.N.Y. 1999); *Bd. of Trs. of Leland Stanford Junior Univ. v. Tyco Int'l. Ltd.*, 253 F.R.D. 524, 526-27 (C.D. Cal. 2008); 4/25/2014 Judge Donato's Standing Order Regarding Civil Discovery at ¶ 13 (http://www.cand.uscourts.gov/jdorders); *In re Anonymous Member of S.C. Bar*, 552 S.E.2d 10, 16-17 (S.C. 2001) (citing S.C. R. Civ. P. 30(j)(5)); Del. Super. Ct. Civ. R. 30(d)(1); *cf. Perrymond v. Lockheed Martin Corp.*, 2011 WL 13269787 at *3 (N.D. Ga. Feb. 18, 2011) (ruling that a brief conference during a five-minute bathroom break was improper but not sanctionable because it did not frustrate the fair examination of the deponent); *compare Morales v. Zondo*, 204 F.R.D. 50, 53 (S.D.N.Y. 2001) ("[A] deponent and the deponent's attorney have no right to confer during a deposition, except for the purpose of determining whether a privilege shall be asserted.") (citation omitted), *and* Local Civ. R. E.D.N.Y. & S.D.N.Y. 30.4 (amended 2018) (prohibiting a deponent's attorney from initiating a private conference "while a deposition question is pending" except for the privilege exception), *with Gavrity v. City of N.Y.*, 2014 WL 4678027 at *2 (E.D.N.Y. Sept. 19, 2014) ("The rules of this Court do not prohibit 'discussions between counsel and client during a deposition other than when a question is pending,'" applying Local Civ. R. E.D.N.Y. & S.D.N.Y 30.4, which prohibits a deponent's attorney from initiating a conference while a question is pending), *and Okoumou v. Horizon*, 2004 WL 2149118 at *2 (S.D.N.Y Sept. 23, 2004) ("A witness is generally free to consult with counsel at any time during a deposition.").

11 *Hall*, 150 F.R.D. at 529.

deposing attorney to ascertain whether there has been any coaching and, if so, what."[12]

Stratosphere *Standard: Attorney-Client Conferences Permissible During Unrequested Breaks*

An alternative standard, found in *In re Stratosphere Securities Litigation*, allows the defending lawyer to confer with his or her client during regularly scheduled breaks or unscheduled breaks *that the defending lawyer did not request*:

> This Court will not preclude an attorney, during a recess *that he or she did not request,* from making sure that his or her client did not misunderstand or misinterpret questions or documents, or attempt to help rehabilitate the client by fulfilling an attorney's ethical duty to prepare a witness. So long as attorneys do not demand a break in the questions, or demand a conference between question and answers, the Court is confident that the search for the truth will adequately prevail.[13]

The *Stratosphere* court stated that recess conferences were consistent with Fed. R. Civ. P 30(c)(1), requiring depositions to proceed as they would at trial:

> It is this Court's experience, at the bar and on the bench, that attorney's [sic] and clients regularly confer during trial and even during the client's testimony, while the court is in recess, be it mid morning or mid afternoon, the lunch recess, [or] the

---

12   *Hall,* 150 F.R.D. at 529 n.7.

13   *In re Stratosphere Corp. Sec. Litig.*, 182 F.R.D. 614, 621 (D. Nev. 1998) (emphasis added); *see Cordova v. United States*, 2006 WL 4109659 at *5 (D.N.M. July 30, 2006); *Odone v. Croda Int'l PLC*, 170 F.R.D. 66, 67-69 (D.D.C. 1997); *Pia v. Supernova Media Inc.*, 2011 WL 6069271 at *3 (D. Utah Dec. 6, 2011); *McKinley Infuser Inc. v. Zdeb*, 200 F.R.D. 648, 650 (D. Colo. 2001); *Ginardi v. Frontier Gas Servs., LLC*, 2012 WL 13028126 at *2 (E.D. Ark. Jan. 6, 2012); *Murray v. Nationwide Better Health*, 2012 WL 3683397 at *4-5 (C.D. Ill. Aug. 24, 2012); *Pain Ctr. of SE Ind., LLC. v. Origin Healthcare Sols. LLC*, 2015 WL 4548528 at *5 (S.D. Ind. July 28, 2015); *Cullen v. Nissan N. Am., Inc.*, 2010 WL 11579750 at *8 (M.D. Tenn. Feb. 2, 2010); *Coyote Springs Inv., LLC v. Eighth Judicial Dist. Court of State ex rel. Cty. of Clark*, 347 P.3d 267, 273 (Nev. 2015); *State ex rel. Means v. King*, 520 S.E.2d 875, 882-83 (W. Va. 1999); *In re Domestic Air Transp. Antitrust Litig.*, 1990 WL 358009 at *9 (N.D. Ga. Dec. 21, 1990); *Few v. Yellowpages.com*, 2014 WL 3507366 at *1-2 (S.D.N.Y. July 14, 2014); Local Civ. R. E.D.N.Y. & S.D.N.Y 30.4; Tex. R. Civ. P. 199.5(d) (allowing conferences during scheduled recesses).

evening recess. The right to prepare a witness is not different before the questions begin than it is during (or after, since a witness may be recalled for rebuttal, etc., during trial).[14]

However, if the defending lawyer requests a recess in the deposition during an active line of questioning or while a question is pending, the recess should be delayed until the question is answered and the interrogating attorney has had a reasonable amount of time to pursue the line of questioning.[15]

Variations of Hall *and* Stratosphere

Some courts have been hesitant both to adopt *Hall*'s strict prohibition on conferencing and to allow the carte blanche conferences during unrequested recesses that *Stratosphere* permitted. While no collective rule has developed from these jurisdictions, courts have considered the duration of the break[16] and when the break occurred.[17]

For most courts, the length of a recess during a single-day deposition does not affect their decision-making on the conferences' appropriateness.[18] However, when depositions become multiple-day affairs, some courts following the *Hall* standard relax their strict prohibition on counseling.[19] For example, in *United States v. Phillip Morris, Inc.*, the court ruled that a prohibition on attorney-client communications during a multiple-day deposition was appropriate as long as the deposition occurred on "a day-to-day basis with no intervening passage of time," but that it

---

14 *In re Stratosphere Corp. Sec. Litig.*, 182 F.R.D. at 621.

15 *In re Stratosphere Corp. Sec. Litig.*, 182 F.R.D. at 621; *see Cordova*, 2006 WL 4109659 at *5.

16 *Odone*, 170 F.R.D. at 67-69; *Phillip Morris*, 212 F.R.D. at 420.

17 *Odone*, 170 F.R.D. at 67-69; *Ecker v. Wis. Cent. Ltd.*, 2008 WL 1777222 at *3 (E.D. Wis. Apr. 16, 2008); *Diebold, Inc. v. Cont'l Cas. Co.*, 2009 WL 10677801 at *1-2 (D.N.J. Aug. 20, 2009).

18 *Odone*, 170 F.R.D. at 67-69.

19 *Phillip Morris*, 212 F.R.D. at 420; *Potashnick v. Port City Constr. Co.*, 609 F.2d 1101, 1119 (5th Cir. 1980) (relaxing the prohibition on consultations between a witness and counsel during an overnight recess during trial).

infringed on the deponent's right to counsel if the deposition could not be held on consecutive days.[20]

Some courts have considered the conference's timing. In *Odone v. Croda International PLC*, the court decided it was not sanctionable for counsel to confer with his client *after* the deposing counsel's examination ceased and before the defending counsel's examination began.[21] "Th[is] Court . . . cannot penalize an attorney for utilizing a five-minute recess that he did not request to learn whether his client misunderstood or misinterpreted the questions and then for attempting to rehabilitate his client on the record."[22]

Following this reasoning, the court in *Ecker v. Wisconsin Central Ltd.* approved of an off-the-record conference before the defending lawyer's examination of his own client because the lawyer "did not interrupt the questioning of plaintiff's counsel or try to steer the witness to a different answer, but instead waited until plaintiff's counsel had completed his examination before attempting to clear up what he apparently thought was a misunderstanding on the part of the witness."[23]

Changes in Testimony Following an Attorney-Client Conference

In *Hall* jurisdictions, any change in testimony following an off-the-record conference is subject to inquiry by the deposing attorney, because attorney-client privilege is automatically waived following an improper conference.[24] However, in *Stratosphere* jurisdictions, a change in testimony following an off-the-record conference necessitates a multiple-step process to ascertain the reasons for the change.

---

20 *Phillip Morris*, 212 F.R.D. at 420.

21 *Odone*, 170 F.R.D. at 69 (noting, however, that "it would have been preferable for the plaintiff's attorney to ascertain on the record whether his client misinterpreted a document."); *Ecker*, 2008 WL 1777222 at *3; *Diebold*, 2009 WL 10677801 at *1-2.

22 *Odone*, 170 F.R.D. at 69.

23 *Ecker*, 2008 WL 1777222 at *3.

24 *Hall*, 150 F.R.D. at 529 n.7.

Immediately Following the Recess in Stratosphere *Jurisdictions*

When the deposition resumes after an unrequested recess and deponents make substantive changes to their testimony, the deposing attorney should establish a clear record of the reasons for the changed testimony. A clear record gives the court a factual basis to rule on a motion to compel.

Technique: Build a Record of Discussions During Breaks

A defending lawyer's improper manipulation of testimony during breaks can be exposed by building a record of the conference and the subsequent change in testimony.

- Q Are you ready to proceed with questions?
- Q Did you have an opportunity to meet with your lawyer during the break?
- Q Is there any part of your testimony you want to change?
- Q What do you want to change?

Once you have established that the witness changed his or her testimony following an attorney-client conference, at trial, the jury will assume the defending attorney directed the change.[25] The next step is to establish on the record that you are attempting to identify the factual basis for the change.

- Q Why are you changing your answer?
- Q Why didn't you tell us that when I asked you the questions the first time?
- Q What did your lawyer say to cause you to change your answer?
- Q Why didn't you have that information the first time you were providing testimony?

If an instruction not to answer based on privilege arises, you now have a record on which to base your motion to compel a response to your question.

---

25 See Greg Cusimano & David Wenner, *Overcoming Jury Bias* (paper and lecture at meeting of the National College of Advocacy, Feb. 12-16, 2003) (identifying jurors' distrust of information they believe lawyers have manipulated).

Moving to Reopen the Deposition

If the defending attorney instructs the deponent not to answer questions that would explain the reasons for changing testimony, the remedy is to bring a motion to compel additional testimony to explain the basis for the change in testimony. The court must decide whether the record warrants reopening the deposition and, if so, the permissible extent of inquiry by the deposing lawyer when resuming the deposition. Little jurisprudence specifically addresses how courts should handle changes in testimony resulting from attorney-client conferences in non-*Hall* jurisdictions, but a few decisions, as well as an analogous rule, provide guidance.

Existing Jurisprudence: Testimony Changed After an Attorney-Client Conference

Courts are most likely to reopen a deposition for further questioning if an improper attorney-client conference occurs while a question is pending, and the conference appears to cause a change in testimony. In *Cordova v. United States*, the court reopened the deposition and ordered the deponent to give direct answers to questions she refused to answer after an improper meeting with her counsel while a question was pending.[26] The deposing attorney was allowed to ask "limited, reasonable follow-up questions" to the deponent's answers. In *Pia v. Supernova Media Inc.*, the court ruled that the deponent was required to answer questions about attorney-client conferences that occurred while a question was pending.[27]

Conversely, other courts have tried to balance the effect that impermissible witness coaching has on ascertaining the truth with the witness's right to counsel.[28] In these instances, some courts have ruled that addressing a witness's changed testimony after a recess conference with his or her counsel is "best handled by allowing the ultimate fact-finder to consider

---

26 *Cordova*, 2006 WL 4109659 at *5-7 (presuming that the deponent's counsel had coached her to refuse to answer questions on specific topics during an improper conference).

27 *Pia v. Supernova Media Inc.*, 2011 WL 6069271 at *3 (D. Utah Dec. 6, 2011).

28 *Potashnick*, 609 F.2d at 1118-19; *Odone*, 170 F.R.D. at 67-69; *Diebold*, 2009 WL 10677801 at *2.

the circumstances of the [conference] itself and counsel's conversation with the witness[ ] in assessing the witness['s] credibility."[29]

Analogous Rule: Errata Sheet Changes

Because so few judicial opinions deal with reopening the deposition to address a change in testimony resulting from an attorney-client conference, no definitive authority exists on how courts should address this issue. When crafting a remedy for altered testimony, courts should recognize that a deposition's primary purpose is to determine the facts as understood by the witness. The deposition should not be a vehicle for a defending attorney to mold the testimony to create a legally convenient record.[30] Therefore, the logical approach is to look to the analogous jurisprudence governing errata sheet changes for guidance. Rule 30(e) allows a deponent to make errata sheet changes to form and substance of their deposition testimony within 30 days of the transcript's delivery.[31] Regardless of whether a change in testimony occurs during the deposition or up to 30 days afterward in an errata sheet, there is no real substantive difference—the testimony has been changed.

When a changed answer in an errata sheet is a significant departure from what was said on the record, most courts permit parties to ask questions about the basis for changes to testimony and determine "whether such changes originate with the attorney or the deponent."[32] If the errata sheet contains a substantive change to the deposition testimony, courts use a materiality test to determine whether the deposition may be reopened to inquire into the basis for the change.[33] The materiality standard to reopen a deposition is whether the changes contained in the errata sheets "make

---

29 *Ecker*, 2008 WL 1777222 at *1; *see also Diebold*, 2009 WL 10677801 at *1-2.

30 *See Hall*, 150 F.R.D. at 528.

31 Fed. R. Civ. P. 30(e); For in-depth analysis, see Mark Kosieradzki, 30(b)(6): Deposing Corporations, Organizations & the Government, ch. 16 (Trial Guides 2015).

32 *Tingley Sys., Inc. v. CSC Consulting, Inc.*, 152 F. Supp. 2d 95, 121 (D. Mass. 2001); *see Luhman v. Dalkon Shield Claimants Tr.*, 1994 WL 542048 at *1 (D. Kan. Oct. 3, 1994).

33 *Tingley Sys.*, 152 F. Supp. 2d at 120.

the deposition incomplete or useless without further testimony."[34] If the court decides that the change from the errata sheet is material, it will allow the deposition to be reopened. The logical extension of the errata sheet rule is to order the deposition reopened to inquire about the basis of changed testimony following an attorney-client conference.

Summary

- Rule 30(c)(1) requires depositions to proceed as they would at trial.

- A lawyer is absolutely prohibited from coaching his or her client during a deposition.

- A client may confer with his or her lawyer while a question is pending for the purpose of determining whether to assert a privilege.

- When asserting a privilege, defending counsel must create a record of the existence of the conference, as well as its subject matter.

- *Hall* standard: All attorney-client conferences during a deposition are prohibited except to decide whether to assert a privilege.

- *Stratosphere* standard: Attorney-client conferences are permissible during recesses *not requested by defending counsel* so long as no question is pending and no active line of questioning is open.

- If a witness a changes his or her testimony based on a conversation with a lawyer, courts have the authority to determine that the attorney-client privilege is waived on the subject.

---

34 *Tingley Sys.*, 152 F. Supp. 2d at 120.

CHAPTER 9
SANCTIONS

"[T]he Court has a lot of arrows in its quiver. And the bow is strung."

—The Hon. George R. Smith[1]

---

1 Zottola v. Anesthesia Consultants of Savannah, P.C., 2012 WL 6824150 at *7 (S.D. Ga. June 7, 2012).

Introduction

Deposition obstruction is sanctionable. Rules 30 and 32 establish the standards for deposition conduct.[2] Rule 37 creates the framework that courts use to impose sanctions when those standards have been violated. Rule 37(a) details the procedure to file a motion to compel discovery and the corresponding sanctions when such a motion is granted. Rule 37(b) details the harsher sanctions that are available if a party fails to obey a discovery-related court order.

In addition to the sanctions identified in the Rules of Civil Procedure, courts also have the inherent power to police those appearing before them.[3] "Taken together, Rules 26(f), 30, and 37(a), along with Rule 16, which gives the court control over pre-trial case management, vest the court with broad authority and discretion to control discovery, including the conduct of depositions."[4] In their equitable power, courts have extremely broad discretion to ensure a just outcome.

Deposition Obstruction Is Sanctionable

Fed. R. Civ. P. 30(d)(2) authorizes sanctions for the different types of deposition misconduct discussed throughout this book. The rule states:

> **Sanction.** The court may impose an appropriate sanction—including the reasonable expenses and attorney's fees incurred by any party—on a person who impedes, delays, or frustrates the fair examination of the deponent.[5]

Rule 30(d)(2) sanctions apply to "any person responsible for an impediment that frustrated the fair examination of the deponent."[6] This includes anyone involved in the deposition, whether it is the deponent,

---

2 Fed. R. Civ. P. 30 & 32.

3 *Sciarretta v. Lincoln Nat'l Life Ins. Co.*, 778 F.3d 1205, 1213 (2015) (citing *Chambers v. NASCO, Inc.*, 501 U.S. 32, 46 (1991)).

4 *Hall v. Clifton Precision*, 150 F.R.D. 525, 527 (E.D. Pa. 1993).

5 Fed. R. Civ. P. 30(d)(2).

6 Fed. R. Civ. P. 30, 2000 committee notes subd. d.

lawyers attending the deposition, a party to the lawsuit, or anybody else who is involved.[7]

The Advisory Committee Notes to the 1993 amendments make it absolutely clear that lawyers defending depositions are subject to sanctions under Rule 30(d)(2) for any form of deposition obstruction:

> [Rule 30(d)(2)] authorizes appropriate sanctions not only when a deposition is unreasonably prolonged, but also when an attorney engages in other practices that improperly frustrate the fair examination of the deponent, such as *making improper objections or giving [prohibited] instructions not to answer.* . . . In general, counsel should not engage in any conduct during a deposition that would not be allowed in the presence of a judicial officer.[8]

Rule 30(d)(2) sanctions are appropriate for all the different types of deposition misconduct discussed throughout this book. This sanctionable conduct includes:

- speaking objections[9]
- excessive unnecessary objections[10]
- abusive conduct[11]
- impermissible instructions not to answer[12]
- a deponent's unilateral refusal not to answer[13]
- impermissible off-the-record attorney-client conferences[14]

---

7 Fed. R. Civ. P. 30, 2000 committee notes subd. d.
8 Fed. R. Civ. P. 30, 1993 committee notes subd. d (emphasis added).
9 *See* Chapter 5 of this book.
10 *See* Chapter 5 of this book.
11 *See* Chapter 4 of this book.
12 *See* Chapter 6 of this book.
13 *See* Chapter 6 of this book.
14 *See* Chapter 8 of this book.

producing a 30(b)(6) designee who is unprepared to answer the matters of examination listed in the 30(b)(6) deposition notice[15]

Regardless of the offending attorney's intentions, all the above misconduct is sanctionable if it frustrates the deponent's fair examination. The court in *Sicurelli v. Jeneric/Pentron, Inc.* explained that demonstrating "bad faith" is not the threshold to impose Rule 30(d)(2) sanctions:

> [F]or purposes of [Rule 30(d)(2)], a clear showing of bad faith on the part of the attorney against whom sanctions are sought is not required. Instead, the imposition of sanctions under [Rule 30(d)(2)] requires only that the attorney's conduct frustrated the fair examination of the deponent.[16]

Although bad faith is not a condition required to impose sanctions, it is hard to imagine a scenario where the disruptions listed above could be made in good faith.

Remedies for Deposition Obstruction

Rule 30(d)(2) expressly authorizes sanctions for deposition misconduct. The request for sanctions, brought pursuant to Rule 30(d)(2), should request a specific remedy for the court to evaluate.[17] Possible remedies for deposition misconduct include:

- a motion to reopen the deposition pursuant to Rule 37(a)
- a motion requesting that the court admonish the offending party for his or her deposition misconduct

---

15   *Arctic Cat, Inc. v. Injection Research Specialists, Inc.*, 210 F.R.D. 680, 683 (D. Minn. 2002); *Black Horse Lane Assoc., L.P. v. Dow Chem. Corp.*, 228 F.3d 275, 304 (3rd Cir. 2000); *Starlight Int'l, Inc. v. Herlihy*, 186 F.R.D. 626, 649 (D. Kan. 1999); *Bank of N.Y. v. Meridien BIAO Bank Tanzania Ltd.*, 171 F.R.D. 135, 171 (S.D.N.Y. 1997); *see* Chapter 7 of this book; *see also* Mark Kosieradzki, 30(b)(6): Deposing Corporations, Organizations & the Government (Trial Guides 2015) (for a comprehensive analysis of 30(b)(6) depositions).

16   *Sicurelli v. Jeneric/Pentron, Inc.*, 2005 WL 3591701 at *8 (E.D.N.Y. Dec. 30, 2005); *GMAC Bank v. HTFC Corp.*, 248 F.R.D. 182, 196 (E.D. Pa. 2008).

17   Kosieradzki 330.

- a motion requesting that the court issue an order for protocol
- such economic sanctions as the court sees fit

If bad faith is demonstrated, the court can impose additional punitive sanctions in the interest of justice.[18]

"Meet and Confer" Requirement

Parties are required to work together to attempt to resolve discovery disputes before seeking resolution from the court. Rule 37(a)(1) requires the moving party to include certification that they conferred or attempted to confer with the non-moving party to resolve the discovery dispute before filing a motion to compel:

> The motion [to compel] must include a certification that the movant has in good faith conferred or attempted to confer with the person or party failing to make disclosure or discovery in an effort to obtain it without court action.[19]

This requirement exists because "meaningful consultation can lead to informal resolution and thus conservation of court resources."[20] In *Shuffle Master, Inc. v. Progressive Games, Inc.*, the court explained the requirements of a proper certification:

> [A] moving party must include more than a cursory recitation that counsel have been "unable to resolve the matter." Counsel . . . must adequately set forth in the motion essential facts sufficient to enable the court to pass a preliminary judgment on the adequacy and sincerity of the good faith conferment between the parties. That is, a certificate must include, *inter alia*, the names of the parties who conferred or attempted to confer, the manner by which they communicated, the dispute

---

18 See *Sciarretta*, 778 F.3d 1205.

19 Fed. R. Civ. P. 37(a)(1).

20 *Hernandez v. Hendrix Produce, Inc.*, 297 F.R.D. 538, 540 n.3 (S.D. Ga. 2014); *see* Fed. R. Civ. P. 37, 1993 committee notes subd. a ("This requirement [of Rule 37(a)(1)] is based on successful experience with similar local rules of court. . . .").

at issue, as well as the dates, times, and results of their discussions, if any.[21]

The specific actions that satisfy the requirement to meet and confer depend on the local jurisdiction's rules. However, the *Shuffle Master* court laid out universal "meet and confer" principles that apply to all Rule 37(a) motions:

> "Good faith" under [37(a)(1)] contemplates, among other things, honesty in one's purpose to meaningfully discuss the discovery dispute, freedom from intention to defraud or abuse the discovery process, and faithfulness to one's obligation to secure information without court action. . . . "Good faith" is tested by the court according to the nature of the dispute, the reasonableness of the positions held by the respective parties, and the means by which both sides conferred. Accordingly, good faith cannot be shown merely through the perfunctory parroting of statutory language on the certificate to secure court intervention; rather it mandates a *genuine attempt to resolve the discovery dispute through non-judicial means.*
>
> . . . [I]n order to bring a proper motion to compel under Rule [37(a)(1)], a moving party must personally engage in two-way communication with the nonresponding party to meaningfully discuss each contested discovery dispute in a genuine effort to avoid judicial intervention.[22]

The sufficiency of the 37(a)(1) "meet and confer" prerequisite is determined on a case-by-case basis. "Neither face-to-face nor telephone contact is necessarily essential to the 'good faith' certification requirement in every case. Sometimes letters, emails, or faxes will suffice."[23]

Motion to Compel

If a witness refuses to answer a deposition question adequately, whether independently or through his or her lawyer's coaching, Rule 37(a) allows the examining party to ask the court to compel an answer to the deposition

---

21 *Shuffle Master, Inc. v. Progressive Games, Inc.*, 170 F.R.D. 166, 171 (D. Nev. 1996).

22 *Shuffle Master,* 170 F.R.D. at 171 (emphasis added).

23 *Scruggs v. Int'l Paper Co.*, 2012 WL 1899405 at *2 (S.D. Ga. May 24, 2012).

question.[24] Rule 37(a)(1) establishes the general right to seek a motion to compel discovery:

> **(1) In General.** On notice to other parties and all affected persons, a party may move for an order compelling disclosure or discovery.[25]

Rule 37(a)(3)(B)(i) authorizes motions to compel answers to deposition questions:

> **(B)** *To Compel a Discovery Response.* A party seeking discovery may move for an order compelling an answer, designation, production, or inspection. This motion may be made if:
>
> > **(i)** a deponent fails to answer a question asked under Rule 30 or 31.[26]

An incomplete or evasive answer to a deposition question constitutes a valid reason to file a motion to compel. Rule 37(a)(4) states:

> ***Evasive or Incomplete Disclosure, Answer, or Response.*** For purposes of [Rule 37(a)], an evasive or incomplete disclosure, answer, or response must be treated as a failure to disclose, answer, or respond.[27]

Whether an answer is considered incomplete or evasive is a fact question to be determined by the court. Building a record with clear, precise questions is important, so the court can evaluate the answers objectively.

All the misconduct discussed in this book can necessitate a motion to compel. If the misconduct impeded the deponent's fair examination—causing important questions to go unanswered or insufficiently

---

[24] Fed. R. Civ. P. 37(a)(3)(C) states the proper sequence for filing a motion to compel: "When taking an oral deposition, the party asking a question may complete or adjourn the examination before moving for an order."

[25] Fed. R. Civ. P. 37(a)(1); Fed. R. Civ. P. 37(a)(2) establishes the proper jurisdiction for a motion to compel: "A motion for an order to a party must be made in the court where the action is pending. A motion for an order to a nonparty must be made in the court where the discovery is or will be taken."

[26] Fed. R. Civ. P. 37(a)(3)(B)(i).

[27] Fed. R. Civ. P. 37(a)(4).

answered—the misconduct directly violates Rule 30(d)(2) and is sanctionable under a Rule 37(a)(3)(B)(i) motion to compel.

Motion for Admonishment & Order for Deposition Protocol

Independent of a 37(a) motion to compel, a party can file a motion requesting that the court admonish the offending party's deposition misconduct and issue additional Rule 30(d)(2) sanctions. The court's broad authority and discretion to control discovery allows it to order appropriate sanctions to prevent discovery abuse, which includes admonishing the offending attorney.[28] The court also may issue an order specifying proper protocol in future depositions.[29]

Payment of Expenses and Attorney Fees

Rule 30(d)(2) and Rules 37(a)(5)(A-B) all generally require the court to award to the prevailing party the reasonable fees and expenses related to the motion. Rule 37(a)(5)(A) details the procedure when the court grants a motion to compel:

> *If the Motion Is Granted (or Disclosure or Discovery Is Provided After Filing).* If the motion is granted—or if the disclosure or requested discovery is provided after the motion was filed—the court must, after giving an opportunity to be heard, require the party or deponent whose conduct necessitated the motion, the party or attorney advising that conduct, or both to pay the movant's reasonable expenses incurred in making the motion, including attorney's fees. But the court must not order this payment if:

---

28   See *Hall*, 150 F.R.D. at 527; *Redwood v. Dobson*, 476 F.3d 462, 470 (7th Cir. 2007); *Rojas v. X Motorsport, Inc.*, 275 F. Supp. 3d 898, 910 (N.D. Ill. 2017); *BNSF Ry. Co. v. San Joaquin Valley R.R. Co.*, 2009 WL 3872043 at *4 (E.D. Cal. Nov. 17, 2009); *Jadwin v. Abraham*, 2008 WL 4057921 at *7 (E.D. Cal. Aug. 22, 2008); *Clay v. Consol Penn. Coal Co., LLC*, 2013 WL 5408064 at *5 (N.D. W.Va. Sept. 25, 2013).

29   See *In re Stratosphere Corp. Sec. Litig.*, 182 F.R.D. 614, 618 (D. Nev. 1998); *In re St. Jude Med., Inc.*, 2002 WL 1050311 at *5 (D. Minn. May 24, 2002).

(i) the movant filed the motion before attempting in good faith to obtain the disclosure or discovery without court action;

(ii) the opposing party's nondisclosure, response, or objection was substantially justified; or

(iii) other circumstances make an award of expenses unjust.[30]

Rule 37(a)(5)(B) details the procedure when the court denies a motion to compel:

If the Motion Is Denied. If the motion is denied, the court may issue any protective order authorized under Rule 26(c) and must, after giving an opportunity to be heard, require the movant, the attorney filing the motion, or both to pay the party or deponent who opposed the motion its reasonable expenses incurred in opposing the motion, including attorney's fees. But the court must not order this payment if the motion was substantially justified or other circumstances make an award of expenses unjust.[31]

Both rules require the court to give the offending party notice and an opportunity to be heard before awarding reasonable expenses.[32] Although both rules also require the court to award reasonable expenses and fees to the prevailing party, the court can choose not to award these expenses if the losing party's conduct was "substantially justified,"[33] or "other circumstances make an award of expenses unjust."[34] Ultimately, the courts have broad discretion to determine whether either exception applies to the motion at hand, and they can use this discretion to award reasonable expenses as they see fit.[35]

---

30 Fed. R. Civ. P. 37(a)(5)(A).

31 Fed. R. Civ. P. 37(a)(5)(B).

32 Fed. R. Civ. P. 37(a)(5)(A-B).

33 Fed. R. Civ. P. 37(a)(5)(A)(ii).

34 Fed. R. Civ. P. 37(a)(5)(A)(iii).

35 If a motion to compel is granted in part and denied in part, Fed. R. Civ. P. 37(a)(5)(C) allows the court to apportion reasonable expenses.

Failure to Comply With a Court Order

If a party violates a discovery-related court order, the court may issue harsher sanctions than the payment of fees and expenses incurred from the violation. These sanctions are non-monetary and instead affect the merits of the pending action. Rule 37(b)(2)(A) states:

> *For Not Obeying a Discovery Order.* If a party or a party's officer, director, or managing agent—or a witness designated under Rule 30(b)(6) or 31(a)(4)—fails to obey an order to provide or permit discovery, including an order under Rule 26(f), 35, or 37(a), the court where the action is pending may issue further just orders.[36]

Sanctions the court may impose for violating a discovery-related court order include, but are not limited to,[37] the following expressly listed in Rule 37(b)(2)(A)(i-vii):

- adverse inferences of facts against the offending party
- prohibiting specific claims or defenses
- striking pleadings
- staying proceedings until the order is obeyed
- dismissing the action
- rendering a default judgment
- holding the offending party in contempt of court[38]

Collectively, these sanctions are more severe because they affect the case's merits through judicial intervention.

Rule 37(b)(2)(C) requires that the disobedient party pay the reasonable expenses caused by violating the court order, subject to the standard

---

36 Fed. R. Civ. P. 37(b)(2).

37 *See Shcherbakovskiy v. Da Capo Al Fine, Ltd.*, 490 F.3d 130, 135 (2nd Cir. 2007); *United States v. One 1999 Forty Seven Foot Fountain Motor Vessel*, 240 F.R.D. 695, 697 (S.D. Fla. 2007); *Nat'l Hockey League v. Metro. Hockey Club, Inc.*, 427 U.S. 639 (1976) (per curiam).

38 Fed. R. Civ. P. 37(b)(2)(A)(i-vii); Kosieradzki 352.

exceptions of the violation being substantially justified or other circumstances making the award of expenses unjust.[39]

Rule 37(b)(1) provides the procedure when a nonparty violates a court order in the district where the deposition is located but the pending action is not.[40] In these instances, the court can hold the offending nonparty in contempt of court or transfer the motion to the court where the action is pending, allowing that court to hold the nonparty in contempt.[41] Rule 37(b)(1) is the only section of Rule 37(b) that applies to nonparties.

A Party's Failure to Attend Its Own Deposition

Under the express language of Rule 37, a party that refuses to attend a deposition will be sanctioned.[42] Rule 37(d)(1)(A)(i) states,

> *Motion; Grounds for Sanctions.* The court where the action is pending may, on motion, order sanctions if:
>
> > **(i)** a party or a party's officer, director, or managing agent—or a person designated under Rule 30(b)(6) or 31(a)(4)—fails, after being served with proper notice, to appear for that person's deposition.[43]

Objecting to the deposition notice is not a permissible basis to refuse to attend a deposition, even if the notice is properly objectionable.[44] Rule 37(d)(2) states:

---

39   Fed. R. Civ. P. 37(b)(2)(C); *see* Fed. R. Civ. P. 37(a)(5)(A).

40   Fed. R. Civ. P. 37(b)(1).

41   Fed. R. Civ. P. 37(b)(1); see also *Pioneer Drive, LLC v. Nissan Diesel Am., Inc.*, 262 F.R.D. 552, 560–61 (D. Mont. 2009) ("Failure to provide knowledgeable designees who can answer on behalf of Defendant shall be treated as contempt of court pursuant to Fed. R. Civ. P. 37(b), and in such a circumstance Defendant's designee(s) and counsel may be jailed until the matters are testified to properly.").

42   Fed. R. Civ. P. 37(d)(1)(A)(i).

43   Fed. R. Civ. P. 37(d)(1)(A).

44   *Beach Mart, Inc. v. L & L Wings, Inc.*, 302 F.R.D. 396, 406 (E.D. N.C. 2014) (citing *New England Carpenters Health Benefits Fund v. First DataBank, Inc.*, 242 F.R.D. 164, 166 (D. Mass. 2007)); *Mitsui & Co. (U.S.A.), Inc. v. P.R. Water Res. Auth.*, 93 F.R.D. 62, 67 (D. P.R. 1981) (citing 8A C. Wright, A. Miller & R. Marcus, Fed. Prac. & Proc. Civ. § 2035, at 262); Fed. R. Civ. P. 37(d), 1970 committee notes subd. d.

(2) *Unacceptable Excuse for Failing to Act.* A failure described in Rule 37(d)(1)(A) is not excused on the ground that the discovery sought was objectionable, unless the party failing to act has a pending motion for a protective order under Rule 26(c).[45]

If a party does not want to comply with a notice of deposition, it is that party's responsibility to seek a protective order.[46] If it does not, it will be sanctioned for not appearing at the deposition.

The permissible sanctions for violating a discovery-related court order may include any of the Rule 37(b)(2)(A) sanctions on the case's merits and must include paying expenses to the non-offending party resulting from the failure to attend.[47]

Courts Have Broad Discretion to Control Discovery by Imposing Sanctions

The function of discovery sanctions is not only to punish offending parties for committing discovery abuses but also—equally important—to deter parties from committing discovery abuses in the first place.[48] In *National Hockey League v. Metropolitan Hockey Club*, the U.S. Supreme Court endorsed the use of sanctions to deter discovery abuse, saying that sanctions to deter discovery abuse would be more effective if they were diligently applied "not merely to penalize those whose conduct may be deemed to warrant such a sanction, but to deter those who might be tempted to such conduct in the absence of such a deterrent."[49]

---

45 Fed. R. Civ. P. 37(d)(2).

46 Fed. R. Civ. P. 37(d), 1970 committee notes subd. d.

47 Fed. R. Civ. P. 37(d)(3) (subject to the same exceptions as Fed. R. Civ. P. 37(a)(5)(A)).

48 *See* Fed. R. Civ. P. 26, 1993 committee notes subd. g (quoting *Nat'l Hockey League v. Metro. Hockey Club*, 427 U.S. at 643).

49 Fed. R. Civ. P. 26(g), 1983 committee notes subd. g (quoting *Nat'l Hockey League*, 427 U.S. at 643).

Accordingly, in addition to the authority that the Rules of Civil Procedure enumerate, courts are empowered to use their broad discretion to police the parties to a suit to ensure just outcomes in discovery.[50]

If the court determines that a party acted in bad faith, the court is not limited to the minimum statutory standard of awarding payment of reasonable expenses and fees.[51] As the U.S. Supreme Court explained in *Chambers v. NASCO, Inc.*:

> [A] federal court [is not] forbidden to sanction bad-faith conduct by means of the inherent power simply because that conduct could also be sanctioned under the statute or the Rules. . . . [W]hen there is bad-faith conduct in the course of litigation that could be adequately sanctioned under the Rules, the court ordinarily should rely on the Rules rather than the inherent power. But if in the informed discretion of the court, neither the statute nor the Rules are up to the task, the court may safely rely on its inherent power.[52]

In *Sciarretta v. Lincoln National Life Insurance Co.*, the U.S. Court of Appeals for the Eleventh Circuit affirmed the trial court's $850,000 sanction against a nonparty for selectively preparing a designated 30(b)(6) corporate witness.[53] The court found that preparing a 30(b)(6) designee with only the self-serving half of the story was not acting in good faith.[54]

If the court discovers that a person or entity appearing in a deposition acted in bad faith, the court has the inherent power to raise the

---

50 *Sciarretta*, 778 F.3d at 1213 (citing *Chambers v. NASCO, Inc.*, 501 U.S. 32, 46 (1991)).

51 See *Chambers*, 501 U.S. at 50; *F.J. Hanshaw Enters., Inc. v. Emerald River Develop., Inc.*, 244 F.3d 1128, 1136-37 (9th Cir. 2001); *Zottola*, 2012 WL 6824150 at *7.

52 *Chambers*, 501 U.S. at 50.

53 *Sciarretta*, 778 F.3d 1205.

54 *Sciarretta*, 778 F.3d at 1213.

issue of obstruction on its own (sua sponte) and impose appropriate sanctions on the offending party.[55]

Summary

- Deposition conduct is sanctionable under Rules 30, 32, and 37.

- Courts have broad discretion to control discovery in pending actions.

- Conduct by any individual that impedes the fair examination of the deponent is sanctionable.

- A finding of bad faith *is not* required to impose sanctions for deposition misconduct.

- Parties must confer and make a good-faith attempt to resolve discovery disputes before involving the court.

- If a deponent refuses to adequately answer a deposition question, a motion to compel an answer is appropriate.

- The losing party in a discovery motion is required to pay the prevailing party's reasonable fees and expenses incurred because of the motion, unless the losing party's conduct was substantially justified or other circumstances make the award of expenses unjust.

- Courts have inherent power and broad discretion to impose sanctions to ensure just outcomes in discovery.

- Courts may impose sanctions sua sponte (on their own) if they discover bad-faith discovery conduct.

---

55   *Sciarretta*, 778 F.3d at 1212 (citing *Roadway Express, Inc. v. Piper*, 447 U.S. 752, 765–66 (1980)); *Sec. Nat'l Bank of Sioux City, IA v. Day*, 800 F.3d 936, 942 (8th Cir. 2015) ("Courts may nonetheless impose Rule 30(d)(2) sanctions on their own accord in order to deter ongoing and future misconduct.").

- If a court determines a party acted in bad faith, the court is not limited to imposing the corresponding sanctions enumerated in the Federal Rules. It may impose any appropriate sanction in the interest of justice.
- When a party violates a discovery-related court order, in addition to reasonable fees and expenses, that party can be subject to sanctions that affect the merits of the case through judicial intervention.

EPILOGUE

Our civil courts enable every citizen to demand accountability for being wronged. They give every citizen the right to face his or her accusers. Truth is the bedrock of our democratic civil justice system. Our courts have carefully designed rules of discovery that guarantee equal access to the facts for everyone, ensuring that all sides have equal access to the truth. Disputes can then be resolved by applying legal principles to those facts.

These rules aren't aspirational. They are rules of engagement designed to get to the truth. They recognize the reality of human conflict, and they channel the passions of those conflicts into controlled forums. If these rules are ignored, litigation becomes nothing more than an adolescent food fight.

I didn't go to law school to become a loophole lawyer. I didn't study day and night to learn how to weasel out of the truth. I went to law school because I thought I could make a difference. The problem we face today is that many lawyers have decided that the rule of law is not about getting to the truth. Rather than using the rules to ensure that disputes are resolved based on the application of legal principles to a set of facts, many lawyers have concluded that winning at all costs is all that matters. To do so, they obstruct access to information instead of engaging on the merits. Litigation, for them, is a game of cat-and-mouse. A game of *catch me if you can*.

This is not what we, as lawyers, should be about. I wrote this book as a guide to how we must conduct ourselves professionally in deposition discovery. The rules apply to everyone, regardless of which side we represent. In the end, I have learned that all our clients are best served if we follow the rules. It really does work.

I join trial teams throughout the country. I've lectured in almost every state. Wherever I go, people say, "Mark, your presentation is great, but our judges never enforce those rules." I always encourage them to try it! Take the high ground. Be patient. Be persistent. Don't get sucked into the vortex. Let the obstructionists show who they really are, as their obstruction unfolds across the pages of the deposition record. If the record shows obstruction, as detailed throughout this book, we have found that 9 times out of 10, the court agrees. Lawyers throughout the country who have exposed obstruction have told me afterward that they were surprised it worked, and that they now feel like they can stand up to the bullies.

Charlie Chan had it right. "If strength were all, tiger would not fear scorpion."[1] You can do it. Go out there, use the rules, and find the truth.

—MRK

---

[1] Charlie Chan's Secret (Twentieth Century Fox 1936).

APPENDIX A:
FEDERAL RULES OF CIVIL PROCEDURE 1, 26, 30, 32 & 37

Rule 1. Scope and Purpose[1]

These rules govern the procedure in all civil actions and proceedings in the United States district courts, except as stated in Rule 81. They should be construed, administered, and employed by the court and the parties to secure the just, speedy, and inexpensive determination of every action and proceeding.

---

1   Fed. R. Civ. P. 1. (As amended Dec. 29, 1948, eff. Oct. 20, 1949; Feb. 28, 1966, eff. July 1, 1966; Apr. 22, 1993, eff. Dec. 1, 1993; Apr. 30, 2007, eff. Dec. 1, 2007; Apr. 29, 2015, eff. Dec. 1, 2015.)

Rule 26. Duty to Disclose; General Provisions Governing Discovery[2]

a) **REQUIRED DISCLOSURES.**

1) Initial Disclosure.

A) In General. Except as exempted by Rule 26(a)(1)(B) or as otherwise stipulated or ordered by the court, a party must, without awaiting a discovery request, provide to the other parties:

(i) the name and, if known, the address and telephone number of each individual likely to have discoverable information—along with the subjects of that information—that the disclosing party may use to support its claims or defenses, unless the use would be solely for impeachment;

(ii) a copy—or a description by category and location—of all documents, electronically stored information, and tangible things that the disclosing party has in its possession, custody, or control and may use to support its claims or defenses, unless the use would be solely for impeachment;

(iii) a computation of each category of damages claimed by the disclosing party—who must also make available for inspection and copying as under Rule 34 the documents or other evidentiary material, unless privileged or protected from disclosure, on which each computation is based, including materials bearing on the nature and extent of injuries suffered; and

(iv) for inspection and copying as under Rule 34, any insurance agreement under which an insurance business may be liable to satisfy all or part of a possible judgment in the action or to indemnify or reimburse for payments made to satisfy the judgment.

---

2   Fed. R. Civ. P. 26. (As amended Dec. 27, 1946, eff. Mar. 19, 1948; Jan. 21, 1963, eff. July 1, 1963; Feb. 28, 1966, eff. July 1, 1966; Mar. 30, 1970, eff. July 1, 1970; Apr. 29, 1980, eff. Aug. 1, 1980; Apr. 28, 1983, eff. Aug. 1, 1983; Mar. 2, 1987, eff. Aug. 1, 1987; Apr. 22, 1993, eff. Dec. 1, 1993; Apr. 17, 2000, eff. Dec. 1, 2000; Apr. 12, 2006, eff. Dec. 1, 2006; Apr. 30, 2007, eff. Dec. 1, 2007; Apr. 28, 2010, eff. Dec. 1, 2010; Apr. 29, 2015, eff. Dec. 1, 2015.)

B) Proceedings Exempt from Initial Disclosure. The following proceedings are exempt from initial disclosure:

   (i) an action for review on an administrative record;

   (ii) a forfeiture action in rem arising from a federal statute;

   (iii) a petition for habeas corpus or any other proceeding to challenge a criminal conviction or sentence;

   (iv) an action brought without an attorney by a person in the custody of the United States, a state, or a state subdivision;

   (v) an action to enforce or quash an administrative summons or subpoena;

   (vi) an action by the United States to recover benefit payments;

   (vii) an action by the United States to collect on a student loan guaranteed by the United States;

   (viii) a proceeding ancillary to a proceeding in another court; and

   (ix) an action to enforce an arbitration award.

C) Time for Initial Disclosures—In General. A party must make the initial disclosures at or within 14 days after the parties' Rule 26(f) conference unless a different time is set by stipulation or court order, or unless a party objects during the conference that initial disclosures are not appropriate in this action and states the objection in the proposed discovery plan. In ruling on the objection, the court must determine what disclosures, if any, are to be made and must set the time for disclosure.

D) Time for Initial Disclosures—For Parties Served or Joined Later. A party that is first served or otherwise joined after the Rule 26(f) conference must make the initial disclosures within 30 days after being served or joined, unless a different time is set by stipulation or court order.

E) Basis for Initial Disclosure; Unacceptable Excuses. A party must make its initial disclosures based on the information then reasonably available to it. A party is not excused from making its disclosures because it has not fully investigated the case or because it challenges the sufficiency of another party's disclosures or because another party has not made its disclosures.

2) *Disclosure of Expert Testimony*.

A) In General. In addition to the disclosures required by Rule 26(a)(1), a party must disclose to the other parties the identity of any witness it may use at trial to present evidence under Federal Rule of Evidence 702, 703, or 705.

B) Witnesses Who Must Provide a Written Report. Unless otherwise stipulated or ordered by the court, this disclosure must be accompanied by a written report—prepared and signed by the witness—if the witness is one retained or specially employed to provide expert testimony in the case or one whose duties as the party's employee regularly involve giving expert testimony. The report must contain:

(i) a complete statement of all opinions the witness will express and the basis and reasons for them;

(ii) the facts or data considered by the witness in forming them;

(iii) any exhibits that will be used to summarize or support them;

(iv) the witness's qualifications, including a list of all publications authored in the previous 10 years;

(v) a list of all other cases in which, during the previous 4 years, the witness testified as an expert at trial or by deposition; and

(vi) a statement of the compensation to be paid for the study and testimony in the case.

C) Witnesses Who Do Not Provide a Written Report. Unless otherwise stipulated or ordered by the court, if the witness is not required to provide a written report, this disclosure must state:

(i) the subject matter on which the witness is expected to present evidence under Federal Rule of Evidence 702, 703, or 705; and

(ii) a summary of the facts and opinions to which the witness is expected to testify.

D) *Time to Disclose Expert Testimony.* A party must make these disclosures at the times and in the sequence that the court orders. Absent a stipulation or a court order, the disclosures must be made:

(i) at least 90 days before the date set for trial or for the case to be ready for trial; or

(ii) if the evidence is intended solely to contradict or rebut evidence on the same subject matter identified by another party under Rule 26(a)(2)(B) or (C), within 30 days after the other party's disclosure.

E) *Supplementing the Disclosure.* The parties must supplement these disclosures when required under Rule 26(e).

3) **Pretrial Disclosures.**

A) *In General.* In addition to the disclosures required by Rule 26(a)(1) and (2), a party must provide to the other parties and promptly file the following information about the evidence that it may present at trial other than solely for impeachment:

(i) the name and, if not previously provided, the address and telephone number of each witness—separately identifying those the party expects to present and those it may call if the need arises;

(ii) the designation of those witnesses whose testimony the party expects to present by deposition and, if not taken stenographically, a transcript of the pertinent parts of the deposition; and

(iii) an identification of each document or other exhibit, including summaries of other evidence—separately identifying those items the party expects to offer and those it may offer if the need arises.

B) *Time for Pretrial Disclosures; Objections.* Unless the court orders otherwise, these disclosures must be made at least 30 days before trial. Within 14 days after they are made, unless the court sets a different time, a party may serve and promptly file a list of the following objections: any objections to the use under Rule 32(a) of a deposition designated by another party under Rule 26(a)(3)(A)(ii); and any objection, together with the grounds for it, that may be made to the admissibility of materials identified under Rule 26(a)(3)(A)(iii). An objection not so made—except for one under Federal Rule of Evidence 402 or 403—is waived unless excused by the court for good cause.

4) *Form of Disclosures.* Unless the court orders otherwise, all disclosures under Rule 26(a) must be in writing, signed, and served.

b) DISCOVERY SCOPE AND LIMITS.

1) *Scope in General.* Unless otherwise limited by court order, the scope of discovery is as follows: Parties may obtain discovery regarding any nonprivileged matter that is relevant to any party's claim or defense and proportional to the needs of the case, considering the importance of the issues at stake in the action, the amount in controversy, the parties' relative access to relevant information, the parties' resources, the importance of the discovery in resolving the issues, and whether the burden or expense of the proposed discovery outweighs its likely benefit. Information within this scope of discovery need not be admissible in evidence to be discoverable.

2) *Limitations on Frequency and Extent.*

A) When Permitted. By order, the court may alter the limits in these rules on the number of depositions and interrogatories or on the length of depositions under Rule 30. By order or local rule, the court may also limit the number of requests under Rule 36.

B) Specific Limitations on Electronically Stored Information. A party need not provide discovery of electronically stored information from sources that the party identifies as not reasonably accessible because of undue burden or cost. On motion to compel discovery or for a protective order, the party from whom discovery is sought must show that the information is not reasonably accessible because of undue burden or cost. If that showing is made, the court may nonetheless order discovery from such sources if the requesting party shows good cause, considering the limitations of Rule 26(b)(2)(C). The court may specify conditions for the discovery.

C) When Required. On motion or on its own, the court must limit the frequency or extent of discovery otherwise allowed by these rules or by local rule if it determines that:

(i) the discovery sought is unreasonably cumulative or duplicative, or can be obtained from some other source that is more convenient, less burdensome, or less expensive;

(ii) the party seeking discovery has had ample opportunity to obtain the information by discovery in the action; or

(iii) the proposed discovery is outside the scope permitted by Rule 26(b)(1).

3) *Trial Preparation: Materials.*

A) Documents and Tangible Things. Ordinarily, a party may not discover documents and tangible things that are prepared in anticipation of litigation or for trial by or for another party or its representative (including the other party's attorney, consultant, surety, indemnitor, insurer, or agent). But, subject to Rule 26(b)(4), those materials may be discovered if:

(i) they are otherwise discoverable under Rule 26(b)(1); and

(ii) the party shows that it has substantial need for the materials to prepare its case and cannot, without undue hardship, obtain their substantial equivalent by other means.

B) Protection Against Disclosure. If the court orders discovery of those materials, it must protect against disclosure of the mental impressions, conclusions, opinions, or legal theories of a party's attorney or other representative concerning the litigation.

C) Previous Statement. Any party or other person may, on request and without the required showing, obtain the person's own previous statement about the action or its subject matter. If the request is refused, the person may move for a court order, and Rule 37(a)(5) applies to the award of expenses. A previous statement is either:

(i) a written statement that the person has signed or otherwise adopted or approved; or

(ii) a contemporaneous stenographic, mechanical, electrical, or other recording—or a transcription of it—that recites substantially verbatim the person's oral statement.

4) Trial Preparation: Experts.

A) Deposition of an Expert Who May Testify. A party may depose any person who has been identified as an expert whose opinions may be presented at trial. If Rule 26(a)(2)(B) requires a report from the expert, the deposition may be conducted only after the report is provided.

B) Trial-Preparation Protection for Draft Reports or Disclosures. Rules 26(b)(3)(A) and (B) protect drafts of any report or disclosure required under Rule 26(a)(2), regardless of the form in which the draft is recorded.

C) Trial-Preparation Protection for Communications Between a Party's Attorney and Expert Witnesses. Rules 26(b)(3)(A) and (B) protect communications between the party's attorney and any witness required to provide a report under Rule 26(a)(2)(B), regardless of the form of the communications, except to the extent that the communications:

(i) relate to compensation for the expert's study or testimony;

(ii) identify facts or data that the party's attorney provided and that the expert considered in forming the opinions to be expressed; or

(iii) identify assumptions that the party's attorney provided and that the expert relied on in forming the opinions to be expressed.

D) Expert Employed Only for Trial Preparation. Ordinarily, a party may not, by interrogatories or deposition, discover facts known or opinions held by an expert who has been retained or specially employed by another party in anticipation of litigation or to prepare for trial and who is not expected to be called as a witness at trial. But a party may do so only:

>   (i) as provided in Rule 35(b); or

>   (ii) on showing exceptional circumstances under which it is impracticable for the party to obtain facts or opinions on the same subject by other means.

> E) *Payment.* Unless manifest injustice would result, the court must require that the party seeking discovery:

>   (i) pay the expert a reasonable fee for time spent in responding to discovery under Rule 26(b)(4)(A) or (D); and

>   (ii) for discovery under (D), also pay the other party a fair portion of the fees and expenses it reasonably incurred in obtaining the expert's facts and opinions.

5) ***Claiming Privilege or Protecting Trial-Preparation Materials.***

> A) *Information Withheld.* When a party withholds information otherwise discoverable by claiming that the information is privileged or subject to protection as trial-preparation material, the party must:

>   (i) expressly make the claim; and

>   (ii) describe the nature of the documents, communications, or tangible things not produced or disclosed—and do so in a manner that, without revealing information itself privileged or protected, will enable other parties to assess the claim.

> B) *Information Produced.* If information produced in discovery is subject to a claim of privilege or of protection as trial-preparation material, the party making the claim may notify any party that received the information of the claim and the basis for it. After being notified, a party must promptly return, sequester, or destroy the specified information and any copies it has; must not use or disclose the information until the claim is resolved; must take reasonable steps to retrieve the information if the party disclosed it before being notified; and may promptly present the information to the court under seal for a determination of the

claim. The producing party must preserve the information until the claim is resolved.

c) **PROTECTIVE ORDERS.**

1) In General. A party or any person from whom discovery is sought may move for a protective order in the court where the action is pending—or as an alternative on matters relating to a deposition, in the court for the district where the deposition will be taken. The motion must include a certification that the movant has in good faith conferred or attempted to confer with other affected parties in an effort to resolve the dispute without court action. The court may, for good cause, issue an order to protect a party or person from annoyance, embarrassment, oppression, or undue burden or expense, including one or more of the following:

A) forbidding the disclosure or discovery;

B) specifying terms, including time and place or the allocation of expenses, for the disclosure or discovery;

C) prescribing a discovery method other than the one selected by the party seeking discovery;

D) forbidding inquiry into certain matters, or limiting the scope of disclosure or discovery to certain matters;

E) designating the persons who may be present while the discovery is conducted;

F) requiring that a deposition be sealed and opened only on court order;

G) requiring that a trade secret or other confidential research, development, or commercial information not be revealed or be revealed only in a specified way; and

H) requiring that the parties simultaneously file specified documents or information in sealed envelopes, to be opened as the court directs.

2) Ordering Discovery. If a motion for a protective order is wholly or partly denied, the court may, on just terms, order that any party or person provide or permit discovery.

3) Awarding Expenses. Rule 37(a)(5) applies to the award of expenses

d) TIMING AND SEQUENCE OF DISCOVERY.

1) Timing. A party may not seek discovery from any source before the parties have conferred as required by Rule 26(f), except in a proceeding exempted from initial disclosure under Rule 26(a)(1)(B), or when authorized by these rules, by stipulation, or by court order.

2) Early Rule 34 Requests.

   A) *Time to Deliver.* More than 21 days after the summons and complaint are served on a party, a request under Rule 34 may be delivered:

   (i) to that party by any other party, and

   (ii) by that party to any plaintiff or to any other party that has been served.

   B) *When Considered Served.* The request is considered to have been served at the first Rule 26(f) conference.

3) Sequence. Unless the parties stipulate or the court orders otherwise for the parties' and witnesses' convenience and in the interests of justice:

   (i) methods of discovery may be used in any sequence; and

   (ii) discovery by one party does not require any other party to delay its discovery.

e) SUPPLEMENTING DISCLOSURES AND RESPONSES.

1) In General. A party who has made a disclosure under Rule 26(a)—or who has responded to an interrogatory, request for production, or request for admission—must supplement or correct its disclosure or response:

   A) in a timely manner if the party learns that in some material respect the disclosure or response is incomplete or incorrect, and if the additional or corrective information has not otherwise been made known to the other parties during the discovery process or in writing; or

   B) as ordered by the court.

2) Expert Witness. For an expert whose report must be disclosed under Rule 26(a)(2)(B), the party's duty to supplement extends both to information included in the report and to information given during the expert's deposition. Any additions or changes to this information must be disclosed by the time the party's pretrial disclosures under Rule 26(a)(3) are due.

f) CONFERENCE OF THE PARTIES; PLANNING FOR DISCOVERY.

1) Conference Timing. Except in a proceeding exempted from initial disclosure under Rule 26(a)(1)(B) or when the court orders otherwise, the parties must confer as soon as practicable—and in any event at least 21 days before a scheduling conference is to be held or a scheduling order is due under Rule 16(b).

2) Conference Content; Parties' Responsibilities. In conferring, the parties must consider the nature and basis of their claims and defenses and the possibilities for promptly settling or resolving the case; make or arrange for the disclosures required by Rule 26(a)(1); discuss any issues about preserving discoverable information; and develop a proposed discovery plan. The attorneys of record and all unrepresented parties that have appeared in the case are jointly responsible for arranging the conference, for attempting in good faith to agree on the proposed discovery plan, and for submitting to the court within 14 days after the conference a written report outlining the plan. The court may order the parties or attorneys to attend the conference in person.

3) Discovery Plan. A discovery plan must state the parties' views and proposals on:

A) what changes should be made in the timing, form, or requirement for disclosures under Rule 26(a), including a statement of when initial disclosures were made or will be made;

B) the subjects on which discovery may be needed, when discovery should be completed, and whether discovery should be conducted in phases or be limited to or focused on particular issues;

C) any issues about disclosure, discovery, or preservation of electronically stored information, including the form or forms in which it should be produced;

D) any issues about claims of privilege or of protection as trial-preparation materials, including—if the parties agree on a procedure to assert these claims after production—whether to ask the court to include their agreement in an order under Federal Rule of Evidence 502;

E) what changes should be made in the limitations on discovery imposed under these rules or by local rule, and what other limitations should be imposed; and

F) any other orders that the court should issue under Rule 26(c) or under Rule 16(b) and (c).

4) Expedited Schedule. If necessary to comply with its expedited schedule for Rule 16(b) conferences, a court may by local rule:

A) require the parties' conference to occur less than 21 days before the scheduling conference is held or a scheduling order is due under Rule 16(b); and

B) require the written report outlining the discovery plan to be filed less than 14 days after the parties' conference, or excuse the parties from submitting a written report and permit them to report orally on their discovery plan at the Rule 16(b) conference.

g) SIGNING DISCLOSURES AND DISCOVERY REQUESTS, RESPONSES, AND OBJECTIONS.

1) Signature Required; Effect of Signature. Every disclosure under Rule 26(a)(1) or (a)(3) and every discovery request, response, or objection must be signed by at least one attorney of record in the attorney's own name—or by the party personally, if unrepresented—and must state the signer's address, e-mail address, and telephone number. By signing, an attorney or party certifies that to the best of the person's knowledge, information, and belief formed after a reasonable inquiry:

A) with respect to a disclosure, it is complete and correct as of the time it is made; and

B) with respect to a discovery request, response, or objection, it is:

(i) consistent with these rules and warranted by existing law or by a nonfrivolous argument for extending, modifying, or reversing existing law, or for establishing new law;

(ii) not interposed for any improper purpose, such as to harass, cause unnecessary delay, or needlessly increase the cost of litigation; and

(iii) neither unreasonable nor unduly burdensome or expensive, considering the needs of the case, prior discovery in the case, the amount in controversy, and the importance of the issues at stake in the action.

2) Failure to Sign. Other parties have no duty to act on an unsigned disclosure, request, response, or objection until it is signed, and the court must strike it unless a signature is promptly supplied after the omission is called to the attorney's or party's attention.

3) Sanction for Improper Certification. If a certification violates this rule without substantial justification, the court, on motion or on its own, must impose an appropriate sanction on the signer, the party on whose behalf the signer was acting, or both. The sanction may include an order to pay the reasonable expenses, including attorney's fees, caused by the violation.

Rule 30. Depositions by Oral Examination[3]

a) WHEN A DEPOSITION MAY BE TAKEN.

1) Without Leave. A party may, by oral questions, depose any person, including a party, without leave of court except as provided in Rule 30(a)(2). The deponent's attendance may be compelled by subpoena under Rule 45.

2) With Leave. A party must obtain leave of court, and the court must grant leave to the extent consistent with Rule 26(b)(1) and (2):

A) if the parties have not stipulated to the deposition and:

(i) the deposition would result in more than 10 depositions being taken under this rule or Rule 31 by the plaintiffs, or by the defendants, or by the third-party defendants;

(ii) the deponent has already been deposed in the case; or

---

[3] Fed. R. Civ. P. 30. (As amended Jan. 21, 1963, eff. July 1, 1963; Mar. 30, 1970, eff. July 1, 1970; Mar. 1, 1971, eff. July 1, 1971; Nov. 20, 1972, eff. July 1, 1975; Apr. 29, 1980, eff. Aug. 1, 1980; Mar. 2, 1987, eff. Aug. 1, 1987; Apr. 22, 1993, eff. Dec. 1, 1993; Apr. 17, 2000, eff. Dec. 1, 2000; Apr. 30, 2007, eff. Dec. 1, 2007; Apr. 29, 2015, eff. Dec. 1, 2015.)

(iii) the party seeks to take the deposition before the time specified in Rule 26(d), unless the party certifies in the notice, with supporting facts, that the deponent is expected to leave the United States and be unavailable for examination in this country after that time; or

B) if the deponent is confined in prison.

b) NOTICE OF THE DEPOSITION; OTHER FORMAL REQUIREMENTS.

1) Notice in General. A party who wants to depose a person by oral questions must give reasonable written notice to every other party. The notice must state the time and place of the deposition and, if known, the deponent's name and address. If the name is unknown, the notice must provide a general description sufficient to identify the person or the particular class or group to which the person belongs.

2) Producing Documents. If a subpoena duces tecum is to be served on the deponent, the materials designated for production, as set out in the subpoena, must be listed in the notice or in an attachment. The notice to a party deponent may be accompanied by a request under Rule 34 to produce documents and tangible things at the deposition.

3) Method of Recording.

A) *Method Stated in the Notice.* The party who notices the deposition must state in the notice the method for recording the testimony. Unless the court orders otherwise, testimony may be recorded by audio, audiovisual, or stenographic means. The noticing party bears the recording costs. Any party may arrange to transcribe a deposition.

B) *Additional Method.* With prior notice to the deponent and other parties, any party may designate another method for recording the testimony in addition to that specified in the original notice. That party bears the expense of the additional record or transcript unless the court orders otherwise.

4) By Remote Means. The parties may stipulate—or the court may on motion order—that a deposition be taken by telephone or other remote means. For the purpose of this rule and Rules 28(a), 37(a)(2), and 37(b)(1), the deposition takes place where the deponent answers the questions.

5) ***Officer's Duties.***

A) *Before the Deposition.* Unless the parties stipulate otherwise, a deposition must be conducted before an officer appointed or designated under Rule 28. The officer must begin the deposition with an on-the-record statement that includes:

(i) the officer's name and business address;

(ii) the date, time, and place of the deposition;

(iii) the deponent's name;

(iv) the officer's administration of the oath or affirmation to the deponent; and

(v) the identity of all persons present.

B) *Conducting the Deposition; Avoiding Distortion.* If the deposition is recorded non-stenographically, the officer must repeat the items in Rule 30(b)(5)(A)(i)-(iii) at the beginning of each unit of the recording medium. The deponent's and attorneys' appearance or demeanor must not be distorted through recording techniques.

C) *After the Deposition.* At the end of a deposition, the officer must state on the record that the deposition is complete and must set out any stipulations made by the attorneys about custody of the transcript or recording and of the exhibits, or about any other pertinent matters.

6) ***Notice or Subpoena Directed to an Organization.*** In its notice or subpoena, a party may name as the deponent a public or private corporation, a partnership, an association, a governmental agency, or other entity and must describe with reasonable particularity the matters for examination. The named organization must then designate one or more officers, directors, or managing agents, or designate other persons who consent to testify on its behalf; and it may set out the matters on which each person designated will testify. A subpoena must advise a nonparty organization of its duty to make this designation. The persons designated must testify about information known or reasonably available to the organization. This paragraph (6) does not preclude a deposition by any other procedure allowed by these rules.

c) **EXAMINATION AND CROSS-EXAMINATION; RECORD OF THE EXAMINATION; OBJECTIONS; WRITTEN QUESTIONS.**

1) Examination and Cross-Examination. The examination and cross-examination of a deponent proceed as they would at trial under the Federal Rules of Evidence, except Rules 103 and 615. After putting the deponent under oath or affirmation, the officer must record the testimony by the method designated under Rule 30(b)(3)(A). The testimony must be recorded by the officer personally or by a person acting in the presence and under the direction of the officer.

2) Objections. An objection at the time of the examination—whether to evidence, to a party's conduct, to the officer's qualifications, to the manner of taking the deposition, or to any other aspect of the deposition—must be noted on the record, but the examination still proceeds; the testimony is taken subject to any objection. An objection must be stated concisely in a nonargumentative and nonsuggestive manner. A person may instruct a deponent not to answer only when necessary to preserve a privilege, to enforce a limitation ordered by the court, or to present a motion under Rule 30(d)(3).

3) Participating Through Written Questions. Instead of participating in the oral examination, a party may serve written questions in a sealed envelope on the party noticing the deposition, who must deliver them to the officer. The officer must ask the deponent those questions and record the answers verbatim.

d) **DURATION; SANCTION; MOTION TO TERMINATE OR LIMIT.**

1) Duration. Unless otherwise stipulated or ordered by the court, a deposition is limited to one day of 7 hours. The court must allow additional time consistent with Rule 26(b)(1) and (2) if needed to fairly examine the deponent or if the deponent, another person, or any other circumstance impedes or delays the examination.

2) Sanction. The court may impose an appropriate sanction—including the reasonable expenses and attorney's fees incurred by any party—on a person who impedes, delays, or frustrates the fair examination of the deponent.

3) Motion to Terminate or Limit.

A) Grounds. At any time during a deposition, the deponent or a party may move to terminate or limit it on the ground that it is being conducted in bad faith or in a manner that unreasonably annoys, embarrasses, or oppresses the deponent or party. The motion may be filed in the court where the action is pending or the deposition is being taken. If the objecting deponent or party so demands, the deposition must be suspended for the time necessary to obtain an order.

B) Order. The court may order that the deposition be terminated or may limit its scope and manner as provided in Rule 26(c). If terminated, the deposition may be resumed only by order of the court where the action is pending.

C) Award of Expenses. Rule 37(a)(5) applies to the award of expenses.

e) REVIEW BY THE WITNESS; CHANGES.

1) Review; Statement of Changes. On request by the deponent or a party before the deposition is completed, the deponent must be allowed 30 days after being notified by the officer that the transcript or recording is available in which:

A) to review the transcript or recording; and

B) if there are changes in form or substance, to sign a statement listing the changes and the reasons for making them.

2) Changes Indicated in the Officer's Certificate. The officer must note in the certificate prescribed by Rule 30(f)(1) whether a review was requested and, if so, must attach any changes the deponent makes during the 30-day period.

f) CERTIFICATION AND DELIVERY; EXHIBITS; COPIES OF THE TRANSCRIPT OR RECORDING; FILING.

1) Certification and Delivery. The officer must certify in writing that the witness was duly sworn and that the deposition accurately records the witness's testimony. The certificate must accompany the record of the deposition. Unless the court orders otherwise, the officer must seal the deposition in an envelope or package bearing the title of the action and marked "Deposition of [witness's name]" and must promptly send it to the attorney who arranged for the transcript or recording. The attorney must store it under conditions that will protect it against loss, destruction, tampering, or deterioration.

2) Documents and Tangible Things.

A) *Originals and Copies.* Documents and tangible things produced for inspection during a deposition must, on a party's request, be marked for identification and attached to the deposition. Any party may inspect and copy them. But if the person who produced them wants to keep the originals, the person may:

(i) offer copies to be marked, attached to the deposition, and then used as originals—after giving all parties a fair opportunity to verify the copies by comparing them with the originals; or

(ii) give all parties a fair opportunity to inspect and copy the originals after they are marked—in which event the originals may be used as if attached to the deposition.

B) *Order Regarding the Originals.* Any party may move for an order that the originals be attached to the deposition pending final disposition of the case.

3) Copies of the Transcript or Recording. Unless otherwise stipulated or ordered by the court, the officer must retain the stenographic notes of a deposition taken stenographically or a copy of the recording of a deposition taken by another method. When paid reasonable charges, the officer must furnish a copy of the transcript or recording to any party or the deponent.

4) Notice of Filing. A party who files the deposition must promptly notify all other parties of the filing.

g) **FAILURE TO ATTEND A DEPOSITION OR SERVE A SUBPOENA; EXPENSES.**

A party who, expecting a deposition to be taken, attends in person or by an attorney may recover reasonable expenses for attending, including attorney's fees, if the noticing party failed to:

1) attend and proceed with the deposition; or

2) serve a subpoena on a nonparty deponent, who consequently did not attend.

Rule 32. Use of Depositions in Court proceedings[4]

a) **USING DEPOSITIONS.**

1) In General. At a hearing or trial, all or part of a deposition may be used against a party on these conditions:

A) The party was present or represented at the taking of the deposition or had reasonable notice of it;

B) it is used to the extent it would be admissible under the Federal Rules of Evidence if the deponent were present and testifying; and

C) the use is allowed by Rule 32(a)(2) through (8).

2) Impeachment and Other Uses. Any party may use a deposition to contradict or impeach the testimony given by the deponent as a witness, or for any other purpose allowed by the Federal Rules of Evidence.

3) Deposition of Party, Agent, or Designee. An adverse party may use for any purpose the deposition of a party or anyone who, when deposed, was the party's officer, director, managing agent, or designee under Rule 30(b)(6) or 31(a)(4).

4) Unavailable Witness. A party may use for any purpose the deposition of a witness, whether or not a party, if the court finds:

A) that the witness is dead;

---

[4] Fed. R. Civ. P. 32. (As amended Mar. 30, 1970, eff. July 1, 1970; Nov. 20, 1972, eff. July 1, 1975; Apr. 29, 1980, eff. Aug. 1, 1980; Mar. 2, 1987, eff. Aug. 1, 1987; Apr. 22, 1993, eff. Dec. 1, 1993; Apr. 30, 2007, eff. Dec. 1, 2007; Mar. 26, 2009, eff. Dec. 1, 2009.)

B) that the witness is more than 100 miles from the place of hearing or trial or is outside the United States, unless it appears that the witness's absence was procured by the party offering the deposition;

C) that the witness cannot attend or testify because of age, illness, infirmity, or imprisonment;

D) that the party offering the deposition could not procure the witness's attendance by subpoena; or

E) on motion and notice, that exceptional circumstances make it desirable—in the interest of justice and with due regard to the importance of live testimony in open court—to permit the deposition to be used.

5) **Limitations on Use.**

A) Deposition Taken on Short Notice. A deposition must not be used against a party who, having received less than 14 days' notice of the deposition, promptly moved for a protective order under Rule 26(c)(1)(B) requesting that it not be taken or be taken at a different time or place—and this motion was still pending when the deposition was taken.

B) Unavailable Deponent; Party Could Not Obtain an Attorney. A deposition taken without leave of court under the unavailability provision of Rule 30(a)(2)(A)(iii) must not be used against a party who shows that, when served with the notice, it could not, despite diligent efforts, obtain an attorney to represent it at the deposition.

6) **Using Part of a Deposition.** If a party offers in evidence only part of a deposition, an adverse party may require the offeror to introduce other parts that in fairness should be considered with the part introduced, and any party may itself introduce any other parts.

7) **Substituting a Party.** Substituting a party under Rule 25 does not affect the right to use a deposition previously taken.

8) **Deposition Taken in an Earlier Action.** A deposition lawfully taken and, if required, filed in any federal- or state-court action may be used in a later action involving the same subject matter between the same parties, or their representatives or successors in interest, to the same extent as if

taken in the later action. A deposition previously taken may also be used as allowed by the Federal Rules of Evidence.

b) OBJECTIONS TO ADMISSIBILITY.

Subject to Rules 28(b) and 32(d)(3), an objection may be made at a hearing or trial to the admission of any deposition testimony that would be inadmissible if the witness were present and testifying.

c) FORM OF PRESENTATION.

Unless the court orders otherwise, a party must provide a transcript of any deposition testimony the party offers, but may provide the court with the testimony in nontranscript form as well. On any party's request, deposition testimony offered in a jury trial for any purpose other than impeachment must be presented in nontranscript form, if available, unless the court for good cause orders otherwise.

d) WAIVER OF OBJECTIONS.

1) To the Notice. An objection to an error or irregularity in a deposition notice is waived unless promptly served in writing on the party giving the notice.

2) To the Officer's Qualification. An objection based on disqualification of the officer before whom a deposition is to be taken is waived if not made:

    A) before the deposition begins; or

    B) promptly after the basis for disqualification becomes known or, with reasonable diligence, could have been known.

3) To the Taking of the Deposition.

    A) Objection to Competence, Relevance, or Materiality. An objection to a deponent's competence—or to the competence, relevance, or materiality of testimony—is not waived by a failure to make the objection before or during the deposition, unless the ground for it might have been corrected at that time.

    B) Objection to an Error or Irregularity. An objection to an error or irregularity at an oral examination is waived if:

        (i) it relates to the manner of taking the deposition, the form of a question or answer, the oath or affirmation, a party's conduct, or other matters that might have been corrected at that time; and

(ii) it is not timely made during the deposition.

C) *Objection to a Written Question.* An objection to the form of a written question under Rule 31 is waived if not served in writing on the party submitting the question within the time for serving responsive questions or, if the question is a recross-question, within 7 days after being served with it.

4) *To Completing and Returning the Deposition.* An objection to how the officer transcribed the testimony—or prepared, signed, certified, sealed, endorsed, sent, or otherwise dealt with the deposition—is waived unless a motion to suppress is made promptly after the error or irregularity becomes known or, with reasonable diligence, could have been known.

Rule 37. Failure to Make Disclosures or to Cooperate in Discovery; Sanctions[5]

a) <u>MOTION FOR AN ORDER COMPELLING DISCLOSURE OR DISCOVERY.</u>

1) In General. On notice to other parties and all affected persons, a party may move for an order compelling disclosure or discovery. The motion must include a certification that the movant has in good faith conferred or attempted to confer with the person or party failing to make disclosure or discovery in an effort to obtain it without court action.

2) Appropriate Court. A motion for an order to a party must be made in the court where the action is pending. A motion for an order to a nonparty must be made in the court where the discovery is or will be taken.

3) Specific Motions.

A) *To Compel Disclosure.* If a party fails to make a disclosure required by Rule 26(a), any other party may move to compel disclosure and for appropriate sanctions.

---

5   Fed. R. Civ. P. 37. (As amended Dec. 29, 1948, eff. Oct. 20, 1949; Mar. 30, 1970, eff. July 1, 1970; Apr. 29, 1980, eff. Aug. 1, 1980; Pub. L. 96-481, §205(a), Oct. 21, 1980, 94 Stat. 2330, eff. Oct. 1, 1981; Mar. 2, 1987, eff. Aug. 1, 1987; Apr. 22, 1993, eff. Dec. 1, 1993; Apr. 17, 2000, eff. Dec. 1, 2000; Apr. 12, 2006, eff. Dec. 1, 2006; Apr. 30, 2007, eff. Dec. 1, 2007; Apr. 16, 2013, eff. Dec. 1, 2013; Apr. 29, 2015, eff. Dec. 1, 2015.)

B) To Compel a Discovery Response. A party seeking discovery may move for an order compelling an answer, designation, production, or inspection. This motion may be made if:

(i) a deponent fails to answer a question asked under Rule 30 or 31;

(ii) a corporation or other entity fails to make a designation under Rule 30(b)(6) or 31(a)(4);

(iii) a party fails to answer an interrogatory submitted under Rule 33; or

(iv) a party fails to produce documents or fails to respond that inspection will be permitted—or fails to permit inspection—as requested under Rule 34.

C) Related to a Deposition. When taking an oral deposition, the party asking a question may complete or adjourn the examination before moving for an order.

4) Evasive or Incomplete Disclosure, Answer, or Response. For purposes of this subdivision (a), an evasive or incomplete disclosure, answer, or response must be treated as a failure to disclose, answer, or respond.

5) Payment of Expenses; Protective Orders.

A) If the Motion Is Granted (or Disclosure or Discovery Is Provided After Filing). If the motion is granted—or if the disclosure or requested discovery is provided after the motion was filed—the court must, after giving an opportunity to be heard, require the party or deponent whose conduct necessitated the motion, the party or attorney advising that conduct, or both to pay the movant's reasonable expenses incurred in making the motion, including attorney's fees. But the court must not order this payment if:

(i) the movant filed the motion before attempting in good faith to obtain the disclosure or discovery without court action;

(ii) the opposing party's nondisclosure, response, or objection was substantially justified; or

(iii) other circumstances make an award of expenses unjust.

B) If the Motion Is Denied. If the motion is denied, the court may issue any protective order authorized under Rule 26(c) and must, after giving an opportunity to be heard, require the movant, the attorney filing the motion, or both to pay the party or deponent who opposed the motion its reasonable expenses incurred in opposing the motion, including attorney's fees. But the court must not order this payment if the motion was substantially justified or other circumstances make an award of expenses unjust.

C) If the Motion Is Granted in Part and Denied in Part. If the motion is granted in part and denied in part, the court may issue any protective order authorized under Rule 26(c) and may, after giving an opportunity to be heard, apportion the reasonable expenses for the motion.

b) FAILURE TO COMPLY WITH A COURT ORDER.

1) Sanctions Sought in the District Where the Deposition Is Taken. If the court where the discovery is taken orders a deponent to be sworn or to answer a question and the deponent fails to obey, the failure may be treated as contempt of court. If a deposition-related motion is transferred to the court where the action is pending, and that court orders a deponent to be sworn or to answer a question and the deponent fails to obey, the failure may be treated as contempt of either the court where the discovery is taken or the court where the action is pending.

2) Sanctions Sought in the District Where the Action Is Pending.

A) For Not Obeying a Discovery Order. If a party or a party's officer, director, or managing agent—or a witness designated under Rule 30(b)(6) or 31(a)(4)—fails to obey an order to provide or permit discovery, including an order under Rule 26(f), 35, or 37(a), the court where the action is pending may issue further just orders. They may include the following:

(i) directing that the matters embraced in the order or other designated facts be taken as established for purposes of the action, as the prevailing party claims;

(ii) prohibiting the disobedient party from supporting or opposing designated claims or defenses, or from introducing designated matters in evidence;

(iii) striking pleadings in whole or in part;

(iv) staying further proceedings until the order is obeyed;

(v) dismissing the action or proceeding in whole or in part;

(vi) rendering a default judgment against the disobedient party; or

(vii) treating as contempt of court the failure to obey any order except an order to submit to a physical or mental examination.

B) For Not Producing a Person for Examination. If a party fails to comply with an order under Rule 35(a) requiring it to produce another person for examination, the court may issue any of the orders listed in Rule 37(b)(2)(A)(i)-(vi), unless the disobedient party shows that it cannot produce the other person.

C) Payment of Expenses. Instead of or in addition to the orders above, the court must order the disobedient party, the attorney advising that party, or both to pay the reasonable expenses, including attorney's fees, caused by the failure, unless the failure was substantially justified or other circumstances make an award of expenses unjust.

c) **FAILURE TO DISCLOSE, TO SUPPLEMENT AN EARLIER RESPONSE, OR TO ADMIT.**

1) Failure to Disclose or Supplement. If a party fails to provide information or identify a witness as required by Rule 26(a) or (e), the party is not allowed to use that information or witness to supply evidence on a motion, at a hearing, or at a trial, unless the failure was substantially justified or is harmless. In addition to or instead of this sanction, the court, on motion and after giving an opportunity to be heard:

A) may order payment of the reasonable expenses, including attorney's fees, caused by the failure;

B) may inform the jury of the party's failure; and

C) may impose other appropriate sanctions, including any of the orders listed in Rule 37(b)(2)(A)(i)-(vi).

2) Failure to Admit. If a party fails to admit what is requested under Rule 36 and if the requesting party later proves a document to be genuine or the matter true, the requesting party may move that the party who failed to admit pay the reasonable expenses, including attorney's fees, incurred in making that proof. The court must so order unless:

A) the request was held objectionable under Rule 36(a);

B) the admission sought was of no substantial importance;

C) the party failing to admit had a reasonable ground to believe that it might prevail on the matter; or

D) there was other good reason for the failure to admit.

d) PARTY'S FAILURE TO ATTEND ITS OWN DEPOSITION, SERVE ANSWERS TO INTERROGATORIES, OR RESPOND TO A REQUEST FOR INSPECTION.

1) In General.

A) *Motion; Grounds for Sanctions.* The court where the action is pending may, on motion, order sanctions if:

(i) a party or a party's officer, director, or managing agent—or a person designated under Rule 30(b)(6) or 31(a)(4)—fails, after being served with proper notice, to appear for that person's deposition; or

(ii) a party, after being properly served with interrogatories under Rule 33 or a request for inspection under Rule 34, fails to serve its answers, objections, or written response.

B) *Certification.* A motion for sanctions for failing to answer or respond must include a certification that the movant has in good faith conferred or attempted to confer with the party failing to act in an effort to obtain the answer or response without court action.

2) Unacceptable Excuse for Failing to Act. A failure described in Rule 37(d)(1)(A) is not excused on the ground that the discovery sought was objectionable, unless the party failing to act has a pending motion for a protective order under Rule 26(c).

3) *Types of Sanctions.* Sanctions may include any of the orders listed in Rule 37(b)(2)(A)(i)-(vi). Instead of or in addition to these sanctions, the court must require the party failing to act, the attorney advising that party, or both to pay the reasonable expenses, including attorney's fees, caused by the failure, unless the failure was substantially justified or other circumstances make an award of expenses unjust.

e) FAILURE TO PRESERVE ELECTRONICALLY STORED INFORMATION.

If electronically stored information that should have been preserved in the anticipation or conduct of litigation is lost because a party failed to take reasonable steps to preserve it, and it cannot be restored or replaced through additional discovery, the court:

1) upon finding prejudice to another party from loss of the information, may order measures no greater than necessary to cure the prejudice; or

2) only upon finding that the party acted with the intent to deprive another party of the information's use in the litigation may:

   A) presume that the lost information was unfavorable to the party;

   B) instruct the jury that it may or must presume the information was unfavorable to the party; or

   C) dismiss the action or enter a default judgment.

f) FAILURE TO PARTICIPATE IN FRAMING A DISCOVERY PLAN.

If a party or its attorney fails to participate in good faith in developing and submitting a proposed discovery plan as required by Rule 26(f), the court may, after giving an opportunity to be heard, require that party or attorney to pay to any other party the reasonable expenses, including attorney's fees, caused by the failure.

APPENDIX B
COMPARING RELEVANT PORTIONS OF RULES 30 & 32

State courts have rules of procedure governing deposition conduct that are substantially similar to the Federal Rules or are intended accomplish the same goals. When a state rule is based on its federal counterpart, those states often look to federal authority for guidance in interpreting their state rule.

This appendix focuses only on Rules 30 and 32 and their state counterparts because these are the rules that directly proscribe the standards for proper deposition conduct—the main subject of this book. The relevant portions of Rules 30 and 32 are listed below:

Trial Standards: Fed. R. Civ. P. 30(c)(1)

> The examination and cross-examination of a deponent proceed as they would at trial under the Federal Rules of Evidence. . . .

Continuing Testimony: Fed. R. Civ. P. 30(c)(2)

> An objection at the time of the examination . . . must be noted on the record, but the examination still proceeds; the testimony is taken subject to any objection.

Nonsuggestive Objections: Fed. R. Civ. P. 30(c)(2)

An objection must be stated concisely in a nonargumentative and nonsuggestive manner.

Instructions Not to Answer: Fed. R. Civ. P. 30(c)(2)

A person may instruct a deponent not to answer only when necessary to preserve a privilege, to enforce a limitation ordered by the court, or to present a motion under Rule 30(d)(3).

Durational Limit: Fed. R. Civ. P. 30(d)(1)

[A] deposition is limited to 1 day of 7 hours.

Obstruction Sanctions: Fed. R. Civ. P. 30(d)(2)

The court may impose an appropriate sanction—including the reasonable expenses and attorney's fees incurred by any party—on a person who impedes, delays, or frustrates the fair examination of the deponent.

Suspending the Deposition: Fed. R. Civ. P. 30(d)(3)(A)

At any time during a deposition, the deponent or a party may move to terminate or limit it on the ground that it is being conducted in bad faith or in a manner that unreasonably annoys, embarrasses, or oppresses the deponent or party. . . . If the objecting deponent or party so demands, the deposition must be suspended for the time necessary to obtain an order.

Trial Admissibility: Fed. R. Civ. P. 32(b)

[A]n objection may be made at a hearing or trial to the admission of any deposition testimony that would be inadmissible if the witness were present and testifying.

Objections to Evidentiary Errors: Fed. R. Civ. P. 32(d)(3)(A)

An objection to a deponent's competence—or to the competence, relevance, or materiality of testimony—is not waived by a failure to make the objection before or during the deposition, unless the ground for it might have been corrected at that time.

Objections to Other Correctable Errors: Fed. R. Civ. P. 32(d)(3)(B)

An objection to an error or irregularity at an oral examination is waived if: (i) it relates to the manner of taking the deposition, the form of a question or answer, the oath or affirmation, a party's conduct, or other matters that might have been corrected at that time; and (ii) it is not timely made during the deposition.

What follows is a comparison of these operative clauses in the Federal Rules and their state counterparts. This appendix uses five categories to describe a state rule's resemblance to its federal counterpart: "virtually identical," "substantially similar," "conceptually similar," "significantly different," and "no comparable rule."

- **Virtually identical:** The state rule mirrors the federal rule, and the only differences are geographic terms, minor articles, corresponding rule sections, or the addition of minor clarifying words.

- **Substantially similar:** The state rule is functionally the same as the federal rule but uses slightly different language in some parts or is ordered differently.

- **Conceptually similar:** The state rule serves the same functional purpose as the federal rule but is either structured differently or uses different terms of art.

- **Significantly different:** The state rule establishes different standards from the federal rule or directly contradicts the federal rule's purpose.

- **No comparable rule:** The state has no rule comparable to the federal rule.

Any important differences between the rules, as well as any additional state-specific standards of deposition conduct, are discussed for each rule comparison. Finally, this appendix also provides case law for each state that discusses the use of federal precedent when interpreting the respective state rules.

ALABAMA

TRIAL STANDARDS: Fed. R. Civ. P. 30(c)(1)

Ala. R. Civ. P. 30(c) is substantially similar:

> Examination and cross-examination of witnesses may proceed as permitted at the trial under the Alabama Rules of Evidence. . . .

CONTINUING TESTIMONY: Fed. R. Civ. P. 30(c)(2)

Ala. R. Civ. P. 30(c) is substantially similar:

> All objections made at the time of the examination . . . shall be noted by the officer upon the deposition. Evidence objected to shall be taken subject to the objections.

NONSUGGESTIVE OBJECTIONS: Fed. R. Civ. P. 30(c)(2)

> Alabama has no comparable rule requiring deposition objections to be concise, nonargumentative, or nonsuggestive.

INSTRUCTIONS NOT TO ANSWER: Fed. R. Civ. P. 30(c)(2)

> Alabama has no comparable rule prohibiting an attorney from instructing a witness not to answer a question.

DURATIONAL LIMIT: Fed. R. Civ. P. 30(d)(1)

> Alabama has no comparable rule establishing a presumptive time limit for depositions.

OBSTRUCTION SANCTIONS: Fed. R. Civ. P. 30(d)(2)

> Alabama has no comparable rule establishing sanctions for frustrating the fair examination of the deponent.

SUSPENDING THE DEPOSITION: Fed. R. Civ. P. 30(d)(3)(A)

Ala. R. Civ. P. 30(d) is conceptually similar:

> At any time during the taking of the deposition, on motion of a party or of the deponent and upon a showing that the examination is being conducted in bad faith or in such manner as unreasonably to annoy, embarrass, or oppress the deponent or party, the court in which the action is pending or the court in the circuit where the deposition is being taken may order the officer conducting the examination to cease forthwith from taking the deposition.... Upon demand of the objecting party or deponent, the taking of the deposition shall be suspended for the time necessary to make a motion for an order.

TRIAL ADMISSIBILITY: Fed. R. Civ. P. 32(b)

Ala. R. Civ. P. 32(b) is substantially similar:

> [O]bjection[s] may be made at the trial or hearing to receiving in evidence any deposition or part thereof for any reason which would require the exclusion of the evidence if the witness were then present and testifying.

OBJECTIONS TO EVIDENTIARY ERRORS: Fed. R. Civ. P. 32(d)(3)(A)

Ala. R. Civ. P. 32(d)(3)(A) is substantially similar:

> Objections to the competency of a witness or to the competency, relevancy, or materiality of testimony are not waived by failure to make them before or during the taking of the

deposition, unless the ground of the objection is one which might have been obviated or removed if presented at that time.

OBJECTIONS TO OTHER CORRECTABLE ERRORS: Fed. R. Civ. P. 32(d)(3)(B)(i-ii)

Ala. R. Civ. P. 32(d)(3)(B) is substantially similar:

> Errors and irregularities occurring at the oral examination in the manner of taking the deposition, in the form of the questions or answers, in the oath or affirmation, or in the conduct of parties, and errors of any kind which might be obviated, removed, or cured if promptly presented, are waived unless seasonable objection thereto is made at the taking of the deposition.

The Alabama Supreme Court has held that, "[b]ecause the Alabama and Federal rules are virtually verbatim, 'a presumption arises that cases construing the Federal Rules are authority for construction of the Alabama Rules.'"[1]

ALASKA

TRIAL STANDARDS: Fed. R. Civ. P. 30(c)(1)

Alaska R. Civ. P. 30(c) is substantially similar:

> Examination and cross-examination of witnesses may proceed as permitted at the trial under provisions of the Rules of Evidence.

CONTINUING TESTIMONY: Fed. R. Civ. P. 30(c)(2)

Alaska R. Civ. P. 30(c) is substantially similar:

> All objections made at the time of the examination . . . shall be noted by the officer upon the record of the deposition; but

---

[1] *Smith v. Wilcox Cty. Board of Educ.*, 365 So. 2d 659, 661 (Ala. 1978).

the examination shall proceed, with the testimony being taken subject to the objections.

NONSUGGESTIVE OBJECTIONS: Fed. R. Civ. P. 30(c)(2)

Alaska R. Civ. P. 30(d)(1) is substantially similar:

> Any objection to evidence during a deposition shall be stated concisely and in a non-argumentative and non-suggestive manner.

However, Alaska R. Civ. P. 30(d)(1) also requires:

> No specification of the defect in the form of the question or the answer shall be stated unless requested by the party propounding the question.

INSTRUCTIONS NOT TO ANSWER: Fed. R. Civ. P. 30(c)(2)

Alaska R. Civ. P. 30(d)(1) is substantially similar:

> A party may instruct a deponent not to answer only when necessary to preserve a privilege, to enforce a limitation on evidence directed by the court, or to present a motion under paragraph (3).

In addition, Alaska R. Civ. P. 30(c)(3) explicitly prohibits off-the-record attorney-client conferences while a question is pending, which the Federal Rules do not address:

> Continual and unwarranted off the record conferences between the deponent and counsel following the propounding of questions and prior to the answer or at any time during the deposition are prohibited.

DURATIONAL LIMIT: Fed. R. Civ. P. 30(d)(1)

Alaska R. Civ. P. 30(d)(2) is significantly different:

> Oral depositions shall not, except pursuant to stipulation of the parties or order of the court, exceed six hours in length for

parties, independent expert witnesses, and treating physicians and three hours in length for other deponents.

This is significantly different because Alaska reduces the presumptive deposition time limit from seven hours to either six hours or three hours, depending on the deponent.

OBSTRUCTION SANCTIONS: Fed. R. Civ. P. 30(d)(2)

Alaska R. Civ. P. 30(d)(2) is substantially similar:

> If the court finds that there has been an impediment, delay, or other conduct that has frustrated the fair examination of the deponent, it may impose upon the persons responsible an appropriate sanction, including the reasonable costs and attorney's fees incurred by any parties as a result thereof.

SUSPENDING THE DEPOSITION: Fed. R. Civ. P. 30(d)(3)(A)

Alaska R. Civ. P. 30(d)(3) is substantially similar:

> At any time during a deposition, on motion of a party or of the deponent and upon a showing that the examination is being conducted in bad faith or in such manner as unreasonably to annoy, embarrass, or oppress the deponent or party. . . . Upon demand of the objecting party or deponent, the taking of the deposition shall be suspended for the time necessary to make a motion for an order.

TRIAL ADMISSIBILITY: Fed. R. Civ. P. 32(b)

Alaska R. Civ. P. 32(b) is substantially similar:

> [O]bjection[s] may be made at the trial or hearing to receiving in evidence any deposition or part thereof for any reason which would require the exclusion of the evidence if the witness were then present and testifying.

OBJECTIONS TO EVIDENTIARY ERRORS: Fed. R. Civ. P. 32(d)(3)(A)

Alaska R. Civ. P. 32(d)(3)(A) is substantially similar:

> Objections to the competency of a witness or to the competency, relevancy, or materiality of testimony are not waived by failure to make them before or during the taking of the deposition, unless the ground of the objection is one which might have been obviated or removed if presented at that time.

OBJECTIONS TO OTHER CORRECTABLE ERRORS: Fed. R. Civ. P. 32(d)(3)(B)(i-ii)

Alaska R. Civ. P. 32(d)(3)(B) is substantially similar:

> Errors and irregularities occurring at the oral examination in the manner of taking the deposition, in the form of the questions or answers, in the oath or affirmation, or in the conduct of parties, and errors of any kind which might be obviated, removed, or cured if promptly presented, are waived unless seasonable objection thereto is made at the taking of the deposition.

The Alaska Supreme Court has held that "in interpreting our civil rules we have often looked to identical federal counterparts for guidance."[2]

ARIZONA

TRIAL STANDARDS: Fed. R. Civ. P. 30(c)(1)

16 A.R.S. R. Civ. P. 30(c)(1) is virtually identical:

> The examination and cross-examination of a deponent proceed as they would at trial under the Arizona Rules of Evidence. . . .

---

[2] *Brown v. Lange*, 21 P.3d 822, 825 (Alaska 2001).

CONTINUING TESTIMONY: Fed. R. Civ. P. 30(c)(2)

16 A.R.S. R. Civ. P. 30(c)(2) is substantially similar:

> The officer must note on the record any objection made during the deposition. . . . [T]estimony is taken subject to any objection.

NONSUGGESTIVE OBJECTIONS: Fed. R. Civ. P. 30(c)(2)

16 A.R.S. R. Civ. P. 30(c)(2) is substantially similar:

> An objection must be stated concisely, in a nonargumentative manner, and without suggesting an answer to the deponent.

However, 16 A.R.S. R. Civ. P. 30(c)(2) also requires that:

> Unless requested by the person who asked the question, an objecting person must not specify the defect in the form of a question or answer.

INSTRUCTIONS NOT TO ANSWER: Fed. R. Civ. P. 30(c)(2)

16 A.R.S. R. Civ. P. 30(c)(2) is substantially similar:

> Counsel may instruct a deponent not to answer—or a deponent may refuse to answer—only when necessary to preserve a privilege, to enforce a limit ordered by the court, or to present a motion under Rule 30(d)(3).

Additionally, 16 A.R.S. R. Civ. P. 30(c)(3) explicitly prohibits off-the-record attorney-client conferences while a question is pending, which the Federal Rules do not address:

> The deponent and his or her counsel may not engage in continuous and unwarranted conferences off the record during the deposition. Unless necessary to preserve a privilege, the deponent and his or her counsel may not confer off the record while a question is pending.

DURATIONAL LIMIT: Fed. R. Civ. P. 30(d)(1)

16 A.R.S. R. Civ. P. 30(d)(1) is significantly different:

> [A] deposition is limited to 4 hours and must be completed in a single day.

This is significantly different because Arizona reduces the presumptive deposition time limit from seven hours to four hours. Additionally, Arizona uses a three-tiered system based on the amount of damages sought in an action to limit the total combined hours of fact witness depositions for each side. These tiers are defined in 16 A.R.S. R. Civ. P. 26.2(b-c), and the corresponding combined hour limit is listed in 16. A.R.S. R. Vi. P. 26.2(f).

OBSTRUCTION SANCTIONS: Fed. R. Civ. P. 30(d)(2)

16 A.R.S. R. Civ. P. 30(d)(2) is conceptually similar:

> The court may impose appropriate sanctions—including any order under Rule 16(h)—against a party or attorney who has engaged in unreasonable, groundless, abusive, or obstructionist conduct in connection with a deposition, including an unreasonable refusal to agree to extend a deposition beyond 4 hours.

This is conceptually similar because it authorizes sanctions for deposition misconduct, but it differs in that it does not require the conduct to frustrate the fair examination of the deponent. It also establishes sanctions for an unreasonable refusal to extend the time limit of a deposition.

SUSPENDING THE DEPOSITION: Fed. R. Civ. P. 30(d)(3)(A)

16 A.R.S. R. Civ. P. 30(d)(3)(A) is virtually identical:

> At any time during a deposition, the deponent or a party may move to terminate or limit the deposition on the ground that it is being conducted in bad faith or in a manner that unreasonably annoys, embarrasses, or oppresses the deponent or party. . . . If the objecting deponent or party so demands, the

deposition must be suspended for the time necessary to obtain an order.

TRIAL ADMISSIBILITY: Fed. R. Civ. P. 32(b)

16 A.R.S. R. Civ. P. 32(b) is virtually identical:

> [A]n objection may be made at a hearing or trial to the admission of any deposition testimony that would be inadmissible if the witness were present and testifying.

OBJECTIONS TO EVIDENTIARY ERRORS: Fed. R. Civ. P. 32(d)(3)(A)

16 A.R.S. R. Civ. P. 32(d)(3)(A) is conceptually similar:

> A party objecting to a deponent's competence—or to the competence, relevance, or materiality of the testimony—must make the objection before or during the deposition if the ground for the objection could have been corrected at that time.

This is conceptually similar because it requires attorneys to raise objections to correctable evidentiary errors at the deposition, but it does not explicitly mention that these objections are waived for trial if they are not raised. It also does not explicitly mention that objections to noncorrectable evidentiary errors are preserved for trial.

OBJECTIONS TO OTHER CORRECTABLE ERRORS: Fed. R. Civ. P. 32(d)(3)(B)(i-ii)

16 A.R.S. R. Civ. P. 32(d)(3)(B) is conceptually similar:

> A party objecting to the manner of taking the deposition, the form of a question or answer, the oath or affirmation, a party's conduct, or other matters that could be corrected at that time must timely make the objection during the deposition.

This is conceptually similar because it requires attorneys to raise objections to correctable errors of form and other matters at the deposition, but it does not explicitly mention that these objections are waived for trial if they are not raised.

The Arizona Supreme Court has held that, "[b]ecause Arizona has substantially adopted the Federal Rules of Civil Procedure, we give great weight to the federal interpretations of the rules."[3]

ARKANSAS

TRIAL STANDARDS: Fed. R. Civ. P. 30(c)(1)

Ark. R. Civ. P. 30(c) is substantially similar:

> Examination and cross-examination of witnesses may proceed as permitted at the trial under the provisions of the Arkansas Rules of Evidence. . . .

CONTINUING TESTIMONY: Fed. R. Civ. P. 30(c)(2)

Ark. R. Civ. P. 30(c) is substantially similar:

> All objections made at the time of the examination . . . shall be noted by the officer upon the record of the deposition; but the examination shall proceed, with the testimony being taken subject to the objections.

NONSUGGESTIVE OBJECTIONS: Fed. R. Civ. P. 30(c)(2)

Ark. R. Civ. P. 30(d)(1) is virtually identical:

> Any objection during a deposition must be stated concisely and in a non-argumentative and non-suggestive manner.

---

3 *Edwards v. Young*, 486 P.2d 181, 182 (Ariz. 1971).

INSTRUCTIONS NOT TO ANSWER: Fed. R. Civ. P. 30(c)(2)

Ark. R. Civ. P. 30(d)(1) is virtually identical:

> A person may instruct a deponent not to answer only when necessary to preserve a privilege, to enforce a limitation directed by the court, or to present a motion under paragraph (4).

DURATIONAL LIMIT: Fed. R. Civ. P. 30(d)(1)

Arkansas has <u>no comparable rule</u> establishing a presumptive time limit. The reporter's notes to the 2005 amendments clarify this difference:

> The Federal Rule's presumptive limitation on the duration of any deposition to one seven-hour day has not been incorporated into the Arkansas Rule.[4]

OBSTRUCTION SANCTIONS: Fed. R. Civ. P. 30(d)(2)

Ark. R. Civ. P. 30(d)(3) is substantially similar:

> If the court finds that any impediment, delay, or other conduct has frustrated the fair examination of the deponent, it may impose upon the persons responsible an appropriate sanction, including the reasonable costs and attorneys' fees incurred by any parties as a result thereof.

SUSPENDING THE DEPOSITION: Fed. R. Civ. P. 30(d)(3)(A)

Ark. R. Civ. P. 30(d)(4) is conceptually similar:

> At any time during a deposition, on motion of a party or of the deponent and upon a showing that the examination is being conducted in bad faith or in such manner as unreasonably to annoy, embarrass, or oppress the deponent or party, the court in which the action is pending may order the officer conducting the examination to cease forthwith from taking the deposition. . . . Upon demand of the objecting party or deponent,

---

[4] Ark. R. Civ. P. 30, reporter's note to 2005 amendments.

the taking of the deposition must be suspended for the time necessary to make a motion for an order.

TRIAL ADMISSIBILITY: Fed. R. Civ. P. 32(b)

Ark. R. Civ. P. 32(b) is substantially similar:

> [An] objection may be made at the trial or hearing to receiving in evidence any deposition or part thereof for any reason which would require the exclusion of the evidence if the witness were then present and testifying.

OBJECTIONS TO EVIDENTIARY ERRORS: Fed. R. Civ. P. 32(d)(3)(A)

Ark. R. Civ. P. 32(d)(3)(A) is substantially similar:

> Objections to the competency of a witness or to the competency, relevancy or materiality of testimony are not waived by failure to make them before or during the taking of the deposition, unless the ground of the objection is one which might have been obviated or removed if presented at that time.

OBJECTIONS TO OTHER CORRECTABLE ERRORS: Fed. R. Civ. P. 32(d)(3)(B)(i-ii)

Ark. R. Civ. P. 32(d)(3)(B) is substantially similar:

> Errors and irregularities occurring at the oral examination in the manner of taking the deposition, in the form of the questions or answers, in the oath or affirmation, or in the conduct of parties, and errors of any kind which might be obviated, removed, or cured if promptly presented, are waived unless seasonable objection thereto is made at the taking of the deposition.

The Arkansas Supreme Court has held that, "[b]ased upon the similarities of our rules with the Federal Rules of Civil Procedure, we consider the interpretation of these rules by federal courts to be of a significant precedential value."[5]

CALIFORNIA

TRIAL STANDARDS: Fed. R. Civ. P. 30(c)(1)

Cal. Code Civ. Proc. § 2025.330(d) is substantially similar:

> Examination and cross-examination of the deponent shall proceed as permitted at trial under the provisions of the Evidence Code.

CONTINUING TESTIMONY: Fed. R. Civ. P. 30(c)(2)

Cal. Code Civ. Proc. § 2025.460(b) is conceptually similar:

> Unless the objecting party demands that the taking of the deposition be suspended to permit a motion for a protective order under Sections 2025.420 and 2025.470, the deposition shall proceed subject to the objection.

This is conceptually similar because it stipulates that deposition testimony proceeds subject to any objection, but it differs in that it fails to specify that the objection be noted on the record.

NONSUGGESTIVE OBJECTIONS: Fed. R. Civ. P. 30(c)(2)

California has no comparable rule requiring deposition objections to be concise, nonargumentative, or nonsuggestive.

INSTRUCTIONS NOT TO ANSWER: Fed. R. Civ. P. 30(c)(2)

California has no comparable rule prohibiting instructions not to answer. However, Cal. Code Civ. Proc. § 2025.460(a) states:

---

[5] *City of Fort Smith v. Carter*, 216 S.W.3d 594, 598 (Ark. 2005).

> The protection of information from discovery on the ground that it is privileged or that it is a protected work product ... is waived unless a specific objection to its disclosure is timely made during the deposition.

This does not explicitly mention instructions not to answer, but it implies that an instruction not to answer is necessary to protect a privilege.

DURATIONAL LIMIT: Fed. R. Civ. P. 30(d)(1)

Cal. Code Civ. Proc. § 2025.290(a) is conceptually similar:

> [A] deposition examination of the witness by all counsel, other than the witness' counsel of record, shall be limited to seven hours of total testimony.

This is conceptually similar because it adopts the same standard time limit for depositions as the federal rule, but it differs by allowing the deponent's own counsel to depose him or her for longer.

OBSTRUCTION SANCTIONS: Fed. R. Civ. P. 30(d)(2)

California has <u>no comparable rule</u> establishing sanctions for frustrating the fair examination of a deponent.

SUSPENDING THE DEPOSITION: Fed. R. Civ. P. 30(d)(3)(A)

Cal. Code Civ. Proc. § 2025.470 is conceptually similar:

> The deposition officer may not suspend the taking of testimony without the stipulation of all parties present unless any party attending the deposition, including the deponent, demands that the deposition officer suspend taking the testimony to enable that party or deponent to move for a protective order under Section 2025.420 on the ground that the examination is being conducted in bad faith or in a manner that unreasonably annoys, embarrasses, or oppresses that deponent or party.

OBJECTIONS TO EVIDENTIARY ERRORS: Fed. R. Civ. P. 32(d)(3)(A)

TRIAL ADMISSIBILITY: Fed. R. Civ. P. 32(b)

Cal. Code Civ. Proc. § 2025.460(c) is significantly different:

> Objections to the competency of the deponent, or to the relevancy, materiality, or admissibility at trial of the testimony or of the materials produced are unnecessary and are not waived by failure to make them before or during the deposition.

This combines objections at the deposition to evidentiary errors and objections at trial to the admissibility of deposition testimony into a single rule. The important difference is that there is no requirement to raise objections to errors that could be immediately corrected at the deposition.

OBJECTIONS TO OTHER CORRECTABLE ERRORS: Fed. R. Civ. P. 32(d)(3)(B)(i-ii)

Cal. Code Civ. Proc. § 2025.460(b) is conceptually similar:

> Errors and irregularities of any kind occurring at the oral examination that might be cured if promptly presented are waived unless a specific objection to them is timely made during the deposition. These errors and irregularities include, but are not limited to, those relating to the manner of taking the deposition, to the oath or affirmation administered, to the conduct of a party, attorney, deponent, or deposition officer, or to the form of any question or answer.

This is conceptually similar because it requires objections to errors that are correctable at the deposition. However, its requirement of objecting to errors "of any kind... that might be cured" contradicts CCP § 2025.460(c), which uniformly deems competency objections unnecessary (even though some competency errors, such as a lack of foundation, are curable at the deposition).

The author has been unable to locate any jurisprudence from the Supreme Court of California that considers the Federal Rules of Civil Procedure persuasive when interpreting California's Code of Civil Procedure.

COLORADO

TRIAL STANDARDS: Fed. R. Civ. P. 30(c)(1)

Colo. R. Civ. P. 30(c) is substantially similar:

> Examination and cross-examination of witnesses may proceed as permitted at the trial under the provisions of the Colorado Rules of Evidence. . . .

CONTINUING TESTIMONY: Fed. R. Civ. P. 30(c)(2)

Colo. R. Civ. P. 30(c) is substantially similar:

> All objections made at the time of the examination . . . shall be noted by the officer upon the record of the deposition. Evidence objected to shall be taken subject to the objections.

NONSUGGESTIVE OBJECTIONS: Fed. R. Civ. P. 30(c)(2)

Colo. R. Civ. P. 30(d)(1) is virtually identical:

> Any objection during a deposition shall be stated concisely and in a non-argumentative and non-suggestive manner.

INSTRUCTIONS NOT TO ANSWER: Fed. R. Civ. P. 30(c)(2)

Colo. R. Civ. P. 30(d)(1) is virtually identical:

> An instruction not to answer may be made during a deposition only when necessary to preserve a privilege, to enforce a limitation directed by the court, or to present a motion pursuant to subsection (d)(3) of this Rule.

DURATIONAL LIMIT: Fed. R. Civ. P. 30(d)(1)

Colo. R. Civ. P. 30(d)(2)(A) is significantly different:

> [A] deposition of a person other than a retained expert . . . whose opinions may be offered at trial is limited to one day of 6 hours.

This is significantly different because Colorado reduces the presumptive deposition time limit from seven hours to six hours unless the deponent is an expert witness.

OBSTRUCTION SANCTIONS: Fed. R. Civ. P. 30(d)(2)

Colorado has <u>no comparable rule</u> establishing sanctions for frustrating the fair examination of a deponent.

SUSPENDING THE DEPOSITION: Fed. R. Civ. P. 30(d)(3)(A)

Colo. R. Civ. P. 30(d)(3) is conceptually similar:

> At any time during the taking of the deposition, on motion of any party or of the deponent and upon a showing that the examination is being conducted in bad faith or in such manner as unreasonably to annoy, embarrass, or oppress the deponent or party, the court in which the action is pending or the court in the district where the deposition is being taken may order the officer conducting the examination to cease forthwith from taking the deposition. . . . Upon demand of the objecting party or deponent, the taking of the deposition shall be suspended for the time necessary to make a motion for an order.

TRIAL ADMISSIBILITY: Fed. R. Civ. P. 32(b)

Colo. R. Civ. P. 32(b) is substantially similar:

> [O]bjection[s] may be made at the trial or hearing to receiving in evidence any deposition or part thereof for any reason

which would require the exclusion of the evidence if the witness were then present and testifying.

OBJECTIONS TO EVIDENTIARY ERRORS: Fed. R. Civ. P. 32(d)(3)(A)

Colo. R. Civ. P. 32(d)(3)(A) is substantially similar:

> Objections to the competency of a witness or to the competency, relevancy, or materiality of testimony are not waived by failure to make them before or during the taking of the deposition, unless the ground of the objection is one which might have been obviated or removed if presented at that time.

OBJECTIONS TO OTHER CORRECTABLE ERRORS: Fed. R. Civ. P. 32(d)(3)(B)(i-ii)

Colo. R. Civ. P. 32(d)(3)(B) is substantially similar:

> Errors and irregularities occurring at the oral examination in the manner of taking the deposition, in the form of the questions or answers, in the oath or affirmation, or in the conduct of parties and errors of any kind which might be obviated, removed, or cured if promptly presented, are waived unless seasonable objection thereto is made at the taking of the deposition.

The Colorado Supreme Court has held that, "[b]ecause the Colorado Rules of Civil Procedure are patterned on the federal rules, we may also look to the federal rules and decisions for guidance."[6]

---

6   *Garrigan v. Bowen*, 243 P.3d 231, 235 (Colo. 2010).

CONNECTICUT

TRIAL STANDARDS: Fed. R. Civ. P. 30(c)(1)

Conn. Prac. Book § 13-30(a) is substantially similar:

> Examination and cross-examination of deponents may proceed as permitted at trial.

CONTINUING TESTIMONY: Fed. R. Civ. P. 30(c)(2)

Conn. Prac. Book § 13-30(b) is substantially similar:

> All objections made at the time of the examination . . . shall be noted by the officer upon the deposition. Evidence objected to shall be taken subject to the objections.

NONSUGGESTIVE OBJECTIONS: Fed. R. Civ. P. 30(c)(2)

Conn. Prac. Book § 13-30(b) is substantially similar:

> Every objection raised during a deposition shall be stated succinctly and framed so as not to suggest an answer to the deponent. . . .

However, Conn. Prac. Book § 13-30(b) also requires that:

> [A]t the request of the questioning attorney, [an objection] shall include a clear statement as to any defect in form or other basis of error or irregularity.

INSTRUCTIONS NOT TO ANSWER: Fed. R. Civ. P. 30(c)(2)

Conn. Prac. Book § 13-30(b) is virtually identical:

> A person may instruct a deponent not to answer only when necessary to preserve a privilege, to enforce a limitation directed by the court, or to present a motion under subsection (c) of this section.

DURATIONAL LIMIT: Fed. R. Civ. P. 30(d)(1)

Connecticut has no comparable rule establishing a presumptive time limit.

OBSTRUCTION SANCTIONS: Fed. R. Civ. P. 30(d)(2)

Connecticut has no comparable rule establishing sanctions for frustrating the fair examination of a deponent.

SUSPENDING THE DEPOSITION: Fed. R. Civ. P. 30(d)(3)(A)

Conn. Prac. Book § 13-30(c) is conceptually similar:

> At any time during the taking of the deposition, on motion of a party or of the deponent and upon a showing that the examination is being conducted in bad faith or in such manner as unreasonably to annoy, embarrass, or oppress the deponent or party, the court in which the action is pending may order the officer conducting the examination forthwith to cease taking the deposition. . . .

This rule is conceptually similar because it authorizes the court to terminate a deposition on motion of a party, but it differs because it does not explicitly grant a party the right to suspend the deposition to make the motion.

TRIAL ADMISSIBILITY: Fed. R. Civ. P. 32(b)

Conn. Prac. Book § 13-31(b) is substantially similar:

> [O]bjection[s] may be made at the trial or hearing to receiving in evidence any deposition or part thereof for any reason which would require the exclusion of the evidence if the witness were then present and testifying.

OBJECTIONS TO EVIDENTIARY ERRORS: Fed. R. Civ. P. 32(d)(3)(A)

Conn. Prac. Book § 13-31(c)(3)(A) is substantially similar:

> Objections to the competency of a witness or to the competency, relevancy or materiality of testimony are not waived by failure to make them before or during the taking of the deposition, unless the ground of the objection is one which might have been obviated or removed if presented at that time.

OBJECTIONS TO OTHER CORRECTABLE ERRORS: Fed. R. Civ. P. 32(d)(3)(B)(i-ii)

Conn. Prac. Book § 13-31(c)(3)(B) is substantially similar:

> Errors and irregularities occurring at the oral examination in the manner of taking the deposition, in the form of the questions or answers, in the oath or affirmation, or in the conduct of parties, and errors of any kind which might be obviated, removed, or cured if promptly presented, are waived unless seasonable objection thereto is made at the taking of the deposition.

The Connecticut Supreme Court has not yet provided a general rule allowing for the use of federal case law to interpret the state's rules of civil procedure. When interpretive issues involving civil procedure have arisen, the court has applied federal case law about specific rules, including Fed R. Civ. P. 23,[7] Fed R. Civ. P. 32(a)(2),[8] and Fed R. Civ. P. 56,[9] to construe the state's corresponding rules of civil procedure. However, the general applicability of federal case law to the Connecticut rules has been provided by the Appellate Court of Connecticut, which has held that, "[w]here a state

---

7 *Collins v. Anthem Health Plans, Inc.*, 836 A.2d 1124, 1135 (Conn. 2003).

8 *Gateway Co. v. DiNoia*, 654 A.2d 342, 350 (Conn. 1995).

9 *Mac's Car City, Inc. v. Am. Nat. Bank*, 532 A.2d 1302, 1304 (Conn. 1987).

rule is similar to a federal rule, we review the federal case law to assist our interpretation of our rule."[10]

DELAWARE

TRIAL STANDARDS: Fed. R. Civ. P. 30(c)(1)

Del. R. Civ. P. 30(c) is substantially similar:

> Examination and cross-examination of witnesses may proceed as permitted at the trial under the provisions of Delaware Uniform Rules of Evidence. . . .

CONTINUING TESTIMONY: Fed. R. Civ. P. 30(c)(2)

Del. R. Civ. P. 30(c) is substantially similar:

> All objections made at the time of the examination . . . shall be noted by the officer upon the record of the deposition; but the evidence shall proceed with the testimony being taken subject to the objections.

NONSUGGESTIVE OBJECTIONS: Fed. R. Civ. P. 30(c)(2)

Del. R. Civ. P. 30(d)(1) is conceptually similar:

> [A]ttorney(s) for the deponent shall not . . . suggest to the deponent the manner in which any question should be answered.

This is conceptually similar because it implicitly prohibits attorneys from making objections that coach the witness, but it differs in that it does not explicitly require objections to be concise.

Del. R. Civ. P. 30(d)(1) also places a strict limit on attorney-client conferencing during the deposition:

> From the commencement until the conclusion of a deposition, including any recesses or continuances thereof of less than five calendar days, the attorney(s) for the deponent shall not: (A) consult or confer with the deponent regarding the substance of

---

10   *Pelarinos v. Henderson*, 643 A.2d 894, 897 (Conn. 1994).

the testimony already given or anticipated to be given except for the purpose of conferring on whether to assert a privilege against testifying or on how to comply with a court order. . . .

INSTRUCTIONS NOT TO ANSWER: Fed. R. Civ. P. 30(c)(2)

Del. R. Civ. P. 30(d)(1) is virtually identical:

> A party may instruct a deponent not to answer only when necessary to preserve a privilege, to enforce a limitation on evidence directed by the Court, or to present a motion under paragraph (d)(3).

DURATIONAL LIMIT: Fed. R. Civ. P. 30(d)(1)

Delaware has no comparable rule establishing a presumptive time limit.

OBSTRUCTION SANCTIONS: Fed. R. Civ. P. 30(d)(2)

Del. R. Civ. P. 30(d)(2) is substantially similar:

> If the Court finds such an impediment, delay or other conduct that has frustrated the fair examination of the deponent, it may impose upon the persons responsible an appropriate sanction, including the reasonable costs and attorney's fees incurred by any party as a result thereof.

SUSPENDING THE DEPOSITION: Fed. R. Civ. P. 30(d)(3)(A)

Del. R. Civ. P. 30(d)(3) is conceptually similar:

> At any time during the taking of the deposition, on motion of a party or of the deponent and upon a showing that the examination is being conducted or defended in bad faith or in such manner as unreasonably to annoy, embarrass or oppress the deponent or party, the Court in which the action is pending or a Court of competent jurisdiction in the state where the deposition is being taken may order: (A) that examination

cease forthwith. . . . Upon demand of the objecting party or deponent, the taking of the deposition shall be suspended for the time necessary to make a motion for an order.

TRIAL ADMISSIBILITY: Fed. R. Civ. P. 32(b)

Del. R. Civ. P. 32(b) is substantially similar:

> [O]bjection[s] may be made at the trial or hearing to receiving in evidence any deposition or part thereof for any reason which would require the exclusion of the evidence if the witness were then present and testifying.

OBJECTIONS TO EVIDENTIARY ERRORS: Fed. R. Civ. P. 32(d)(3)(A)

Del. R. Civ. P. 32(d)(3)(A) is substantially similar:

> Objections to the competency of a witness or to the competency, relevancy or materiality of testimony are not waived by failure to make them before or during the taking of the deposition, unless the ground of the objection is one which might have been obviated or removed if presented at that time.

OBJECTIONS TO OTHER CORRECTABLE ERRORS: Fed. R. Civ. P. 32(d)(3)(B)(i-ii)

Del. R. Civ. P. 32(d)(3)(B) is substantially similar:

> Errors and irregularities occurring at the oral examination in the manner of taking the deposition, the form of the questions or answers, in the oath or affirmation, or in the conduct of parties, and errors of any kind which might be obviated, removed, or cured if promptly presented, are waived unless seasonable objection thereto is made at the taking of the deposition.

Relying on previous authority, the Delaware Supreme Court has instructed that "[d]ecisions interpreting the Federal Rules of Civil Procedure are usually of great persuasive weight in the construction of parallel Delaware rules; however, such decisions are not actually binding upon Delaware courts."[11]

FLORIDA

TRIAL STANDARDS: Fed. R. Civ. P. 30(c)(1)

Fla. R. Civ. P. 1.310(c) is substantially similar:

> Examination and cross-examination of witnesses may proceed as permitted at the trial.

CONTINUING TESTIMONY: Fed. R. Civ. P. 30(c)(2)

Fla. R. Civ. P. 1.310(c) is substantially similar:

> All objections made at time of the examination . . . must be noted by the officer on the deposition. . . . [E]vidence objected to must be taken subject to the objections.

NONSUGGESTIVE OBJECTIONS: Fed. R. Civ. P. 30(c)(2)

Fla. R. Civ. P. 1.310(c) is virtually identical:

> Any objection during a deposition must be stated concisely and in a nonargumentative and nonsuggestive manner.

INSTRUCTIONS NOT TO ANSWER: Fed. R. Civ. P. 30(c)(2)

Fla. R. Civ. P. 1.310(c) is virtually identical:

> A party may instruct a deponent not to answer only when necessary to preserve a privilege, to enforce a limitation on

---

[11] *Cede & Co. v. Technicolor, Inc.*, 542 A.2d 1182, 1191 n.11 (Del. 1988) (internal citations omitted).

evidence directed by the court, or to present a motion under subdivision (d).

DURATIONAL LIMIT: Fed. R. Civ. P. 30(d)(1)

Florida has <u>no comparable rule</u> establishing a presumptive time limit.

OBSTRUCTION SANCTIONS: Fed. R. Civ. P. 30(d)(2)

SUSPENDING THE DEPOSITION: Fed. R. Civ. P. 30(d)(3)(A)

Fla. R. Civ. P. 1.310(d) is conceptually similar:

> At any time during the taking of the deposition, on motion of a party or of the deponent and on a showing that the examination is being conducted in bad faith or in such manner as unreasonably to annoy, embarrass, or oppress the deponent or party, or that objection and instruction to a deponent not to answer are being made in violation of rule 1.310(c), the court in which the action is pending or the circuit court where the deposition is being taken may order the officer conducting the examination to cease immediately from taking the deposition. . . . Upon demand of any party or the deponent, the taking of the deposition must be suspended for the time necessary to make a motion for an order. The provisions of rule 1.380(a) apply to the award of expenses incurred in relation to the motion.

This is conceptually similar because it combines elements from both Federal Rules 30(d)(3)(A) and 30(d)(2). The procedure for suspending the deposition is substantially similar, and when the motion to suspend is due to Rule 1.310(c) violations (prohibited objections and instructions not to answer), the corresponding sanctions are conceptually similar to the federal sanctions for frustrating the fair examination of a deponent.

TRIAL ADMISSIBILITY: Fed. R. Civ. P. 32(b)

Fla. R. Civ. P. 1.330(b) is substantially similar:

> [O]bjection[s] may be made at the trial or hearing to receiving in evidence any deposition or part of it for any reason that would require the exclusion of the evidence if the witness were then present and testifying.

OBJECTIONS TO EVIDENTIARY ERRORS: Fed. R. Civ. P. 32(d)(3)(A)

Fla. R. Civ. P. 1.330(d)(3)(A) is substantially similar:

> Objections to the competency of a witness or to the competency, relevancy, or materiality of testimony are not waived by failure to make them before or during the taking of the deposition unless the ground of the objection is one that might have been obviated or removed if presented at that time.

OBJECTIONS TO OTHER CORRECTABLE ERRORS: Fed. R. Civ. P. 32(d)(3)(B)(i-ii)

Fla. R. Civ. P. 1.330(d)(3)(B) is substantially similar:

> Errors and irregularities occurring at the oral examination in the manner of taking the deposition, in the form of the questions or answers, in the oath or affirmation, or in the conduct of parties and errors of any kind that might be obviated, removed, or cured if promptly presented are waived unless timely objection to them is made at the taking of the deposition.

The Florida Supreme Court has provided an instruction that state courts may look to federal case law for guidance when interpreting the state's rules, holding that, "[a]lthough the Federal Rules of Civil Procedure and the Florida Rules of Civil Procedure differ in some respects, 'the objective in promulgating the Florida rules has been to harmonize our rules with the federal rules.' . . . Thus, we look to the federal rules and decisions for guidance in interpreting Florida's civil procedure rules."[12]

GEORGIA

TRIAL STANDARDS: Fed. R. Civ. P. 30(c)(1)

Ga. Code Ann. § 9-11-30(c)(1) is substantially similar:

> Examination and cross-examination of witnesses may proceed as permitted at the trial under the rules of evidence.

CONTINUING TESTIMONY: Fed. R. Civ. P. 30(c)(2)

Ga. Code Ann. § 9-11-30(c)(2) is substantially similar:

> All objections made at the time of the examination . . . shall be noted by the officer upon the deposition. Evidence objected to shall be taken subject to the objections.

NONSUGGESTIVE OBJECTIONS: Fed. R. Civ. P. 30(c)(2)

Georgia has no comparable rule requiring objections to be concise, nonargumentative, or nonsuggestive.

INSTRUCTIONS NOT TO ANSWER: Fed. R. Civ. P. 30(c)(2)

Georgia has no comparable rule prohibiting instructions not to answer a deposition question.

DURATIONAL LIMIT: Fed. R. Civ. P. 30(d)(1)

Ga. Unif. Sup. Ct. R. 5.3 is virtually identical:

> [A] deposition is limited to one day of seven hours.

---

12   *Gleneagle Ship Mgmt. Co. v. Leondakos*, 602 So.2d 1282, 1283-84 (Fla. 1992) (internal citations omitted).

OBSTRUCTION SANCTIONS: Fed. R. Civ. P. 30(d)(2)

Georgia has <u>no comparable rule</u> establishing sanctions for frustrating the fair examination of a deponent.

SUSPENDING THE DEPOSITION: Fed. R. Civ. P. 30(d)(3)(A)

Ga. Code Ann. § 9-11-30(d) is conceptually similar:

> At any time during the taking of the deposition, on motion of a party or of the deponent and upon a showing that the examination is being conducted in bad faith or in such manner as unreasonably to annoy, embarrass, or oppress the deponent or party, the court in which the action is pending or the court in the county where the deposition is being taken may order the officer conducting the examination to cease forthwith from taking the deposition. . . . Upon demand of the objecting party or deponent, the taking of the deposition shall be suspended for the time necessary to make a motion for an order.

TRIAL ADMISSIBILITY: Fed. R. Civ. P. 32(b)

Ga. Code Ann. § 9-11-32(b) is substantially similar:

> [O]bjection[s] may be made at the trial or hearing to receiving in evidence any deposition or part thereof for any reason which would require the exclusion of the evidence if the witness were then present and testifying.

OBJECTIONS TO EVIDENTIARY ERRORS: Fed. R. Civ. P. 32(d)(3)(A)

Ga. Code Ann. § 9-11-32(d)(3)(A) is substantially similar:

> Objections to the competency of a witness or to the competency, relevancy, or materiality of testimony are not waived by failure to make them before or during the taking of the deposition unless the ground of the objection is one

which might have been obviated or removed if presented at that time.

OBJECTIONS TO OTHER CORRECTABLE ERRORS: Fed. R. Civ. P. 32(d)(3)(B)(i-ii)

Ga. Code Ann. § 9-11-32(d)(3)(B) is substantially similar:

> Errors and irregularities occurring at the oral examination in the manner of taking the deposition, in the form of the questions or answers, in the oath or affirmation, or in the conduct of parties, and errors of any kind which might be obviated, removed, or cured if promptly presented are waived unless seasonable objection thereto is made at the taking of the deposition.

The Georgia Supreme Court has not yet provided a general rule allowing for the use of federal case law to interpret the state's rules of civil procedure. When interpretive issues involving civil procedure have arisen, the court has applied federal case law about specific rules, including Fed. R. Civ. P. 9(c),[13] Fed. R. Civ. P. 16,[14] and Fed. R. Civ. P. 25(c),[15] to construe the state's corresponding rules of civil procedure. However, the Court of Appeals of Georgia has provided guidance on this issue, holding that "the Georgia Civil Procedure Act was taken from the Federal Rules of Civil Procedure, and 'with slight immaterial variations, its sections are substantially identical to corresponding rules. Because of this similarity, it is proper that we give consideration and great weight to constructions placed on the Federal Rules by the federal courts.'"[16]

---

[13] *McDonough Const. Co. v. McLendon Elec. Co.*, 250 S.E.2d 424, 429 (Ga. 1978).
[14] *Ambler v. Archer*, 196 S.E.2d 858, 862 (Ga. 1973).
[15] *Nat'l City Mortgage Co. v. Tidwell*, 749 S.E.2d 730, 732 (Ga. 2013).
[16] *Bicknell v. CBT Factors Corp.*, 321 S.E.2d 383, 385 (Ga. App. 1984).

HAWAII

TRIAL STANDARDS: Fed. R. Civ. P. 30(c)(1)

Haw. R. Civ. P. 30(c) is substantially similar:

> Examination and cross-examination of witnesses may proceed as permitted at the trial under the provisions of the Hawai'i Rules of Evidence. . . .

CONTINUING TESTIMONY: Fed. R. Civ. P. 30(c)(2)

Haw. R. Civ. P. 30(c) is substantially similar:

> All objections made at the time of the examination . . . shall be noted by the officer upon the record of the deposition; but the examination shall proceed, with the testimony being taken subject to the objections.

NONSUGGESTIVE OBJECTIONS: Fed. R. Civ. P. 30(c)(2)

Haw. R. Civ. P. 30(d)(1) is virtually identical:

> Any objection during a deposition must be stated concisely and in a non-argumentative and non-suggestive manner.

INSTRUCTIONS NOT TO ANSWER: Fed. R. Civ. P. 30(c)(2)

Haw. R. Civ. P. 30(d)(1) is virtually identical:

> A person may instruct a deponent not to answer only when necessary to preserve a privilege, to enforce a limitation directed by the court, or to present a motion under Rule 30(d)(4).

DURATIONAL LIMIT: Fed. R. Civ. P. 30(d)(1)

Haw. R. Civ. P. 30(d)(2) is virtually identical:

> [A] deposition is limited to one day of seven hours.

OBSTRUCTION SANCTIONS: Fed. R. Civ. P. 30(d)(2)

Haw. R. Civ. P. 30(d)(3) is substantially similar:

> If the court finds that any impediment, delay, or other conduct has frustrated the fair examination of the deponent, it may impose upon the persons responsible an appropriate sanction, including the reasonable costs and attorney's fees incurred by any parties as a result thereof.

SUSPENDING THE DEPOSITION: Fed. R. Civ. P. 30(d)(3)(A)

Haw. R. Civ. P. 30(d)(4) is substantially similar:

> At any time during a deposition, on motion of a party or of the deponent and upon a showing that the examination is being conducted in bad faith or in such manner as unreasonably to annoy, embarrass, or oppress the deponent or party, the court in which the action is pending or the court in the circuit where the deposition is being taken may order the officer conducting the examination to cease forthwith from taking the deposition. . . . Upon demand of the objecting party or deponent, the taking of the deposition must be suspended for the time necessary to make a motion for an order.

TRIAL ADMISSIBILITY: Fed. R. Civ. P. 32(b)

Haw. R. Civ. P. 32(c) is substantially similar:

> [O]bjection[s] may be made at the trial or hearing to receiving in evidence any deposition or part thereof for any reason which would require the exclusion of the evidence if the witness were then present and testifying.

OBJECTIONS TO EVIDENTIARY ERRORS: Fed. R. Civ. P. 32(d)(3)(A)

Haw. R. Civ. P. 32(e)(3)(A) is substantially similar:

> Objections to the competency of a witness or to the competency, relevancy, or materiality of testimony are not waived by failure to make them before or during the taking of the deposition, unless the ground of the objection is one which might have been obviated or removed if presented at that time.

OBJECTIONS TO OTHER CORRECTABLE ERRORS: Fed. R. Civ. P. 32(d)(3)(B)(i-ii)

Haw. R. Civ. P. 32(e)(3)(B) is substantially similar:

> Errors and irregularities occurring at the oral examination in the manner of taking the deposition, in the form of the questions or answers, in the oath or affirmation, or in the conduct of parties, and errors of any kind which might be obviated, removed, or cured if promptly presented, are waived unless seasonable objection thereto is made at the taking of the deposition.

The Supreme Court of Hawaii has held that, "[w]here we have patterned a rule of procedure after an equivalent rule within the FRCP, interpretations of the rule 'by the federal courts are deemed to be highly persuasive in the reasoning of this court.'"[17]

---

17   *Kawamata Farms, Inc. v. United Agri Prods.*, 948 P.2d 1055, 1092-93 (Haw. 1997) (internal citations omitted).

IDAHO

TRIAL STANDARDS: Fed. R. Civ. P. 30(c)(1)

I.R.C.P. 30(c)(1) is substantially similar:

> The examination and cross-examination of a deponent proceed as they would at trial under Rule 43(d) and the Idaho Rules of Evidence.

CONTINUING TESTIMONY: Fed. R. Civ. P. 30(c)(2)

I.R.C.P. 30(c)(2) is virtually identical:

> An objection at the time of the examination . . . must be noted on the record, but the examination still proceeds; the testimony is taken subject to any objection.

NONSUGGESTIVE OBJECTIONS: Fed. R. Civ. P. 30(c)(2)

I.R.C.P. 30(d)(1) is virtually identical:

> An objection must be stated concisely in a nonargumentative and nonsuggestive manner.

INSTRUCTIONS NOT TO ANSWER: Fed. R. Civ. P. 30(c)(2)

I.R.C.P. 30(d)(1) is virtually identical:

> A person may instruct a deponent not to answer only when necessary to preserve a privilege, to enforce a limitation ordered by the court, or to present a motion under Rule 30(d)(4).

DURATIONAL LIMIT: Fed. R. Civ. P. 30(d)(1)

Idaho has <u>no comparable rule</u> limiting the deposition.

OBSTRUCTION SANCTIONS: Fed. R. Civ. P. 30(d)(2)

I.R.C.P. 30(d)(3) is virtually identical:

> The court may impose an appropriate sanction, including the reasonable expenses and attorney's fees incurred by any party, or any other sanction listed in Rule 37(b), on a person who impedes, delays, or frustrates the fair examination of the deponent.

Additionally, I.R.C.P. 30(d)(2) explicitly prohibits any individual present at a deposition from frustrating the deponent's fair examination:

> Counsel or any other person present during the deposition must not impede, delay or frustrate the fair examination of the deponent.

SUSPENDING THE DEPOSITION: Fed. R. Civ. P. 30(d)(3)(A)

I.R.C.P. 30(d)(4)(A) is virtually identical:

> At any time during a deposition, the deponent or a party may move to terminate or limit it on the ground that it is being conducted in bad faith or in a manner that unreasonably annoys, embarrasses, or oppresses the deponent or party. . . . If the objecting deponent or party so demands, the deposition must be suspended for the time necessary to obtain an order.

TRIAL ADMISSIBILITY: Fed. R. Civ. P. 32(b)

I.R.C.P. 32(b) is virtually identical:

> [A]n objection may be made at a hearing or trial to the admission of any deposition testimony that would be inadmissible if the witness were present and testifying.

OBJECTIONS TO EVIDENTIARY ERRORS: Fed. R. Civ. P. 32(d)(3)(A)

I.R.C.P. 32(d)(3)(A) is virtually identical:

> An objection to a deponent's competence, or to the competence, relevance, or materiality of testimony, is not waived by a failure to make the objection before or during the deposition, unless the ground for it might have been corrected at that time.

OBJECTIONS TO OTHER CORRECTABLE ERRORS: Fed. R. Civ. P. 32(d)(3)(B)(i-ii)

I.R.C.P. 32(d)(3)(B) is virtually identical:

> An objection to an error or irregularity at an oral examination is waived if: (i) it relates to the manner of taking the deposition, the form of a question or answer, the oath or affirmation, a party's conduct, or other matters that might have been corrected at that time; and (ii) it is not timely made during the deposition.

The Idaho Supreme Court has commented that "part of the reason for adopting the Federal Rules of Civil Procedure in Idaho, and interpreting our own rules adopted from the federal courts as uniformly as possible with the federal cases, was to establish a uniform practice and procedure in both the federal and state courts in the State of Idaho."[18]

ILLINOIS

TRIAL STANDARDS: Fed. R. Civ. P. 30(c)(1)

Ill. Sup. Ct. R. 206(c)(2) is substantially similar:

> In an evidence deposition the examination and cross-examination shall be the same as though the deponent were testifying at the trial.

---

18   *Chacon v. Sperry Corp.*, 723 P.2d 814, 819 (Idaho 1986).

CONTINUING TESTIMONY: Fed. R. Civ. P. 30(c)(2)

Ill. Sup. Ct. R. 206(f) is conceptually similar:

> Objections made at the time of the examination . . . shall be included in the deposition. Evidence objected to shall be taken subject to the objection.

NONSUGGESTIVE OBJECTIONS: Fed. R. Civ. P. 30(c)(2)

Ill. Sup. Ct. R. 206(c)(3) is conceptually similar:

> Objections at depositions shall be concise, stating the exact legal nature of the objection.

This is conceptually similar because, as clarified by the 1999 committee comments:

> Subparagraph (c)(3) has been added to eliminate speaking objections.

However, the rule does not specify how to properly state "the exact legal nature of the objection."

INSTRUCTIONS NOT TO ANSWER: Fed. R. Civ. P. 30(c)(2)

Illinois has <u>no comparable rule</u> prohibiting instructions not to answer a deposition question.

DURATIONAL LIMIT: Fed. R. Civ. P. 30(d)(1)

Ill. Sup. Ct. R. 206(d) is significantly different:

> No discovery deposition of any party or witness shall exceed three hours regardless of the number of parties involved in the case, except by stipulation of all parties or by order upon showing that good cause warrants a lengthier examination.

This is significantly different because the presumptive limit of a deposition is decreased from seven hours to three hours.

OBSTRUCTION SANCTIONS: Fed. R. Civ. P. 30(d)(2)

Ill. Sup. Ct. R. 219(c) and Ill. Sup. Ct. R. 219(d), when taken together, are conceptually similar.

Ill. Sup. Ct. R. 219(c):

> If a party, or any person at the instance of or in collusion with a party, unreasonably fails to comply with any provision of part E of article II of the rules of this court (Discovery, Requests for Admission, and Pretrial Procedure) . . . the court, on motion, may enter . . . such orders as are just. . . . [T]he court, upon motion or upon its own initiative, may impose upon the offending party or his or her attorney, or both, an appropriate sanction. . . .

Ill. Sup. Ct. R. 219(d):

> If a party willfully . . . abuses these discovery rules, the court may enter any order provided for in paragraph (c) of this rule.

These rules are conceptually similar to the federal rule because they authorize sanctions for abusing and ignoring discovery rules—conduct that usually obstructs the deposition.

SUSPENDING THE DEPOSITION: Fed. R. Civ. P. 30(d)(3)(A)

Ill. Sup. Ct. R. 206(e) is conceptually similar:

> At any time during the taking of the deposition, on motion of any party or of the deponent and upon a showing that the examination is being conducted in bad faith or in any manner that unreasonably annoys, embarrasses, or oppresses the deponent or party, the court may order that the examination cease forthwith. . . . Upon the demand of the objecting party

or deponent, the taking of the deposition shall be suspended for the time necessary to present a motion for an order.

TRIAL ADMISSIBILITY: Fed. R. Civ. P. 32(b)

OBJECTIONS TO EVIDENTIARY ERRORS: Fed. R. Civ. P. 32(d)(3)(A)

Ill. Sup. Ct. R. 211(c)(1) is conceptually similar:

> Grounds of objection to the competency of the deponent or admissibility of testimony which might have been corrected if presented during the taking of the deposition are waived by failure to make them at that time; otherwise objections to the competency of the deponent or admissibility of testimony may be made when the testimony is offered in evidence.

This is conceptually similar because it combines Federal Rules 32(b) and 32(d)(3)(A) into a single rule. Within this combined rule, the corresponding requirements are susbstantially similar to their federal counterparts.

OBJECTIONS TO OTHER CORRECTABLE ERRORS: Fed. R. Civ. P. 32(d)(3)(B)(i-ii)

Ill. Sup. Ct. R. 211(c)(2) is substantially similar:

> Objections to the form of a question or answer, errors and irregularities occurring at the oral examination in the manner of taking the deposition, in the oath or affirmation, or in the conduct of any person, and errors and irregularitites of any kind which might be corrected if promptly presented, are waived unless seasonable objection thereto is made at the taking of the deposition.

The Illinois Supreme Court has not yet provided a general rule allowing for the use of federal case law to interpret the state's rules of civil procedure. When interpretive issues involving civil procedure have arisen, however, the court has applied federal case law about specific rules, including Fed. R. Civ. P. 23[19] and Fed. R. Civ. P. 36,[20] to construe the state's corresponding rules of civil procedure.

INDIANA

TRIAL STANDARDS: Fed. R. Civ. P. 30(c)(1)

Ind. R. Trial P. 30(C) is substantially similar:

> Examination and cross-examination of witnesses may proceed as permitted at the trial under the provisions of Rule 43(B).

CONTINUING TESTIMONY: Fed. R. Civ. P. 30(c)(2)

INSTRUCTIONS NOT TO ANSWER: Fed. R. Civ. P. 30(c)(2)

Ind. R. Trial P. 30(C) is conceptually similar:

> All objections made at the time of the examination . . . shall be noted by the officer upon the deposition. When there is an objection to a question, the objection and reason therefor shall be noted, and the question shall be answered unless the attorney instructs the deponent not to answer, or the deponent refuses to answer, in which case either party may have the question certified by the Reporter, and the question with the objection thereto when so certified shall be delivered to the party requesting the certification who may then proceed under Rule 37(A).

This is conceptually similar because it requires the testimony to continue subject to any objection. However, it differs by not including the standard prohibition on instructions not to answer, and it procedurally facilitates a Rule 37(a) motion to compel by automatically delivering the disputed question to the party requesting certification.

---

19   *Mashal v. City of Chicago*, 981 N.E.2d 951, 959 (Ill. 2012).
20   *P.R.S. Int'l, Inc. v. Shred Pax Corp.*, 703 N.E.2d 71, 77 (Ill. 1998).

NONSUGGESTIVE OBJECTIONS: Fed. R. Civ. P. 30(c)(2)

Indiana has no comparable rule requiring deposition objections to be concise, nonargumentative, or nonsuggestive.

_____

DURATIONAL LIMIT: Fed. R. Civ. P. 30(d)(1)

Indiana has no comparable rule limiting the deposition.

_____

OBSTRUCTION SANCTIONS: Fed. R. Civ. P. 30(d)(2)

Indiana has no comparable rule establishing sanctions for frustrating the fair examination of a deponent.

_____

SUSPENDING THE DEPOSITION: Fed. R. Civ. P. 30(d)(3)(A)

Ind. R. Trial P. 30(D) is conceptually similar:

> At any time during the taking of the deposition, on motion of any party or of the deponent and upon a showing that the examination is being conducted in bad faith or in such manner as unreasonably to annoy, embarrass, or oppress the deponent or party, the court in which the action is pending or the court in the county where the deposition is being taken may order the officer conducting the examination to cease forthwith from taking the deposition. . . . Upon demand of the objecting party or deponent the taking of the deposition shall be suspended for the time necessary to make a motion for an order.

_____

Comparing Relevant Portions of Rules 30 & 32

TRIAL ADMISSIBILITY: Fed. R. Civ. P. 32(b)

Ind. R. Trial P. 32(B) is substantially similar:

> [O]bjection[s] may be made at the trial or hearing to receiving in evidence any depositions or part thereof for any reason which would require the exclusion of the evidence if the witness were then present and testifying.

OBJECTIONS TO EVIDENTIARY ERRORS: Fed. R. Civ. P. 32(d)(3)(A)

Ind. R. Trial P. 32(D)(3)(a) is substantially similar:

> Objections to the competency of a witness or to the competency, relevancy, or materiality of testimony are not waived by failure to make them before or during the taking of the deposition, unless the ground of the objection is one which might have been obviated or removed if presented at that time.

OBJECTIONS TO OTHER CORRECTABLE ERRORS: Fed. R. Civ. P. 32(d)(3)(B)(i-ii)

Ind. R. Trial P. 32(D)(3)(b) is substantially similar:

> Errors and irregularities occurring at the oral examination in the manner of taking the deposition, in the form of the questions or answers, in the oath or affirmation, or in the conduct of parties and errors of any kind which might be obviated, removed, or cured if promptly presented, are waived unless reasonable objection thereto is made at the taking of the deposition.

The Indiana Supreme Court has not yet provided a general rule allowing for the use of federal case law to interpret the state's rules of civil procedure. When interpretive issues involving civil procedure have arisen, the court has applied federal case law about specific rules, including Fed.

R. Civ. P. 23,[21] Fed. R. Civ. P. 41(a)(2),[22] and Fed. R. Civ. P. 60(b),[23] to construe the state's corresponding rules of civil procedure. However, the applicability of federal case law to the Indiana rules has been provided by the Court of Appeals of Indiana in a sweeping holding that states: "In the absence of state law, we look to federal decisions for guidance in interpreting our rules of procedure which are similar to the Federal Rules of Civil Procedure."[24]

IOWA

TRIAL STANDARDS: Fed. R. Civ. P. 30(c)(1)

Iowa R. Civ. P. 1.708(1)(a) is substantially similar:

> Examination and cross-examination of witnesses may proceed as permitted at the trial.

CONTINUING TESTIMONY: Fed. R. Civ. P. 30(c)(2)

Iowa R. Civ. P. 1.708(1)(b) is substantially similar:

> All objections made at the time of the examination . . . shall be noted by the officer upon the deposition. Evidence objected to shall be taken subject to the objections.

NONSUGGESTIVE OBJECTIONS: Fed. R. Civ. P. 30(c)(2)

Iowa R. Civ. P. 1.708(1)(b) is virtually identical:

> An objection must be stated concisely in a nonargumentative and nonsuggestive manner.

---

21 *Associated Med. Networks, Ltd. v. Lewis*, 824 N.E.2d 679, 685 (Ind. 2005).

22 *Highland Realty, Inc. v. Indianapolis Airport Auth.*, 563 N.E.2d 1271, 1273 (Ind. 1990).

23 *Soft Water Utilities, Inc. v. Le Fevre*, 301 N.E.2d 745, 747 (Ind. 1973).

24 *Jackson v. Russell*, 491 N.E.2d 1017, 1018 (Ind. Ct. App. 1986).

Comparing Relevant Portions of Rules 30 & 32

INSTRUCTIONS NOT TO ANSWER: Fed. R. Civ. P. 30(c)(2)

Iowa R. Civ. P. 1.708(1)(b) is virtually identical:

> A person may instruct a deponent not to answer only when necessary to preserve a privilege, to enforce a limitation ordered by the court, or to present a motion under rule 1.708(2).

DURATIONAL LIMIT: Fed. R. Civ. P. 30(d)(1)

Iowa has no comparable rule limiting the deposition.

OBSTRUCTION SANCTIONS: Fed. R. Civ. P. 30(d)(2)

Iowa R. Civ. P. 1.708(2)(a) is virtually identical:

> The court may impose an appropriate sanction, including the reasonable expenses and attorney fees incurred by any party, on a person who impedes, delays, or frustrates the fair examination of the deponent.

SUSPENDING THE DEPOSITION: Fed. R. Civ. P. 30(d)(3)(A)

Iowa R. Civ. P. 1.708(2)(b) is conceptually similar:

> At any time during the taking of the deposition, on motion of a party or of the deponent and upon a showing that the examination is being conducted in bad faith or in such manner as unreasonably to annoy, embarrass, or oppress the deponent or party, the court in which the action is pending or the court in the district where the deposition is being taken may order the officer conducting the examination to cease forthwith from taking the deposition. . . . Upon demand of the objecting party or deponent, the taking of the deposition shall be suspended for the time necessary to make a motion for an order.

TRIAL ADMISSIBILITY: Fed. R. Civ. P. 32(b)

OBJECTIONS TO EVIDENTIARY ERRORS: Fed. R. Civ. P. 32(d)(3)(A)

Iowa R. Civ. 1.717(5) is conceptually similar:

> Except as above provided, testimony taken by deposition may be objected to at the trial on any ground which would require its exclusion if given by a witness in open court, and objections to testimony, or competency of a witness, need not be made prior to or during the deposition, unless the grounds thereof could then have been obviated or removed.

This is conceptually similar to both of these federal rules, but it differs by combining them into a single rule.

OBJECTIONS TO OTHER CORRECTABLE ERRORS: Fed. R. Civ. P. 32(d)(3)(B)(i-ii)

Iowa R. Civ. P. 1.717(4) is substantially similar:

> Errors or irregularities occurring during an oral deposition as to any conduct or manner of taking it, or the oath, or the form of any question or answer, and any other errors which might thereupon have been cured, obviated or removed, are waived unless seasonably objected to during the deposition.

The Iowa Supreme Court has not yet provided a general rule allowing for the use of federal case law to interpret the state's rules of civil procedure. When interpretive issues involving civil procedure have arisen, however, the court has applied federal case law about specific rules, including Fed. R. Civ. P. 11,[25] Fed. R. Civ. P. 13,[26] Fed. R. Civ. P. 26(b),[27]

---

[25] *Barnhill v. Iowa Dist. Court for Polk Cty.*, 765 N.W.2d 267, 273 (Iowa 2009), as corrected (May 14, 2009).

[26] *Harrington v. Polk Cty. Fed. Sav. & Loan Ass'n of Des Moines*, 196 N.W.2d 543, 545 (Iowa 1972).

[27] *Wells Dairy, Inc. v. Am. Indus. Refrigeration, Inc.*, 690 N.W.2d 38 (Iowa 2004).

and Fed. R. Civ. P. 56,[28] to construe the state's corresponding rules of civil procedure.

KANSAS

TRIAL STANDARDS: Fed. R. Civ. P. 30(c)(1)

K.S.A. § 60-230(c)(1) is substantially similar:

> The examination and cross-examination of a deponent proceed as they would at trial under the provisions of K.S.A. 60-243, and amendments thereto.

CONTINUING TESTIMONY: Fed. R. Civ. P. 30(c)(2)

K.S.A. § 60-230(c)(2) is virtually identical:

> An objection at the time of the examination . . . must be noted on the record, but the examination still proceeds; the testimony is taken subject to any objection.

NONSUGGESTIVE OBJECTIONS: Fed. R. Civ. P. 30(c)(2)

K.S.A. § 60-230(c)(2) is virtually identical:

> An objection must be stated concisely in a nonargumentative and nonsuggestive manner.

INSTRUCTIONS NOT TO ANSWER: Fed. R. Civ. P. 30(c)(2)

K.S.A. § 60-230(c)(2) is virtually identical:

> A person may instruct a deponent not to answer only when necessary to preserve a privilege, to enforce a limitation ordered by the court or to present a motion under subsection (d)(3).

---

28 *Brody v. Ruby*, 267 N.W.2d 902, 904 (Iowa 1978).

DURATIONAL LIMIT: Fed. R. Civ. P. 30(d)(1)

Kansas has no comparable rule establishing a presumptive time limit.

OBSTRUCTION SANCTIONS: Fed. R. Civ. P. 30(d)(2)

Kansas has no comparable rule establishing sanctions for frustrating the fair examination of the deponent.

SUSPENDING THE DEPOSITION: Fed. R. Civ. P. 30(d)(3)(A)

K.S.A. § 60-230(d)(1) is virtually identical:

> At any time during a deposition, the deponent or a party may move to terminate or limit it on the ground that it is being conducted in bad faith or in a manner that unreasonably annoys, embarrasses or oppresses the deponent or party. The motion may be filed in the court where the action is pending or where the deposition is being taken. If the objecting deponent or party so demands, the deposition must be suspended for the time necessary to obtain an order.

TRIAL ADMISSIBILITY: Fed. R. Civ. P. 32(b)

K.S.A. § 60-232(b) is virtually identical:

> [A]n objection may be made at a hearing or trial to the admission of any deposition testimony that would be inadmissible if the witness were present and testifying.

OBJECTIONS TO EVIDENTIARY ERRORS: Fed. R. Civ. P. 32(d)(3)(A)

K.S.A. § 60-232(d)(3)(A) is virtually identical:

> An objection to a deponent's competence, or to the competence, relevance or materiality of testimony, is not waived by a failure to make the objection before or during the deposition, unless the ground for it might have been corrected at that time.

OBJECTIONS TO OTHER CORRECTABLE ERRORS: Fed. R. Civ. P. 32(d)(3)(B)(i-ii)

K.S.A. § 60-232(d)(3)(B) is virtually identical:

> An objection to an error or irregularity at an oral examination is waived if: (i) It relates to the manner of taking the deposition, the form of a question or answer, the oath or affirmation, a party's conduct or other matters that might have been corrected at that time; and (ii) it is not timely made during the deposition.

The Kansas Supreme Court has not yet provided a general rule allowing for the use of federal case law to interpret the state's rules of civil procedure. When interpretive issues involving civil procedure have arisen, however, the court has applied federal case law about specific rules, including Fed. R. Civ. P. 12,[29] Fed. R. Civ. P. 23,[30] Fed. R. Civ. P. 24(a)(2),[31] Fed. R. Civ. P. 54(b),[32] Fed. R. Civ. P. 55(b),[33] and Fed. R. Civ. P. 60(b),[34] to construe the state's corresponding rules of civil procedure.

---

[29] *Aeroflex Wichita, Inc. v. Filardo*, 275 P.3d 869, 875-76 (Kan. 2012).

[30] *Newton v. Hornblower, Inc.*, 582 P.2d 1136, 1141 (Kan. 1978).

[31] *Ternes v. Galichia*, 305 P.3d 617, 620 (Kan. 2013).

[32] *Dennis v. Se. Kansas Gas Co.*, 610 P.2d 627, 632 (Kan. 1980).

[33] *Montez v. Tonkawa Vill. Apartments*, 523 P.2d 351, 354 (Kan. 1974).

[34] *Id.*

KENTUCKY

TRIAL STANDARDS: Fed. R. Civ. P. 30(c)(1)

Ky. R. Civ. P. 30.03(1) is substantially similar:

> Examination and cross-examination of witnesses may proceed as permitted at the trial under the provisions of Rules 43.05 and 43.06.

CONTINUING TESTIMONY: Fed. R. Civ. P. 30(c)(2)

Ky. R. Civ. P. 30.03(2) is substantially similar:

> All objections made at the time of the examination . . . shall be noted by the officer upon the deposition. Evidence objected to shall be taken subject to the objections.

NONSUGGESTIVE OBJECTIONS: Fed. R. Civ. P. 30(c)(2)

Ky. R. Civ. P. 30.03(3) is virtually identical:

> Any objection to evidence during a deposition shall be stated concisely and in a nonargumentative and nonsuggestive manner.

INSTRUCTIONS NOT TO ANSWER: Fed. R. Civ. P. 30(c)(2)

Ky. R. Civ. P. 30.03(3) is virtually identical:

> An attorney may instruct his or her client not to answer only when necessary to preserve a privilege, to enforce a limitation on evidence directed by the court, or to present a motion under CR 30.04.

DURATIONAL LIMIT: Fed. R. Civ. P. 30(d)(1)

Kentucky has <u>no comparable rule</u> establishing a presumptive time limit.

OBSTRUCTION SANCTIONS: Fed. R. Civ. P. 30(d)(2)

Ky. R. Civ. P. 30.03(4) is substantially similar:

> If the court finds such an impediment, delay, or other conduct has frustrated the fair examination of the deponent, it may impose upon the persons responsible an appropriate sanction, including the reasonable costs and attorney's fees incurred by any parties as a result thereof.

SUSPENDING THE DEPOSITION: Fed. R. Civ. P. 30(d)(3)(A)

Ky. R. Civ. P. 30.04 is substantially similar:

> At any time during the taking of the deposition, on motion of a party or of the deponent and upon a showing that the examination is being conducted in bad faith or in such manner as unreasonably to annoy, embarrass, or oppress the deponent or party, the court in which the action is pending or the court in the judicial district where the deposition is being taken may order the officer conducting the examination to cease forthwith from taking the deposition. . . . Upon demand of the objecting party or deponent, the taking of the deposition shall be suspended for the time necessary to make a motion for an order.

TRIAL ADMISSIBILITY: Fed. R. Civ. P. 32(b)

Ky. R. Civ. P. 32.02 is substantially similar:

> [O]bjection[s] may be made at the trial or hearing to receiving in evidence any deposition or part thereof for any reason which would require the exclusion of the evidence if the witness were then present and testifying.

OBJECTIONS TO EVIDENTIARY ERRORS: Fed. R. Civ. P. 32(d)(3)(A)

Ky. R. Civ. P. 32.04(3)(a) is substantially similar:

> Objections to the competency of a witness or to the competency, relevancy, or materiality of testimony are not waived by failure to make them before or during the taking of the deposition, unless the ground of the objection is one which might have been obviated or removed if presented at that time.

OBJECTIONS TO OTHER CORRECTABLE ERRORS: Fed. R. Civ. P. 32(d)(3)(B)(i-ii)

Ky. R. Civ. P. 32.04(3)(b) is substantially similar:

> Errors and irregularities occurring at the oral examination in the manner of taking the deposition, in the form of the questions or answers, in the oath or affirmation, or in the conduct of parties and errors of any kind which might be obviated, removed, or cured if promptly presented, are waived unless seasonable objection thereto is made at the taking of the deposition.

The Kentucky Supreme Court has not yet provided a general rule allowing for the use of federal case law to interpret the state's rules of civil procedure. When interpretive issues involving civil procedure have arisen, the court has applied federal case law about specific rules, including Fed. R. Civ. P. 24,[35] Fed. R. Civ. P. 26(b),[36] Fed. R. Civ. P. 35(a),[37] and Fed. R. Civ. P. 54(b),[38] to construe the state's corresponding rules of civil procedure.

---

[35] *Pearman v. Schlaak*, 575 S.W.2d 462, 464 (Ky. 1978).

[36] *O'Connell v. Cowan*, 332 S.W.3d 34, 40 (Ky. 2010), *reh'g granted, opinion modified* (Dec. 16, 2010).

[37] *Perry v. Com., ex rel. Kessinger*, 652 S.W.2d 655, 658 (Ky. 1983).

[38] *Watson v. Best Fin. Servs., Inc.*, 245 S.W.3d 722, 725 (Ky. 2008).

LOUISIANA

TRIAL STANDARDS: Fed. R. Civ. P. 30(c)(1)

La. Code Civ. P. art. 1443(A) is substantially similar:

> Examination and cross-examination of witnesses may proceed as permitted at the trial under the provisions of the Louisiana Code of Evidence.

CONTINUING TESTIMONY: Fed. R. Civ. P. 30(c)(2)

La. Code Civ. P. art. 1443(B) is substantially similar:

> All objections made at the time of the examination . . . shall be noted by the officer upon the deposition. . . . Evidence objected to shall be taken subject to the objections.

NONSUGGESTIVE OBJECTIONS: Fed. R. Civ. P. 30(c)(2)

La. Code Civ. P. art. 1443(B) is virtually identical:

> Any objection during a deposition shall be stated concisely and in a non-argumentative and non-suggestive manner.

INSTRUCTIONS NOT TO ANSWER: Fed. R. Civ. P. 30(c)(2)

Louisiana has <u>no comparable rule</u> prohibiting instructions not to answer a deposition question. However, La. Code Civ. P. art. 1443 provides:

> The officer shall cease or suspend recordation of the testimony, questions, objections, or any other statements only upon agreement of all counsel and parties present at the deposition, or upon termination or suspension of the deposition pursuant to Code of Civil Procedure Article 1444.

This could be construed to imply that an instruction not to answer is permissible only if agreed upon by all parties and counsel present at the deposition. However, this rule explicitly refers to only the officer's recordation of the testimony.

DURATIONAL LIMIT: Fed. R. Civ. P. 30(d)(1)

Louisiana has no comparable rule establishing a presumptive time limit.

OBSTRUCTION SANCTIONS: Fed. R. Civ. P. 30(d)(2)

La. Code Civ. P. art. 1443(B) is conceptually similar:

> Counsel shall cooperate with and be courteous to each other and to the witness and otherwise conduct themselves as required in open court and shall be subject to the power of the court to punish for contempt.

This is conceptually similar because it seeks to hold parties accountable for deposition misconduct, but it differs by not explicitly stating that frustrating the deponent's fair examination is cause for sanctions. It also differs by specifying the sanction of contempt, rather than allowing for the "appropriate sanctions" of the federal rule.

SUSPENDING THE DEPOSITION: Fed. R. Civ. P. 30(d)(3)(A)

La. Code Civ. P. art. 1444 is conceptually similar:

> At any time during the taking of the deposition, on motion of a party or of the deponent and upon a showing that the examination is being conducted in bad faith or in such manner as unreasonably to annoy, embarrass, or oppress the deponent or party, the court in which the action is pending may order the officer conducting the examination to cease forthwith from taking the deposition. . . . Upon demand of the objecting party or deponent, the taking of

the deposition shall be suspended for the time necessary to make a motion for an order.

TRIAL ADMISSIBILITY: Fed. R. Civ. P. 32(b)

La. Code Civ. P. art. 1451 is substantially similar:

> [O]bjection[s] may be made at the trial or hearing to receiving in evidence any deposition or part thereof for any reason which would require the exclusion of the evidence if the witness were then present and testifying.

OBJECTIONS TO EVIDENTIARY ERRORS: Fed. R. Civ. P. 32(d)(3)(A)

La. Code Civ. P. art. 1455 is substantially similar:

> Objections to the competency of a witness or to the competency, relevancy, or materiality of testimony are not waived by failure to make them before or during the taking of the deposition, unless the ground of the objection is one which might have been obviated or removed if presented at that time.

OBJECTIONS TO OTHER CORRECTABLE ERRORS: Fed. R. Civ. P. 32(d)(3)(B)(i-ii)

La. Code Civ. P. art. 1455 is substantially similar:

> Objections to errors and irregularities occurring at the oral examination in the manner of taking the deposition, in the form of the questions or answers, in the oath or affirmation, or in the conduct of parties, and errors of any kind which might be obviated, removed, or cured if promptly presented, are waived unless seasonably made at the taking of the deposition.

The Supreme Court of Louisiana has held: "Since we obtained these discovery rules from the federal rules, we may look for guidance from the federal decisions which have interpreted identical provisions."[39]

MAINE

TRIAL STANDARDS: Fed. R. Civ. P. 30(c)(1)

Me. R. Civ. P. 30(c) is substantially similar:

> Examination and cross-examination of witnesses may proceed as permitted at the trial under the provisions of the Maine Rules of Evidence.

CONTINUING TESTIMONY: Fed. R. Civ. P. 30(c)(2)

Me. R. Civ. P. 30(c) is substantially similar:

> All objections made at the time of the examination . . . shall be noted by the officer upon the deposition. Evidence objected to shall be taken subject to the objections.

NONSUGGESTIVE OBJECTIONS: Fed. R. Civ. P. 30(c)(2)

Me. R. Civ. P. 30(d)(1) is virtually identical:

> Any objection to evidence during a deposition shall be stated concisely and in a non-argumentative and non-suggestive manner.

INSTRUCTIONS NOT TO ANSWER: Fed. R. Civ. P. 30(c)(2)

Me. R. Civ. P. 30(d)(1) is virtually identical:

> A party may instruct a deponent not to answer only when necessary to preserve a privilege, to enforce a limitation on evidence directed by the court, or to present a motion under paragraph (3).

---

39 *Madison v. Travelers Ins. Co.*, 308 So. 2d 784, 786 (La. 1975).

DURATIONAL LIMIT: Fed. R. Civ. P. 30(d)(1)

Me. R. Civ. P. 30(d)(2) is significantly different:

> No deposition shall exceed 8 hours of testimony. . . .

This is significantly different because it extends the federal rule's presumptive time limit of seven hours to eight hours.

OBSTRUCTION SANCTIONS: Fed. R. Civ. P. 30(d)(2)

Me. R. Civ. P. 30(d)(2) is substantially similar:

> If the court finds such an impediment, delay, or other conduct that has frustrated the fair examination of the deponent, it may impose upon the persons responsible an appropriate sanction, including the reasonable costs and attorney fees incurred by any parties as a result thereof.

SUSPENDING THE DEPOSITION: Fed. R. Civ. P. 30(d)(3)(A)

Me. R. Civ. P. 30(d)(3) is conceptually similar:

> At any time during a deposition, on motion of a party or of the deponent and upon a showing that the examination is being conducted in bad faith or in such manner as unreasonably to annoy, embarrass, or oppress the deponent or party, any justice or judge of the court in which the action is pending may order the officer conducting the examination to cease forthwith from taking the deposition. . . . Upon demand of the objecting party or deponent, the taking of the deposition shall be suspended for the time necessary to make a motion for an order.

TRIAL ADMISSIBILITY: Fed. R. Civ. P. 32(b)

Me. R. Civ. P. 32(b) is substantially similar:

> [O]bjection[s] may be made at the trial or hearing to receiving in evidence any deposition or part thereof for any reason

which would require the exclusion of the evidence if the witness were then present and testifying.

OBJECTIONS TO EVIDENTIARY ERRORS: Fed. R. Civ. P. 32(d)(3)(A)

Me. R. Civ. P. 32(d)(3)(A) is substantially similar:

> Objections to the competency of a witness or to the competency, relevancy, or materiality of testimony are not waived by failure to make them before or during the taking of the deposition, unless the ground of the objection is one which might have been obviated or removed if presented at that time.

OBJECTIONS TO OTHER CORRECTABLE ERRORS: Fed. R. Civ. P. 32(d)(3)(B)(i-ii)

Me. R. Civ. P. 32(d)(3)(B) is substantially similar:

> Errors and irregularities occurring at the oral examination in the manner of taking the deposition, in the form of the questions or answers, in the oath or affirmation, or in the conduct of parties, and errors of any kind which might be obviated, removed, or cured if promptly presented, are waived unless seasonable objection thereto is made at the taking of the deposition.

The Supreme Judicial Court of Maine has not yet provided a general rule allowing for the use of federal case law to interpret the state's rules of civil procedure. When interpretive issues involving civil procedure have arisen, however, the court has applied federal case law about specific rules, including Fed. R. Civ. P. 17(a),[40] to construe the state's corresponding rule of civil procedure.

---

40 *Tisdale v. Rawson*, 822 A.2d 1136, 1141 (Me. 2003).

MARYLAND

TRIAL STANDARDS: Fed. R. Civ. P. 30(c)(1)

Md. R. 2-415(b) is substantially similar:

> When a deposition is taken upon oral examination, examination and cross-examination of the deponent may proceed as permitted in the trial of an action in open court.

CONTINUING TESTIMONY: Fed. R. Civ. P. 30(c)(2)

Md. R. 2-145(h) is significantly different:

> All objections made during a deposition shall be recorded with the testimony.

While this rule requires all objections to be recorded, it does not stipulate that the examination shall proceed subject to the objections.

NONSUGGESTIVE OBJECTIONS: Fed. R. Civ. P. 30(c)(2)

Md. R. 2-415(h) is conceptually similar:

> The grounds of an objection need not be stated unless requested by a party. If the ground of an objection is stated, it shall be stated specifically, concisely, and in a non-argumentative and non-suggestive manner. If a party desires to make an objection for the record during the taking of a deposition that reasonably could have the effect of coaching or suggesting to the deponent how to answer, then the deponent, at the request of any party, shall be excused from the deposition during the making of the objection.

This general requirement of stating an objection concisely is substantially similar to the federal rule. However, Maryland also stipulates that stating the ground of an objection is unnecessary unless requested by the examiner, and that if the explanation would be suggestive, then counsel can temporarily excuse the deponent from the deposition.

The committee notes provide more detail describing proper deposition objections:

> During the taking of a deposition, it is presumptively improper for an attorney to make objections that are not consistent with Rule 2-415(h). Objections should be stated as simply, concisely, and non-argumentatively as possible to avoid coaching or making suggestions to the deponent and to minimize interruptions in the questioning of the deponent. Examples include "objection, leading;" "objection, asked and answered;" and "objection, compound question."[41]

INSTRUCTIONS NOT TO ANSWER: Fed. R. Civ. P. 30(c)(2)

Md. R. 2-415(i) is significantly different:

> When a deponent refuses to answer a question, the proponent of the question shall complete the examination to the extent practicable before filing a motion for an order compelling discovery.

This rule does not prohibit instructions not to answer, subject to the standard exceptions. Instead, it stipulates that the examiner should continue the deposition after a deponent refuses to answer a question and then file a motion to compel discovery.

DURATIONAL LIMIT: Fed. R. Civ. P. 30(d)(1)

Md. R. 2-411 is conceptually similar:

> Leave of court must be obtained to take a deposition . . . that is longer than one seven-hour day. . . .

OBSTRUCTION SANCTIONS: Fed. R. Civ. P. 30(d)(2)

Maryland has no comparable rule establishing sanctions for frustrating the fair examination of a deponent.

---

[41] Md. R. 2-415(h), committee note.

SUSPENDING THE DEPOSITION: Fed. R. Civ. P. 30(d)(3)(A)

Maryland has no comparable rule authorizing a party to terminate the deposition if it is being conducted with bad faith or in a manner that harasses a deponent or party.

TRIAL ADMISSIBILITY: Fed. R. Civ. P. 32(b)

Md. R. 2-419(d) is substantially similar:

> [A]n objection may be made at a hearing or trial to receiving in evidence all or part of a deposition for any reason that would require the exclusion of the evidence if the witness were then present and testifying.

OBJECTIONS TO EVIDENTIARY ERRORS: Fed. R. Civ. P. 32(d)(3)(A)

Md. R. 2-415(h) is substantially similar:

> An objection to the competency of a witness or to the competency, relevancy, or materiality of testimony is not waived by failure to make it before or during a deposition unless the ground of the objection is one that might have been obviated or removed if presented at that time.

OBJECTIONS TO OTHER CORRECTABLE ERRORS: Fed. R. Civ. P. 32(d)(3)(B)(i-ii)

Md. R. 2-415(h) is substantially similar:

> An objection to the manner of taking a deposition, to the form of questions or answers, to the oath or affirmation, to the conduct of the parties, or to any other kind of error or irregularity that might be obviated or removed if objected to at the time of its occurrence is waived unless a timely objection is made during the deposition.

The Maryland Court of Appeals has not yet provided a general rule allowing for the use of federal case law to interpret the state's rules of civil procedure. When interpretive issues involving civil procedure have arisen, the court has applied federal case law about specific rules, including Fed. R. Civ. P. 23,[42] Fed. R. Civ. P. 24,[43] Fed. R. Civ. P. 36,[44] and Fed. R. Civ. P. 54(b),[45] to construe the state's corresponding rules of civil procedure.

MASSACHUSETTS

TRIAL STANDARDS: Fed. R. Civ. P. 30(c)(1)

Mass. R. Civ. P. 30(c) is substantially similar:

> Examination and cross-examination of witnesses may proceed as permitted at the trial under the provisions of Rule 43(b).

CONTINUING TESTIMONY: Fed. R. Civ. P. 30(c)(2)

Mass. R. Civ. P. 30(c) is virtually identical:

> All objections made at the time of the examination . . . shall be noted by the officer upon the deposition; but the examination shall proceed. . . . Testimony to which objection is made shall be taken subject to the objections.

NONSUGGESTIVE OBJECTIONS: Fed. R. Civ. P. 30(c)(2)

Mass. R. Civ. P. 30(c) is virtually identical:

> Any objection to testimony during a deposition shall be stated concisely and in a non-argumentative and non-suggestive manner.

---

42 *Philip Morris Inc. v. Angeletti*, 752 A.2d 200, 219 (Md. 2000).
43 *Duckworth v. Deane*, 903 A.2d 883, 891 (Md. 2006).
44 *Murnan v. Joseph J. Hock, Inc.*, 335 A.2d 104, 106 (Md. 1975).
45 *Planning Bd. of Howard Cty. v. Mortimer*, 530 A.2d 1237, 1239-40 (Md. 1987).

INSTRUCTIONS NOT TO ANSWER: Fed. R. Civ. P. 30(c)(2)

Mass. R. Civ. P. 30(c) is conceptually similar:

> Counsel for a witness or a party may not instruct a deponent not to answer except where necessary to assert or preserve a privilege or protection against disclosure, to enforce a limitation on evidence directed by the court or stipulated in writing by the parties, or to terminate the deposition and present a motion to the court pursuant to Rules 30(d) or 37(d).

This rule provides a stipulation between the parties as an additional permissible reason for an instruction not to answer a deposition question.

DURATIONAL LIMIT: Fed. R. Civ. P. 30(d)(1)

Massachusetts has <u>no comparable rule</u> establishing a time limit.

OBSTRUCTION SANCTIONS: Fed. R. Civ. P. 30(d)(2)

Massachusetts has <u>no comparable rule</u> establishing sanctions for frustrating the fair examination of a deponent.

SUSPENDING THE DEPOSITION: Fed. R. Civ. P. 30(d)(3)(A)

Mass. R. Civ. P. 30(d) is conceptually similar:

> At any time during the taking of the deposition, on motion of any party or of the deponent and upon a showing that the examination is being conducted in bad faith or in such manner as unreasonably to annoy, embarrass, or oppress the deponent or party, the court in which the action is pending or the court in the county or judicial district, as the case may be, where the deposition is being taken may order the officer conducting the examination to cease forthwith from taking the deposition. . . . Upon demand of the objecting party or deponent, the taking

of the deposition shall be suspended for the time necessary to make a motion for an order.

―――――――――

TRIAL ADMISSIBILITY: Fed. R. Civ. P. 32(b)

Mass. R. Civ. P. 32(b) is substantially similar:

> [O]bjection[s] may be made at the trial or hearing to receiving in evidence any deposition or part thereof for any reason which would require the exclusion of the evidence if the witness were then present and testifying.

―――――――――

OBJECTIONS TO EVIDENTIARY ERRORS: Fed. R. Civ. P. 32(d)(3)(A)

Mass. R. Civ. P. 32(d)(3)(A) is substantially similar:

> Objections to the competency of a witness or to the competency, relevancy, or materiality of testimony are not waived by failure to make them before or during the taking of the deposition, unless the ground of the objection is one which might have been obviated or removed if presented at that time.

―――――――――

OBJECTIONS TO OTHER CORRECTABLE ERRORS: Fed. R. Civ. P. 32(d)(3)(B)(i-ii)

Mass. R. Civ. P. 32(d)(3)(B) is substantially similar:

> Errors and irregularities occurring at the oral examination in the manner of taking the deposition, in the form of the questions or answers, in the oath or affirmation, or in the conduct of parties, and errors of any kind which might be obviated, removed, or cured if promptly presented, are waived unless seasonable objection thereto is made at the taking of the deposition.

―――――――――

The Massachusetts Supreme Judicial Court has held: "We look to Federal decisions interpreting the Federal Rules of Civil Procedure for guidance."[46]

MICHIGAN

TRIAL STANDARDS: Fed. R. Civ. P. 30(c)(1)

Mich. Ct. R. 2.306(C)(1)(b) is substantially similar:

> Examination and cross-examination of the witness shall proceed as permitted at a trial under the Michigan Rules of Evidence.

CONTINUING TESTIMONY: Fed. R. Civ. P. 30(c)(2)

Mich. Ct. R. 2.306(C)(4)(a) is substantially similar:

> All objections made at the deposition . . . must be noted on the record by the person before whom the deposition is taken. . . . [E]vidence objected to on grounds other than privilege shall be taken subject to the objections.

NONSUGGESTIVE OBJECTIONS: Fed. R. Civ. P. 30(c)(2)

Mich. Ct. R. 2.306(C)(4)(b) is substantially similar:

> An objection during a deposition must be stated concisely in a civil and nonsuggestive manner.

Additionally, Mich. Ct. R. 2.306(C)(4)(c)(i-ii) explicitly requires that deposition objections be limited:

> Objections are limited to (i) objections that would be waived under MCR 2.308(C)(2) or (3), and (ii) those necessary to preserve a privilege or other legal protection or to enforce a limitation ordered by the court.

---

46   *Cronin v. Strayer*, 467 N.E.2d 143, 149 (Mass. 1984).

INSTRUCTIONS NOT TO ANSWER: Fed. R. Civ. P. 30(c)(2)

Mich. Ct. R. 2.306(C)(5)(a) is substantially similar:

> A person may instruct a deponent not to answer only when necessary to preserve a privilege or other legal protection, to enforce a limitation ordered by the court, or to present a motion under MCR 2.306(D)(1).

Additionally, Mich. Ct. R. 2.306(C)(5)(b) explicitly prohibits attorney-client conferences while a question is pending, which is not addressed in the Federal Rules:

> A deponent may not communicate with another person while a question is pending, except to decide whether to assert a privilege or other legal protection.

DURATIONAL LIMIT: Fed. R. Civ. P. 30(d)(1)

Michigan has <u>no comparable rule</u> establishing a time limit.

OBSTRUCTION SANCTIONS: Fed. R. Civ. P. 30(d)(2)

Mich. Ct. R. 2.306(D)(2) is substantially similar:

> On motion, the court may impose an appropriate sanction—including the reasonable expenses and attorney fees incurred by any party—on a person who impedes, delays, or frustrates the fair examination of the deponent or otherwise violates this rule.

SUSPENDING THE DEPOSITION: Fed. R. Civ. P. 30(d)(3)(A)

When taken together, Mich. Ct. R. 2.306(D)(1) and Mich. Ct. R. 2.306(D)(3) are conceptually similar.

Mich. Ct. R. 2.306(D)(3):

> On demand of the objecting party or deponent, the taking of the deposition must be suspended for the time necessary to move for an order.

Mich. Ct. R. 2.306(D)(1):

> At any time during the taking of the deposition, on motion of a party or of the deponent and on a showing that the examination is being conducted in bad faith or in a manner unreasonably to annoy, embarrass, or oppress the deponent or party, or that the matter inquired about is privileged, a court in which the action is pending or the court in the county or district where the deposition is being taken may order the person conducting the examination to cease taking the deposition. . . .

These rules are conceptually similar to the federal rule because they allow a party to suspend a deposition to file a motion if it is being conducted in bad faith.

TRIAL ADMISSIBILITY: Fed. R. Civ. P. 32(b)

Mich. Ct. R. 2.308(B) is substantially similar:

> [O]bjection[s] may be made at the trial or hearing to receiving in evidence a deposition or part of a deposition for any reason that would require the exclusion of the evidence.

OBJECTIONS TO EVIDENTIARY ERRORS: Fed. R. Civ. P. 32(d)(3)(A)

Mich. Ct. R. 2.308(C)(3)(a) is substantially similar:

> Objections to the competency of a witness or to the competency, relevancy, or materiality of testimony are not waived by failure to make them before or during the taking of a deposition, unless the ground of the objection is one which might have been obviated or removed if presented at that time.

OBJECTIONS TO OTHER CORRECTABLE ERRORS: Fed. R. Civ. P. 32(d)(3)(B)(i-ii)

Mich. Ct. R. 2.308(C)(3)(b) is substantially similar:

> Errors and irregularities occurring at the deposition in the manner of taking the deposition, in the form of the questions or answers, in the oath or affirmation, or in the conduct of parties and errors of any other kind which might be cured if promptly presented, are waived unless seasonable objection is made at the taking of the deposition.

The Michigan Supreme Court has held, in reference to the Rules of Civil Procedure, as follows: "Because of the similarity of the state and Federal provisions, we deem it proper to look to the Federal courts for guidance."[47]

MINNESOTA

TRIAL STANDARDS: Fed. R. Civ. P. 30(c)(1)

Minn. R. Civ. P. 30.03 is substantially similar:

> Examination and cross-examination of witnesses may proceed as permitted at the trial under the provisions of the Minnesota Rules of Evidence. . . .

CONTINUING TESTIMONY: Fed. R. Civ. P. 30(c)(2)

Minn. R. Civ. P. 30.03 is substantially similar:

> All objections made at the time of the examination . . . shall be noted by the officer upon the deposition; but the examination shall proceed, with the testimony being taken subject to the objections.

---

47 *D'Agostini v. City of Roseville*, 240 N.W.2d 252, 253 (Mich. 1976).

NONSUGGESTIVE OBJECTIONS: Fed. R. Civ. P. 30(c)(2)

Minn. R. Civ. P. 30.04(a) is virtually identical:

> Any objection to evidence during a deposition shall be stated concisely and in a non-argumentative and non-suggestive manner.

INSTRUCTIONS NOT TO ANSWER: Fed. R. Civ. P. 30(c)(2)

Minn. R. Civ. P. 30.04(a) is virtually identical:

> A person may instruct a deponent not to answer only when necessary to preserve a privilege, to enforce a limitation on evidence directed by the court, or to present a motion under paragraph (d).

DURATIONAL LIMIT: Fed. R. Civ. P. 30(d)(1)

Minn. R. Civ. P. 30.04(b) is virtually identical:

> [A] deposition is limited to one day of seven hours.

OBSTRUCTION SANCTIONS: Fed. R. Civ. P. 30(d)(2)

Minn. R. Civ. P. 30.04(c) is substantially similar:

> If the court finds such an impediment, delay, or other conduct that has frustrated the fair examination of the deponent, it may impose upon the persons responsible an appropriate sanction, including the reasonable costs and attorney's fees incurred by any parties as a result thereof.

SUSPENDING THE DEPOSITION: Fed. R. Civ. P. 30(d)(3)(A)

Minn. R. Civ. P. 30.04(d) is conceptually similar:

> At any time during a deposition, on motion of a party or of the deponent and upon a showing that the examination is being conducted in bad faith or in such manner as unreasonably to

annoy, embarrass, or oppress the deponent or party, the court in which the action is pending or the court in the district where the deposition is being taken may order the officer conducting the examination to cease forthwith from taking the deposition. . . . Upon demand of the objecting party or deponent, the taking of the deposition shall be suspended for the time necessary to make a motion for an order.

TRIAL ADMISSIBILITY: Fed. R. Civ. P. 32(b)

Minn. R. Civ. P. 32.02 is substantially similar:

[O]bjection[s] may be made at the trial or hearing to receiving in evidence any deposition or part thereof for any reason which would require the exclusion of evidence if the witness were then present and testifying.

OBJECTIONS TO EVIDENTIARY ERRORS: Fed. R. Civ. P. 32(d)(3)(A)

Minn. R. Civ. P. 32.04(c)(1) is substantially similar:

Objections to the competency of a witness or to the competency, relevancy, or materiality of testimony are not waived by failure to make them before or during the taking of the deposition, unless the ground of the objection is one which might have been obviated or removed if presented at that time.

OBJECTIONS TO OTHER CORRECTABLE ERRORS: Fed. R. Civ. P. 32(d)(3)(B)(i-ii)

Minn. R. Civ. P. 32.04(c)(2) is substantially similar:

Errors and irregularities occurring at the oral examination in the manner of taking the deposition, in the form of the questions or answers, in the oath or affirmation, or in the conduct of parties, and errors of any kind which might be obviated, removed, or cured if promptly presented, are waived unless seasonable objection thereto is made at the taking of the deposition.

The Minnesota Supreme Court has held that, "[w]here the language of the Federal Rules of Civil Procedure is similar to language in the Minnesota civil procedure rules, federal cases on the issue are instructive."[48]

MISSISSIPPI

TRIAL STANDARDS: Fed. R. Civ. P. 30(c)(1)

Miss. R. Civ. P. 30(c) is substantially similar:

> Examination and cross-examination of witnesses may proceed as permitted at the trial.

CONTINUING TESTIMONY: Fed. R. Civ. P. 30(c)(2)

Miss. R. Civ. P. 30(c) is substantially similar:

> All objections made at the time of the examination to the qualifications of the person taking the deposition, or to the manner of taking it, or to the evidence presented, or to the conduct of any party, and any other objection to the proceedings, shall be noted upon the transcription or recording. Evidence objected to shall be taken subject to the objections.

NONSUGGESTIVE OBJECTIONS: Fed. R. Civ. P. 30(c)(2)

Mississippi has no comparable rule requiring deposition objections to be concise, nonargumentative, or nonsuggestive.

---

48 *T.A. Schifsky & Sons, Inc. v. Bahr Const., LLC*, 773 N.W.2d 783 (Minn. 2009).

INSTRUCTIONS NOT TO ANSWER: Fed. R. Civ. P. 30(c)(2)

Mississippi has no comparable rule prohibiting instructions not to answer a deposition question.

DURATIONAL LIMIT: Fed. R. Civ. P. 30(d)(1)

Mississippi has no comparable rule establishing a maximum length.

OBSTRUCTION SANCTIONS: Fed. R. Civ. P. 30(d)(2)

Mississippi has no comparable rule establishing sanctions for frustrating the fair examination of a deponent.

SUSPENDING THE DEPOSITION: Fed. R. Civ. P. 30(d)(3)(A)

Miss. R. Civ. P. 30(d) is conceptually similar:

> At any time during the taking of the deposition, on motion of a party or of the deponent and upon a showing that the examination is being conducted in bad faith or in such manner as unreasonably to annoy, embarrass, or oppress the deponent or party, the court in which the action is pending may order the officer conducting the examination to cease forthwith from taking the deposition. . . . Upon demand of the objecting party or deponent, the taking of the deposition shall be suspended for the time necessary to make a motion for an order.

TRIAL ADMISSIBILITY: Fed. R. Civ. P. 32(b)

Miss. R. Civ. P. 32(b) is substantially similar:

> [O]bjection[s] may be made at the trial or hearing to receive in evidence any deposition or part thereof for any reason which would require the exclusion of the evidence if the witness were then present and testifying.

OBJECTIONS TO EVIDENTIARY ERRORS: Fed. R. Civ. P. 32(d)(3)(A)

Miss. R. Civ. P. 32(d)(3)(A) is substantially similar:

> Objections to the competency of a witness or to the competency, relevancy, or materiality of testimony are not waived by failure to make them before or during the taking of the deposition, unless the ground of the objection is one which might have been obviated or removed if presented at that time.

OBJECTIONS TO OTHER CORRECTABLE ERRORS: Fed. R. Civ. P. 32(d)(3)(B)(i-ii)

Miss. R. Civ. P. 32(d)(3)(B) is substantially similar:

> Errors and irregularities occurring at the oral examination in the manner of taking the deposition, in the form of the questions or answers, in the oath or affirmation, or in the conduct of the parties, and errors of any kind which might be obviated, removed, or cured if promptly presented, are waived unless seasonable objection thereof is made at the taking of the deposition.

The Mississippi Supreme Court has held that, "[i]n construing our rules, we look for guidance to the federal cases since the MRCP were patterned after the Federal Rules of Procedure."[49]

MISSOURI

TRIAL STANDARDS: Fed. R. Civ. P. 30(c)(1)

Missouri has <u>no comparable rule</u> requiring the examination and cross-examination of a deponent to proceed as they would at trial under the Federal Rules of Evidence.

---

[49] *Bourn v. Tomlinson Interest, Inc.*, 456 So.2d 747, 749 (Miss. 1984).

CONTINUING TESTIMONY: Fed. R. Civ. P. 30(c)(2)

Mo. R. Civ. P. 57.03(d) is substantially similar:

> All objections made at the time of the examination . . . shall be noted by the officer upon the deposition. Evidence objected to shall be taken subject to the objections.

NONSUGGESTIVE OBJECTIONS: Fed. R. Civ. P. 30(c)(2)

Missouri has no comparable rule requiring deposition objections to be concise, nonargumentative, or nonsuggestive.

INSTRUCTIONS NOT TO ANSWER: Fed. R. Civ. P. 30(c)(2)

Missouri has no comparable rule prohibiting instructions not to answer a deposition question. However, Mo. Civ. P. 61.01(g) establishes the procedure when a deponent refuses to answer a question:

> If a witness fails or refuses to testify in response to questions propounded on deposition, the proponent of the question may move for an order compelling an answer. The proponent of the question may complete or adjourn the deposition examination before applying for an order.

DURATIONAL LIMIT: Fed. R. Civ. P. 30(d)(1)

Missouri has no comparable rule establishing a maximum length.

OBSTRUCTION SANCTIONS: Fed. R. Civ. P. 30(d)(2)

Missouri has no comparable rule establishing sanctions for frustrating the fair examination of a deponent.

SUSPENDING THE DEPOSITION: Fed. R. Civ. P. 30(d)(3)(A)

Mo. R. Civ. P. 57.03(e) is conceptually similar:

> At any time during the taking of the deposition, on motion of a party or of the deponent and upon a showing that the examination is being conducted in bad faith or in such manner as unreasonably to annoy, embarrass, or oppress the deponent or party, the court in which the action is pending or a court having general jurisdiction in the place where the deposition is being taken may order the officer conducting the examination to cease forthwith from taking the deposition. . . . Upon demand of the objecting party or deponent, the taking of the deposition shall be suspended for the time necessary to make a motion for an order.

TRIAL ADMISSIBILITY: Fed. R. Civ. P. 32(b)

Missouri has no comparable rule authorizing objections at trial to the admissibility of deposition testimony.

OBJECTIONS TO EVIDENTIARY ERRORS: Fed. R. Civ. P. 32(d)(3)(A)

Mo. R. Civ. P. 57.07(b)(3) is conceptually similar:

> An objection to a deponent's competency is not waived by failing to make an objection before or during the deposition unless the basis for the objection could have been removed if the objection had been presented before or during the deposition.

OBJECTIONS TO OTHER CORRECTABLE ERRORS: Fed. R. Civ. P. 32(d)(3)(B)(i-ii)

Mo. R. Civ. P. 57.07(b)(4) is substantially similar:

> Errors and irregularities in the manner of taking the deposition, in the form of the questions or answers, in the oath or affirmation, or in the conduct of parties and errors of any kind that might be cured if promptly presented are waived unless seasonable objection thereto is made during the deposition.

Both the Missouri Supreme Court and the Missouri Court of Appeals have held that, "while federal interpretations of similar procedural rules can provide us illustrative and useful guidance; they are not controlling, even if the federal rule is nearly identical to Missouri's."[50]

MONTANA

TRIAL STANDARDS: Fed. R. Civ. P. 30(c)(1)

Mont. R. Civ. P. 30(c)(1) is virtually identical:

> The examination and cross-examination of a deponent proceed as they would at trial under the Montana Rules of Evidence. . . .

CONTINUING TESTIMONY: Fed. R. Civ. P. 30(c)(2)

Mont. R. Civ. P. 30(c)(2) is virtually identical:

> An objection at the time of the examination . . . must be noted on the record, but the examination still proceeds; the testimony is taken subject to any objection.

---

50 *Richter v. Union Pac. R.R. Co.*, 265 S.W.3d 294, 299 (Mo. App. 2008); *accord Giddens v. Kansas City So. Ry. Co.*, 29 S.W.3d 813, 820 (Mo. 2000) (en banc).

NONSUGGESTIVE OBJECTIONS: Fed. R. Civ. P. 30(c)(2)

Mont. R. Civ. P. 30(c)(2) is virtually identical:

> An objection must be stated concisely in a nonargumentative and nonsuggestive manner.

INSTRUCTIONS NOT TO ANSWER: Fed. R. Civ. P. 30(c)(2)

Mont. R. Civ. P. 30(c)(2) is virtually identical:

> A person may instruct a deponent not to answer only when necessary to preserve a privilege, to enforce a limitation ordered by the court, or to present a motion under Rule 30(d)(3).

DURATIONAL LIMIT: Fed. R. Civ. P. 30(d)(1)

Mont. R. Civ. P. 30(d)(1) is virtually identical:

> [A] deposition is limited to 1 day of 7 hours. . . .

OBSTRUCTION SANCTIONS: Fed. R. Civ. P. 30(d)(2)

Mont. R. Civ. P. 30(d)(2) is virtually identical:

> The court may impose an appropriate sanction—including the reasonable expenses and attorney fees incurred by any party—on a person who impedes, delays, or frustrates the fair examination of the deponent.

SUSPENDING THE DEPOSITION: Fed. R. Civ. P. 30(d)(3)(A)

Mont. R. Civ. P. 30(d)(3)(A) is virtually identical:

> At any time during a deposition, the deponent or a party may move to terminate or limit it on the ground that it is being conducted in bad faith or in a manner that unreasonably annoys, embarrasses, or oppresses the deponent or party. .

.. If the objecting deponent or party so demands, the deposition must be suspended for the time necessary to obtain an order.

TRIAL ADMISSIBILITY: Fed. R. Civ. P. 32(b)

Mont. R. Civ. P. 32(b) is virtually identical:

> [A]n objection may be made at a hearing or trial to the admission of any deposition testimony that would be inadmissible if the witness were present and testifying.

OBJECTIONS TO EVIDENTIARY ERRORS: Fed. R. Civ. P. 32(d)(3)(A)

Mont. R. Civ. P. 32(d)(3)(A) is virtually identical:

> An objection to a deponent's competence—or to the competence, relevance, or materiality of testimony—is not waived by a failure to make the objection before or during the deposition, unless the ground for it might have been corrected at that time.

OBJECTIONS TO OTHER CORRECTABLE ERRORS: Fed. R. Civ. P. 32(d)(3)(B)(i-ii)

Mont. R. Civ. P. 32(d)(3)(B) is virtually identical:

> An objection to an error or irregularity at an oral examination is waived if: (i) it relates to the manner of taking the deposition, the form of a question or answer, the oath or affirmation, a party's conduct, or other matters that might have been corrected at that time; and (ii) it is not timely made during the deposition.

The Montana Supreme Court has held that when "the language of the state and federal rules is identical, the interpretation of the federal rules have persuasive application to the interpretation of the state rules."[51]

NEBRASKA

TRIAL STANDARDS: Fed. R. Civ. P. 30(c)(1)

Neb. R. Sup. Ct. § 6-330(c)(1) is virtually identical:

> Examination and cross-examination of witnesses may proceed as permitted at the trial under the provisions of the Nebraska Evidence Rules.

CONTINUING TESTIMONY: Fed. R. Civ. P. 30(c)(2)

Neb. R. Sup. Ct. § 6-330(c)(1) is substantially similar:

> All objections made at time of the examination . . . shall be noted by the officer upon the deposition. Evidence objected to shall be taken subject to the objections.

NONSUGGESTIVE OBJECTIONS: Fed. R. Civ. P. 30(c)(2)

Neb. R. Sup. Ct. § 6-330(c)(2) is virtually identical:

> An objection must be stated concisely in a nonargumentative and nonsuggestive manner.

INSTRUCTIONS NOT TO ANSWER: Fed. R. Civ. P. 30(c)(2)

Neb. R. Sup. Ct. § 6-330(c)(2) is virtually identical:

> A person may instruct a deponent not to answer only when necessary to preserve a privilege, to enforce a limitation ordered by the court, or to present a motion under Rule 30(d).

---

[51] *U.S. Fid. & Guar. Co. v. Rodgers*, 882 P.2d 1037, 1039 (Mont. 1994).

DURATIONAL LIMIT: Fed. R. Civ. P. 30(d)(1)

Nebraska has no comparable rule establishing a maximum length.

OBSTRUCTION SANCTIONS: Fed. R. Civ. P. 30(d)(2)

Nebraska has no comparable rule establishing sanctions for frustrating the fair examination of a deponent.

SUSPENDING THE DEPOSITION: Fed. R. Civ. P. 30(d)(3)(A)

Neb. R. Sup. Ct. § 6-330(d) is virtually identical:

> At any time during a deposition, the deponent or a party may move to terminate or limit the deposition on the ground that (1) it is being conducted in bad faith or in a manner that unreasonably annoys, embarrasses, or oppresses the deponent or party. . . . If the objecting deponent or party so demands, the deposition must be suspended for the time necessary to obtain an order.

TRIAL ADMISSIBILITY: Fed. R. Civ. P. 32(b)

Neb. R. Sup. Ct. § 6-332(b) is conceptually similar:

> [O]bjection[s] may be made at the trial or hearing to receiving in evidence any deposition or part thereof for any reason which would require the exclusion of the evidence if the witness were then present and testifying; or if the trial court directs, such objections may be heard and determined prior to trial.

OBJECTIONS TO EVIDENTIARY ERRORS: Fed. R. Civ. P. 32(d)(3)(A)

Neb. R. Sup. Ct. § 6-332(d)(3)(A) is substantially similar:

> Objections to the competency of a witness or to the competency or relevancy of testimony are not waived by failure to make them before or during the taking of the deposition, unless the ground of the objection is one which might have been obviated or removed if presented at that time.

OBJECTIONS TO OTHER CORRECTABLE ERRORS: Fed. R. Civ. P. 32(d)(3)(B)(i-ii)

Neb. R. Sup. Ct. § 6-332(d)(3)(B) is substantially similar:

> Errors and irregularities occurring at the oral examination in the manner of taking the deposition in the form of the questions or answers, in the oath or affirmation, or in the conduct of parties, and errors of any kind which might be obviated, removed, or cured if promptly presented, are waived unless seasonable objection thereto is made at the taking of the depositions.

The Nebraska Supreme Court has held that "[i]nasmuch as the Nebraska Rules of Discovery are generally and substantially patterned after the corresponding discovery rules in the Federal Rules of Civil Procedure, Nebraska courts will look to federal decisions interpreting corresponding federal rules for guidance in construing similar Nebraska rules."[52]

---

[52] *Gernstein v. Lake*, 610 N.W.2d 714, 716 (Neb. 2000).

NEVADA

TRIAL STANDARDS: Fed. R. Civ. P. 30(c)(1)

Nev. R. Civ. P. 30(c) is virtually identical:

> Examination and cross-examination of witnesses may proceed as permitted at the trial under the provisions of Rule 43(b).

CONTINUING TESTIMONY: Fed. R. Civ. P. 30(c)(2)

Nev. R. Civ. P. 30(c) is virtually identical:

> All objections made at the time of the examination . . . shall be noted by the officer upon the record of the deposition; but the examination shall proceed, with the testimony being taken subject to the objections.

NONSUGGESTIVE OBJECTIONS: Fed. R. Civ. P. 30(c)(2)

Nev. R. Civ. P. 30(d)(1) is virtually identical:

> An objection must be stated concisely and in a non-argumentative and non-suggestive manner.

INSTRUCTIONS NOT TO ANSWER: Fed. R. Civ. P. 30(c)(2)

Nev. R. Civ. P. 30(d)(1) is virtually identical:

> Instructing a deponent not to answer shall only be allowed when necessary to preserve a privilege, to enforce a limitation directed by the court, or to file a motion under paragraph (3).

DURATIONAL LIMIT: Fed. R. Civ. P. 30(d)(1)

Nev. R. Civ. P. (d)(1) is virtually identical:

> [A] deposition is limited to 1 day of 7 hours.

OBSTRUCTION SANCTIONS: Fed. R. Civ. P. 30(d)(2)

Nev. R. Civ. P. 30(d)(2) is virtually identical:

> The court may impose an appropriate sanction—including the reasonable expenses and attorney's fees incurred by any party—on a person who impedes, delays, or frustrates the fair examination of the deponent.

SUSPENDING THE DEPOSITION: Fed. R. Civ. P. 30(d)(3)(A)

Nev. R. Civ. P. 30(d)(3)(A) is virtually identical:

> At any time during a deposition, the deponent or a party may move to terminate or limit it on the grounds that it is being conducted in bad faith or in a manner that unreasonably annoys, embarrasses, or oppresses the deponent or party. . . . If the objecting deponent or party so demands, the deposition must be suspended for the time necessary to obtain an order.

TRIAL ADMISSIBILITY: Fed. R. Civ. P. 32(b)

Nev. R. Civ. P. 32(b) is substantially similar:

> [O]bjection[s] may be made at the trial or hearing to receiving in evidence any deposition or part thereof for any reason which would require the exclusion of the evidence if the witness were then present and testifying.

OBJECTIONS TO EVIDENTIARY ERRORS: Fed. R. Civ. P. 32(d)(3)(A)

Nev. R. Civ. P. 32(d)(3)(A) is substantially similar:

> Objections to the competency of a witness or to the competency, relevancy, or materiality of testimony are not waived by failure to make them before or during the taking of the deposition, unless the ground of the objection is one

which might have been obviated or removed if presented at that time.

OBJECTIONS TO OTHER CORRECTABLE ERRORS: Fed. R. Civ. P. 32(d)(3)(B)(i-ii)

Nev. R. Civ. P. 32(d)(3)(B) is substantially similar:
> Errors and irregularities occurring at the oral examination in the manner of taking the deposition, in the form of the questions or answers, in the oath or affirmation, or in the conduct of parties, and errors of any kind which might be obviated, removed, or cured if promptly presented, are waived unless seasonable objection thereto is made at the taking of the deposition.

The Supreme Court of Nevada has held that "[f]ederal cases interpreting the Federal Rules of Civil Procedure 'are strong persuasive authority, because the Nevada Rules of Civil Procedure are based in large part upon their federal counterparts.'"[53]

NEW HAMPSHIRE

TRIAL STANDARDS: Fed. R. Civ. P. 30(c)(1)

New Hampshire has <u>no comparable rule</u> requiring depositions to proceed as they would at trial.

CONTINUING TESTIMONY: Fed. R. Civ. P. 30(c)(2)

N.H. R. Super. Ct. 26(g) is significantly different:
> The stenographer shall cause to be noted any objection to any interrogatory or answer without deciding its competency. If complaint is made of interference with any witness, the

---

53   *Executive Mgmt., Ltd. v. Ticor Title Ins. Co.*, 38 P.3d 872, 876 (Nev. 2002) (internal citations omitted).

stenographer shall cause such complaint to be noted and shall certify the correctness or incorrectness thereof in the caption.

This rule calls for the stenographer to make a determination at the deposition of the validity of complaints of deposition interference on the record. It also does not explicitly stipulate that the examination proceeds subject to any objection.

NONSUGGESTIVE OBJECTIONS: Fed. R. Civ. P. 30(c)(2)

New Hampshire has no comparable rule requiring deposition objections to be concise, nonargumentative, or nonsuggestive.

INSTRUCTIONS NOT TO ANSWER: Fed. R. Civ. P. 30(c)(2)

N.H. R. Super. Ct. 26(j) is conceptually similar:

> (j) The deponent, on deposition or on written interrogatory, shall ordinarily be required to answer all questions not subject to privilege or excused by the statute relating to depositions, and it is not grounds for refusal to answer a particular question that the testimony would be inadmissible at the trial if the testimony sought appears reasonably calculated to lead to the discovery of admissible evidence and does not violate any privilege.

This is conceptually similar because it stipulates that a deponent should ordinarily answer all deposition questions absent a privilege or statutory exception (and there are no other exceptions listed in Rule 26, which governs depositions), but it does not explicitly address when an attorney instructs a deponent not to answer.

DURATIONAL LIMIT: Fed. R. Civ. P. 30(d)(1)

N.H. R. Super. Ct. 26(a) is significantly different:

> A party may take as many depositions as necessary to adequately prepare a case for trial so long as the combined

total of deposition hours does not exceed 20 unless otherwise stipulated by counsel or ordered by the court for good cause shown.

New Hampshire limits deposition length in the aggregate to 20 total hours instead of the federal rule's seven hours per deposition.

OBSTRUCTION SANCTIONS: Fed. R. Civ. P. 30(d)(2)

New Hampshire has no comparable rule establishing sanctions for frustrating the fair examination of a deponent.

SUSPENDING THE DEPOSITION: Fed. R. Civ. P. 30(d)(3)(A)

New Hampshire has no comparable rule establishing procedure for a party to suspend the deposition and move for a protective order if the deposition is being conducted in bad faith or in a manner that harasses a party.

TRIAL ADMISSIBILITY: Fed. R. Civ. P. 32(b)

New Hampshire has no comparable rule authorizing objections at trial to the admission of deposition testimony that would be inadmissible if the witness were present.

OBJECTIONS TO EVIDENTIARY ERRORS: Fed. R. Civ. P. 32(d)(3)(A)

New Hampshire has no comparable rule concerning the preservation or waiver of evidentiary errors at the deposition.

OBJECTIONS TO OTHER CORRECTABLE ERRORS: Fed. R. Civ. P. 32(d)(3)(B)(i-ii)

New Hampshire has no comparable rule concerning the preservation or waiver of other correctable errors at the deposition.

The New Hampshire Supreme Court has not yet provided a general rule allowing for the use of federal case law to interpret the state's rules of civil procedure. When interpretive issues involving civil procedure have arisen, however, the court has applied federal case law to construe the state's corresponding rule of civil procedure. "Because Superior Court Rule 27-A . . . is similar to its federal counterpart, Federal Rule of Civil Procedure 23, we rely upon federal cases interpreting the federal rule as analytic aids."[54]

NEW JERSEY

TRIAL STANDARDS: Fed. R. Civ. P. 30(c)(1)

N.J. Ct. R. 4:14-3(a) is substantially similar:

> Examination and cross-examination of deponents may proceed as permitted in the trial of actions in open court. . . .

CONTINUING TESTIMONY: Fed. R. Civ. P. 30(c)(2)

N.J. Ct. R. 4:14-3(c) is substantially similar:

> All objections made at the time of the examination . . . shall be noted by the officer upon the deposition.

However, it does not explicitly provide that the deposition proceeds subject to any objection. N.J. Ct. R. 4:14-3(c) also strongly discourages raising any objections at a deposition that are not explicitly required by other rules:

> No objection shall be made during the taking of a deposition except those addressed to the form of a question or to assert a

---

54   *In re Bayview Crematory, LLC*, 930 A.2d 1190, 1193 (N.H. 2007).

privilege, a right to confidentiality or a limitation pursuant to a previously entered court order. The right to object on other grounds is preserved and may be asserted at the time the deposition testimony is proffered at trial.

NONSUGGESTIVE OBJECTIONS: Fed. R. Civ. P. 30(c)(2)

N.J. Ct. R. 4:14-3(c) is conceptually similar:

> No objection shall be expressed in language that suggests an answer to the deponent.

INSTRUCTIONS NOT TO ANSWER: Fed. R. Civ. P. 30(c)(2)

N.J. Ct. R. 4:14-3(c) is substantially similar:

> [A]n attorney shall not instruct a witness not to answer a question unless the basis of the objection is privilege, a right to confidentiality or a limitation pursuant to a previously entered court order.

N.J. Ct. R. 4:14-3(f) also prohibits attorney-client conferences during the deposition:

> Once the deponent has been sworn, there shall be no communication between the deponent and counsel during the course of the deposition while testimony is being taken except with regard to the assertion of a claim of privilege, a right to confidentiality or a limitation pursuant to a previously entered court order.

DURATIONAL LIMIT: Fed. R. Civ. P. 30(d)(1)

New Jersey has <u>no comparable rule</u> creating a presumptive time limit on the length of depositions. However, N.J. Ct. R. 4:14-3(d) stipulates that depositions are to be taken continuously:

> Except as otherwise provided by R. 4:14-4 and R. 4:23-1(a) all depositions shall be taken continuously and without

adjournment unless the court otherwise orders or the parties and the deponent stipulate otherwise.

OBSTRUCTION SANCTIONS: Fed. R. Civ. P. 30(d)(2)

New Jersey has <u>no comparable rule</u> establishing sanctions for frustrating the fair examination of a deponent.

SUSPENDING THE DEPOSITION: Fed. R. Civ. P. 30(d)(3)(A)

N.J. Ct. R. 4:14-4 is conceptually similar:

At any time during the taking of the deposition, on formal motion or telephone application to the court of a party or of the deponent and upon a showing that the examination or any part thereof is being conducted or defended in bad faith or in such manner as unreasonably to annoy, embarrass or oppress the deponent or party, or in violation of R. 4:14-3(c) or (f), the court may order the person conducting the examination to cease forthwith from taking the deposition. . . . Upon demand of the objecting party or deponent, the taking of the deposition shall be suspended for the time necessary to make a motion or telephone application for an order.

TRIAL ADMISSIBILITY: Fed. R. Civ. P. 32(b)

N.J. Ct. R. 4:16-2 is substantially similar:

[O]bjection[s] may be made at the trial or hearing to receiving in evidence any deposition or part thereof for any reason which would require the exclusion of the evidence if the witness were then present and testifying.

OBJECTIONS TO EVIDENTIARY ERRORS: Fed. R. Civ. P. 32(d)(3)(A)

N.J. Ct. R. 4:16-4(c)(1) is substantially similar:

> Objections to the competency of a witness or to the competency, relevancy, or materiality of testimony are not waived by failure to make them before or during the taking of the deposition, unless the ground of the objection is one which might have been obviated or removed if presented at that time.

OBJECTIONS TO OTHER CORRECTABLE ERRORS: Fed. R. Civ. P. 32(d)(3)(B)(i-ii)

N.J. Ct. R. 4:16-4(c)(2) is substantially similar:

> [E]rrors and irregularities occurring at the oral examination in the manner of taking the deposition, in the form of the questions or answers, in the oath or affirmation, or in the conduct of parties, and errors of any kind which might be obviated, removed, or cured if promptly presented are waived unless timely objection thereto is made at the taking of the deposition.

The Supreme Court of New Jersey has held that, "[s]ince our court rules are based on the Federal Rules of Civil Procedure, it is appropriate to turn to federal case law for guidance."[55]

NEW MEXICO

TRIAL STANDARDS: Fed. R. Civ. P. 30(c)(1)

N.M. Sup. Ct. R. 1-030(C) is substantially similar:

> Examination and cross-examination of witnesses may proceed as permitted at the trial under the New Mexico Rules of Evidence....

---

55 *Freeman v. Lincoln Beach Motel*, 442 A.2d 650, 651 (N.J. Law Div. 1981).

CONTINUING TESTIMONY: Fed. R. Civ. P. 30(c)(2)

N.M. Sup. Ct. R. 1-030(C) is substantially similar:

> All objections made at the time of the examination . . . shall be noted by the officer upon the record of the deposition; but the examination shall proceed, with the testimony being taken subject to the objections.

NONSUGGESTIVE OBJECTIONS: Fed. R. Civ. P. 30(c)(2)

N.M. Sup. Ct. R. 1-030(D)(1) is substantially similar:

> Any objection during a deposition shall be stated concisely and in a non-argumentative and non-suggestive manner.

N.M. Sup. Ct. R. 1-030(D)(1) also specifies the proper method to raise objections:

> Objections to form or foundation may be made only by stating "objection—form," or "objection—foundation." No specification of the defect in the form or foundation of the question or the answer shall be stated unless requested by the party propounding the question. Argumentative interruptions shall not be permitted.

INSTRUCTIONS NOT TO ANSWER: Fed. R. Civ. P. 30(c)(2)

N.M. Sup. Ct. R. 1-030(D)(1) is conceptually similar:

> When a question is pending, or a document has been presented to the deponent, no one may interrupt the deposition until the answer is given, except when necessary to preserve a privilege, to enforce a limitation directed by the court or to present a motion under Subparagraph (2) of this paragraph.

This is conceptually similar because it forbids an attorney from interrupting the line of questioning to instruct the witness not to answer, but it differs because it does not explicitly prohibit instructions not to answer. This rule also implicitly prohibits off-the-record attorney-client conferences while a question is pending.

DURATIONAL LIMIT: Fed. R. Civ. P. 30(d)(1)

N.M. Sup. Ct. R. 1-030(D)(2) is substantially similar:

> [A] deposition of a person other than an expert witness is limited to one day and lasting no more than seven (7) hours on the record.

OBSTRUCTION SANCTIONS: Fed. R. Civ. P. 30(d)(2)

New Mexico has no comparable rule establishing sanctions for frustrating the fair examination of a deponent.

SUSPENDING THE DEPOSITION: Fed. R. Civ. P. 30(d)(3)(A)

N.M. Sup. Ct. R. 1-030(D)(3) is conceptually similar:

> At any time during a deposition, on motion of a party or of the deponent and upon a showing that the examination is being conducted in bad faith or in such manner as unreasonably to annoy, embarrass or oppress the deponent or party, the court in which the action is pending or the court in the county where the deposition is being taken may order the officer conducting the examination to cease forthwith from taking the deposition. . . . Upon demand of the objecting party or deponent, the taking of the deposition shall be suspended for the time necessary to make a motion for an order.

TRIAL ADMISSIBILITY: Fed. R. Civ. P. 32(b)

N.M. Sup. Ct. R. 1-032(B) is substantially similar:

> [O]bjection[s] may be made at the trial or hearing to receiving in evidence any deposition or part thereof for any reason

which would require the exclusion of the evidence if the witness were then present and testifying.

OBJECTIONS TO EVIDENTIARY ERRORS: Fed. R. Civ. P. 32(d)(3)(A)

N.M. Sup. Ct. R. 1-032(D)(3)(a) is substantially similar:

> Objections to the competency of a witness or to the competency, relevancy or materiality of testimony are not waived by failure to make them before or during the taking of the deposition, unless the ground of the objection is one which might have been obviated or removed if presented at that time.

OBJECTIONS TO OTHER CORRECTABLE ERRORS: Fed. R. Civ. P. 32(d)(3)(B)(i-ii)

N.M. Sup. Ct. R. 1-032(D)(3)(b) is substantially similar:

> Errors and irregularities occurring at the oral examination in the manner of taking the deposition, in the form of the questions or answers, in the oath or affirmation or in the conduct of parties and errors of any kind which might be obviated, removed or cured if promptly presented, are waived unless seasonable objection thereto is made at the taking of the deposition.

The New Mexico Supreme Court has held that, "[w]hen our state court rules closely track the language of their federal counterparts, we have determined that federal construction of the federal rules is persuasive authority for the construction of New Mexico rules."[56]

---

56 *Albuquerque Redi-Mix, Inc. v. Scottsdale Ins. Co.*, 168 P.3d 99, 102 (N.M. 2007).

NEW YORK

TRIAL STANDARDS: Fed. R. Civ. P. 30(c)(1)

N.Y. Civ. Prac. Law & R. 3113(c) is substantially similar:

> Examination and cross-examination of deponents shall proceed as permitted in the trial of actions in open court, except that a non-party deponent's counsel may participate in the deposition and make objections on behalf of his or her client in the same manner as counsel for a party.

This rule establishes the right for a nonparty deponent's counsel to make objections on behalf of their client, which the federal rule does not address.

CONTINUING TESTIMONY: Fed. R. Civ. P. 30(c)(2)

SUSPENDING THE DEPOSITION: Fed. R. Civ. P. 30(d)(3)(A)

N.Y. Civ. Prac. Law & R. 3113(b) is conceptually similar:

> All objections made at the time of the examination . . . shall be noted by the officer upon the deposition and the deposition shall proceed subject to the right of a person to apply for a protective order.

This rule, when combined with N.Y. Civ. Prac. Law & R. 3103(b), explicitly allows a party at a deposition being conducted in bad faith to suspend the deposition to apply for a protective order.

N.Y. Civ. Prac. Law & R. 3103(b) reads:

> Suspension of disclosure pending application for protective order. Service of a notice of motion for a protective order shall suspend disclosure of the particular matter in dispute.

NONSUGGESTIVE OBJECTIONS: Fed. R. Civ. P. 30(c)(2)

New York has <u>no comparable rule</u> requiring deposition objections to be concise, nonargumentative, or nonsuggestive.

Comparing Relevant Portions of Rules 30 & 32

INSTRUCTIONS NOT TO ANSWER: Fed. R. Civ. P. 30(c)(2)

New York has <u>no comparable rule</u> prohibiting attorneys from instructing a deponent not to answer a deposition question.

DURATIONAL LIMIT: Fed. R. Civ. P. 30(d)(1)

New York has <u>no comparable rule</u> limiting deposition length. However, N.Y. Civ. Prac. Law & R. 3113(b) specifies:

> The deposition shall be taken continuously and without unreasonable adjournment, unless the court otherwise orders or the witness and parties present otherwise agree.

OBSTRUCTION SANCTIONS: Fed. R. Civ. P. 30(d)(2)

New York has <u>no comparable rule</u> establishing sanctions for frustrating the fair examination of a deponent. However, N.Y. Civ. Prac. Law & R. 3103(a) authorizes the court to issue a protective order to prevent deposition misconduct:

> The court may at any time on its own initiative, or on motion of any party or of any person from whom or about whom discovery is sought, make a protective order denying, limiting, conditioning or regulating the use of any disclosure device. Such order shall be designed to prevent unreasonable annoyance, expense, embarrassment, disadvantage, or other prejudice to any person or the courts.

TRIAL ADMISSIBILITY: Fed. R. Civ. P. 32(b)

N.Y. Civ. Prac. Law & R. 3115(a) is substantially similar:

> Subject to the other provisions of this rule, objection may be made at the trial or hearing to receiving in evidence any deposition or part thereof for any reason which would require the exclusion of the evidence if the witness were then present and testifying.

OBJECTIONS TO EVIDENTIARY ERRORS: Fed. R. Civ. P. 32(d)(3)(A)

N.Y. Civ. Prac. Law & R. 3115(d) is substantially similar:

> Objections to the competency of a witness or to the admissibility of testimony are not waived by failure to make them before or during the taking of the deposition, unless the ground of the objection is one which might have been obviated or removed if objection had been made at that time.

OBJECTIONS TO OTHER CORRECTABLE ERRORS: Fed. R. Civ. P. 32(d)(3)(B)(i-ii)

N.Y. Civ. Prac. Law & R. 3115(b) is substantially similar:

> Errors and irregularities occurring at the oral examination in the manner of taking the deposition, in the form of the questions or answers, in the oath or affirmation, or in the conduct of persons, and errors of any kind which might be obviated or removed if objection were promptly presented, are waived unless reasonable objection thereto is made at the taking of the deposition.

The author has been unable to locate any jurisprudence from the New York Court of Appeals that considers the Federal Rules of Civil Procedure persuasive when interpreting New York's Civil Practice Laws.

NORTH CAROLINA

TRIAL STANDARDS: Fed. R. Civ. P. 30(c)(1)

N.C. R. Civ. P. 30(c) is substantially similar:

> Examination and cross-examination of witnesses may proceed as permitted at the trial under the provisions of Rule 43(b).

CONTINUING TESTIMONY: Fed. R. Civ. P. 30(c)(2)

N.C. R. Civ. P. 30(c) is substantially similar:

> All objections made at the time of the examination . . . shall be noted upon the deposition by the person before whom the deposition is taken. . . . [E]vidence objected to shall be taken subject to the objections.

NONSUGGESTIVE OBJECTIONS: Fed. R. Civ. P. 30(c)(2)

North Carolina has <u>no comparable rule</u> requiring deposition objections to be concise, nonargumentative, or nonsuggestive.

INSTRUCTIONS NOT TO ANSWER: Fed. R. Civ. P. 30(c)(2)

North Carolina has <u>no comparable rule</u> prohibiting attorneys from instructing a deponent not to answer a deposition question.

DURATIONAL LIMIT: Fed. R. Civ. P. 30(d)(1)

North Carolina has <u>no comparable rule</u> limiting a deposition's length.

OBSTRUCTION SANCTIONS: Fed. R. Civ. P. 30(d)(2)

North Carolina has <u>no comparable rule</u> establishing sanctions for frustrating the fair examination of a deponent.

SUSPENDING THE DEPOSITION: Fed. R. Civ. P. 30(d)(3)(A)

N.C. R. Civ. P. 30(d) is conceptually similar:

> At any time during the taking of the deposition, on motion of a party or of the deponent and upon a showing that the examination is being conducted in bad faith or in such manner as unreasonably to annoy, embarrass, or oppress the deponent or party, a judge of the court in which the action is pending

or any judge in the county where the deposition is being taken may order before whom the examination is being taken to cease forthwith from taking the deposition. . . . Upon demand of the objecting party or deponent, the taking of the deposition shall be suspended for the time necessary to make a motion for an order.

TRIAL ADMISSIBILITY: Fed. R. Civ. P. 32(b)

N.C. R. Civ. P. 32(b) is substantially similar:

[O]bjection[s] may be made at the trial or hearing to receiving in evidence any deposition or part thereof for any reason which would require the exclusion of the evidence if the witness were then present and testifying.

OBJECTIONS TO EVIDENTIARY ERRORS: Fed. R. Civ. P. 32(d)(3)(A)

N.C. R. Civ. P. 32(d)(3)(a) is substantially similar:

Objections to the competency of a witness or to the competency, relevancy, or materiality of testimony are not waived by failure to make them before or during the taking of the deposition, unless the ground of the objection is one which might have been obviated or removed if presented at that time.

OBJECTIONS TO OTHER CORRECTABLE ERRORS: Fed. R. Civ. P. 32(d)(3)(B)(i-ii)

N.C. R. Civ. P. 32(d)(3)(b) is substantially similar:

Errors and irregularities occurring at the oral examination in the manner of taking the deposition, in the form of the questions or answers, in the oath or affirmation, or in the conduct of parties, and errors of any kind which might be obviated, removed, or cured if promptly presented, are waived unless seasonable objection thereto is made at the taking of the deposition.

The North Carolina Supreme Court has held that, "[b]ecause the Federal Rules of Civil Procedure are the source of the North Carolina Rules of Civil Procedure, this Court has said that we will look to decisions under the federal rules 'for enlightenment and guidance as we develop "the philosophy of the new rules."'"[57]

NORTH DAKOTA

TRIAL STANDARDS: Fed. R. Civ. P. 30(c)(1)

N.D. R. Civ. P. 30(c)(1) is substantially similar:

> The examination and cross-examination of a deponent proceed as they would at trial under the North Dakota Rules of Evidence.

CONTINUING TESTIMONY: Fed. R. Civ. P. 30(c)(2)

N.D. R. Civ. P. 30(c)(2) is virtually identical:

> An objection at the time of the examination . . . must be noted on the record, but the examination still proceeds; the testimony is taken subject to any objection.

NONSUGGESTIVE OBJECTIONS: Fed. R. Civ. P. 30(c)(2)

N.D. R. Civ. P. 30(c)(2) is virtually identical:

> An objection must be stated concisely in a nonargumentative and nonsuggestive manner.

INSTRUCTIONS NOT TO ANSWER: Fed. R. Civ. P. 30(c)(2)

N.D. R. Civ. P. 30(c)(2) is virtually identical:

> A person may instruct a deponent not to answer only when necessary to preserve a privilege, to enforce a limitation ordered by the court, or to present a motion under Rule 30(d)(2).

---

[57] *Goins v. Puleo*, 512 S.E.2d 748, 752 (N.C. 1999).

DURATIONAL LIMIT: Fed. R. Civ. P. 30(d)(1)

North Dakota has no comparable rule limiting a deposition's length.

OBSTRUCTION SANCTIONS: Fed. R. Civ. P. 30(d)(2)

N.D. R. Civ. P. 30(d)(1) is virtually identical:

> The court may impose an appropriate sanction—including the reasonable expenses and attorney's fees incurred by any party—on a person who impedes, delays, or frustrates the fair examination of the deponent.

SUSPENDING THE DEPOSITION: Fed. R. Civ. P. 30(d)(3)(A)

N.D. R. Civ. P. 30(d)(2)(A) is virtually identical:

> At any time during a deposition, the deponent or a party may move to terminate it on the ground that it is being conducted in bad faith or in a manner that unreasonably annoys, embarrasses, or oppresses the deponent or party. The motion may be filed in the court where the action is pending or the deposition is being taken. If the objecting deponent or party so demands, the deposition must be suspended for the time necessary to obtain an order.

TRIAL ADMISSIBILITY: Fed. R. Civ. P. 32(b)

N.D. R. Civ. P. 32(b) is virtually identical:

> [A]n objection may be made at a hearing or trial to the admission of any deposition testimony that would be inadmissible if the witness were present and testifying.

OBJECTIONS TO EVIDENTIARY ERRORS: Fed. R. Civ. P. 32(d)(3)(A)

N.D. R. Civ. P. 32(d)(3)(A) is virtually identical:

> An objection to the deponent's competence—or to the competence, relevance, or materiality of the testimony—is not waived by a failure to make the objection before or during the deposition, unless the ground for the objection might have been corrected at that time.

OBJECTIONS TO OTHER CORRECTABLE ERRORS: Fed. R. Civ. P. 32(d)(3)(B)(i-ii)

N.D. R. Civ. P. 32(d)(3)(B) is virtually identical:

> An objection to an error or irregularity at an oral examination is waived if: (i) it relates to the manner of taking the deposition, the form of a question or answer, the oath or affirmation, a party's conduct, or other matters that might have been corrected at that time; and (ii) it is not timely made during the deposition.

The North Dakota Supreme Court has held this standard: "Our Rules of Civil Procedure were derived from the Federal Rules of Civil Procedure and any construction and interpretation given to the federal rules is entitled to appreciable weight by this Court in interpreting and construing our rules."[58]

OHIO

TRIAL STANDARDS: Fed. R. Civ. P. 30(c)(1)

Ohio Civ. P. 30(C)(1) is substantially similar:

> Each party at the deposition may examine the deponent without regard to which party served notice or called the deposition. In all other respects the examination and cross-examination of

---

58 *Larson v. Unlimited Bus. Exch. of N. Dakota, Inc.*, 330 N.W.2d 518, 520 (N.D. 1983).

a deponent may proceed as they would at trial under the Ohio Rules of Evidence. . . .

CONTINUING TESTIMONY: Fed. R. Civ. P. 30(c)(2)

Ohio Civ. P. 30(C)(2) is virtually identical:

> An objection made at the time of the examination . . . shall be noted on the record, but the examination still proceeds, the testimony taken subject to any objection.

NONSUGGESTIVE OBJECTIONS: Fed. R. Civ. P. 30(c)(2)

Ohio Civ. P. 30(C)(2) is virtually identical:

> An objection shall be stated concisely in a nonargumentative and nonsuggestive manner.

INSTRUCTIONS NOT TO ANSWER: Fed. R. Civ. P. 30(c)(2)

Ohio Civ. P. 30(C)(2) is virtually identical:

> A person may instruct a deponent not to answer only when necessary to preserve a privilege, to enforce a limitation ordered by the court, or to present a motion under Civ. R. 30(D).

DURATIONAL LIMIT: Fed. R. Civ. P. 30(d)(1)

Ohio has <u>no comparable rule</u> limiting a deposition's length.

OBSTRUCTION SANCTIONS: Fed. R. Civ. P. 30(d)(2)

Ohio has <u>no comparable rule</u> establishing sanctions for frustrating the fair examination of a deponent.

SUSPENDING THE DEPOSITION: Fed. R. Civ. P. 30(d)(3)(A)

Ohio Civ. P. 30(D) is conceptually similar:

> At any time during the taking of the deposition, on motion of any party or of the deponent and upon a showing that the examination is being conducted in bad faith or in such manner as unreasonably to annoy, embarrass, or oppress the deponent or party, the court in which the action is pending may order the officer conducting the examination to cease forthwith from taking the deposition. . . . Upon demand of the objecting party or deponent, the taking of the deposition shall be suspended for the time necessary to make a motion for an order.

TRIAL ADMISSIBILITY: Fed. R. Civ. P. 32(b)

Ohio Civ. P. 32(B) is substantially similar:

> [O]bjection[s] may be made at the trial or hearing to receiving in evidence any deposition or part thereof for any reason which would require the exclusion of the evidence if the witness were then present and testifying.

OBJECTIONS TO EVIDENTIARY ERRORS: Fed. R. Civ. P. 32(d)(3)(A)

Ohio Civ. P. 32(D)(3)(a) is substantially similar:

> Objections to the competency of a witness or to the competency, relevancy, or materiality of testimony are not waived by failure to make them before or during the taking of the deposition, unless the ground of the objection is one which might have been obviated or removed if presented at that time.

OBJECTIONS TO OTHER CORRECTABLE ERRORS: Fed. R. Civ. P. 32(d)(3)(B)(i-ii)

Ohio Civ. P. 32(D)(3)(b) is virtually identical:

> Errors and irregularities occurring at the oral examination in the manner of taking the deposition, in the form of the questions or answers, in the oath or affirmation, or in the conduct of parties and errors of any kind which might be obviated, removed, or cured if promptly presented, are waived unless reasonable objection thereto is made at the taking of the deposition.

The Ohio Supreme Court has held that, "[b]ecause the Ohio Rules of Civil Procedure are modeled after the Federal Rules of Civil Procedure, federal law interpreting the federal rule is appropriate and persuasive authority in interpreting a similar Ohio rule."[59]

OKLAHOMA

TRIAL STANDARDS: Fed. R. Civ. P. 30(c)(1)

Okla. Stat. Ann. tit. 12 § 3230(D) is substantially similar:

> Examination and cross-examination of witnesses may proceed as permitted at the trial under the provisions of Section 2101 et seq. of this title. . . .

CONTINUING TESTIMONY: Fed. R. Civ. P. 30(c)(2)

Okla. Stat. Ann. tit. 12 § 3230(D) is substantially similar:

> All objections made at the time of the examination . . . shall be noted by the officer upon the record of the deposition; however, the examination shall proceed, with the testimony being taken subject to the objections.

---

59   *Felix v. Ganley Chevrolet, Inc.*, 49 N.E.3d 1224, 1230 (Ohio 2015).

NONSUGGESTIVE OBJECTIONS: Fed. R. Civ. P. 30(c)(2)

Okla. Stat. Ann. tit. 12 § 3230(E)(1) is virtually identical:

> Any objection to evidence during a deposition shall be stated concisely and in a nonargumentative and nonsuggestive manner.

INSTRUCTIONS NOT TO ANSWER: Fed. R. Civ. P. 30(c)(2)

Okla. Stat. Ann. tit. 12 § 3230(E)(1) is substantially similar:

> A party may instruct a deponent not to answer only when necessary to preserve a privilege or work product protection, to enforce a limitation on evidence directed by the court, to present a motion under paragraph 2 of this subsection, or to move for a protective order under subsection C of Section 3226 of this title.

DURATIONAL LIMIT: Fed. R. Civ. P. 30(d)(1)

Okla. Stat. Ann. tit. 12 § 3230(A)(3) is significantly different:

> [A] deposition upon oral examination shall not last more than six (6) hours and shall be taken only between the hours of 8:00 a.m. and 5:00 p.m. on a day other than a Saturday or Sunday and on a date other than a holiday designated in Section 82.1 of Title 25 of the Oklahoma Statutes.

This is significantly different because it changes the presumptive limit of a deposition from seven hours to six hours and institutes constraints on the day and time when a deposition can take place.

OBSTRUCTION SANCTIONS: Fed. R. Civ. P. 30(d)(2)

Okla. Stat. Ann. tit. 12 § 3230(E)(1) is substantially similar:

> If the court finds a person has engaged in conduct which has frustrated the fair examination of the deponent, it may impose upon the persons responsible an appropriate sanction,

including the reasonable costs and attorney fees incurred by any parties as a result thereof.

SUSPENDING THE DEPOSITION: Fed. R. Civ. P. 30(d)(3)(A)

Okla. Stat. Ann. tit. 12 § 3230(E)(2) is conceptually similar:

> At any time during the taking of the deposition, on motion of a party or of the deponent and upon a showing that the examination is being conducted in bad faith or in such manner as unreasonably to annoy, embarrass or oppress the deponent or party, the court in which the action is pending or the court in the county where the deposition is being taken may order the officer conducting the examination to cease taking the deposition. . . . Upon demand of the objecting party or deponent, the taking of the deposition shall be suspended for the time necessary to make a motion for the order provided for in this section.

TRIAL ADMISSIBILITY: Fed. R. Civ. P. 32(b)

Okla. Stat. Ann. tit. 12 § 3232(B) is substantially similar:

> [O]bjection[s] may be made, at the trial or hearing, to receiving in evidence any deposition or part thereof for any reason which would require the exclusion of the evidence if the witness were then present and testifying.

OBJECTIONS TO EVIDENTIARY ERRORS: Fed. R. Civ. P. 32(d)(3)(A)

Okla. Stat. Ann. tit. 12 § 3232(D)(3)(a) is substantially similar:

> Objections to the competency of a witness or to the competency, relevancy or materiality of testimony are not waived by failure to make them before or during the taking of the deposition, unless the ground of the objection is one which might have been obviated or removed if presented at that time.

OBJECTIONS TO OTHER CORRECTABLE ERRORS: Fed. R. Civ. P. 32(d)(3)(B)(i-ii)

Okla. Stat. Ann. tit. 12 § 3232(D)(3)(b) is substantially similar:

> Errors and irregularities occurring in the manner of the oral examination in the taking of the deposition, in the form of the questions or answers, in the oath or affirmation, or in the conduct of parties, and errors of any kind which might be obviated, removed or cured if promptly presented, are waived unless seasonable objection thereto is made at the taking of the deposition.

The Supreme Court of Oklahoma has previously instructed that courts may compare discovery rules to their federal counterparts, holding: "We may look to discovery procedures in the federal rules when construing similar language in the Oklahoma Discovery Code."[60]

OREGON

TRIAL STANDARDS: Fed. R. Civ. P. 30(c)(1)

Or. R. Civ. P. 39(D)(1) is substantially similar:

> Examination and cross-examination of deponents may proceed as permitted at trial.

CONTINUING TESTIMONY: Fed. R. Civ. P. 30(c)(2)

Or. R. Civ. P. 39(D)(3) is substantially similar:

> All objections made at the time of the examination shall be noted on the record. . . . Evidence shall be taken subject to the objection. . . .

---

60   *Crest Infiniti, II, LP v. Swinton*, 174 P.3d 996, 999 (Okla. 2007).

NONSUGGESTIVE OBJECTIONS: Fed. R. Civ. P. 30(c)(2)

Or. R. Civ. P. 39(D)(3) is substantially similar:

> A party or deponent shall state objections concisely and in a non-argumentative and non-suggestive manner.

INSTRUCTIONS NOT TO ANSWER: Fed. R. Civ. P. 30(c)(2)

Or. R. Civ. P. 39(D)(3) is substantially similar:

> [A] party may instruct a deponent not to answer a question, and a deponent may decline to answer a question, only: (a) when necessary to present or preserve a motion under section E of this rule; (b) to enforce a limitation on examination ordered by the court; or (c) to preserve a privilege or constitutional or statutory right.

DURATIONAL LIMIT: Fed. R. Civ. P. 30(d)(1)

Oregon has <u>no comparable rule</u> limiting the length of a deposition.

OBSTRUCTION SANCTIONS: Fed. R. Civ. P. 30(d)(2)

Oregon has <u>no comparable rule</u> establishing sanctions for frustrating the fair examination of a deponent.

SUSPENDING THE DEPOSITION: Fed. R. Civ. P. 30(d)(3)(A)

Or. R. Civ. P. 39(E)(1) is conceptually similar:

> At any time during the taking of a deposition, upon motion and a showing by a party or a deponent that the deposition is being conducted or hindered in bad faith, or in a manner not consistent with these rules, or in such manner as unreasonably to annoy, embarrass, or oppress the deponent or any party, the court may order the officer conducting the examination to cease forthwith from taking the deposition. . . . Upon demand of the moving party or deponent, the

parties shall suspend the taking of the deposition for the time necessary to make a motion under this subsection.

TRIAL ADMISSIBILITY: Fed. R. Civ. P. 32(b)

Oregon has no comparable rule addressing whether objections can be made at hearing or trial to the admission of deposition testimony that would be inadmissible if the witness were present and testifying.

OBJECTIONS TO EVIDENTIARY ERRORS: Fed. R. Civ. P. 32(d)(3)(A)

Or. R. Civ. P. 41(C)(1) is substantially similar:

> Objections to the competency of a witness or to the competency, relevancy, or materiality of testimony are not waived by failure to make them before or during the taking of the deposition, unless the ground of the objection is one which might have been obviated or removed if presented at that time.

OBJECTIONS TO OTHER CORRECTABLE ERRORS: Fed. R. Civ. P. 32(d)(3)(B)(i-ii)

Or. R. Civ. P. 41(C)(2) is substantially similar:

> Errors and irregularities occurring at the oral examination in the manner of taking the deposition, in the form of the questions or answers, in the oath or affirmation, or in the conduct of parties, and errors of any kind which might be obviated, removed, or cured if promptly presented, are waived unless seasonable objection thereto is made at the taking of the deposition.

The Oregon Supreme Court has not yet provided a general rule allowing for the use of federal case law to interpret the state's rules of civil procedure. When interpretive issues involving civil procedure have arisen, however, the court has applied federal case law about specific rules, including Fed. R. Civ. P. 42(a), (b),[61] Fed. R. Civ. P. 54(b),[62] and Fed. R. Civ. P. 56,[63] to construe the state's corresponding rules of civil procedure.

PENNSYLVANIA

The Pennsylvania Rules of Civil Procedure have no rules comparable to any of the rules analyzed in this appendix. Instead, most of the applicable rules governing proper deposition conduct in Pennsylvania have developed from local case law.

RHODE ISLAND

TRIAL STANDARDS: Fed. R. Civ. P. 30(c)(1)

R.I. Ct. R. 30(c) is substantially similar:

> Examination and cross-examination of witnesses may proceed as permitted at the trial under the provisions of the applicable Rhode Island Rules of Evidence.

CONTINUING TESTIMONY: Fed. R. Civ. P. 30(c)(2)

R.I. Ct. R. 30(c) is substantially similar:

> All objections made at the time of the examination . . . shall be noted by the officer upon the record of the deposition, but the examination shall proceed with the testimony being taken subject to the objections.

---

[61] *Vander Veer v. Toyota Motor Distributors, Inc.*, 577 P.2d 1343, 1349 (Or. 1978).

[62] *State ex rel. Zidell v. Jones*, 720 P.2d 350, 356 (Or. 1986).

[63] *Taylor v. Baker*, 566 P.2d 884, 886 (Or. 1977).

NONSUGGESTIVE OBJECTIONS: Fed. R. Civ. P. 30(c)(2)

R.I. Ct. R. 30(d)(1) is substantially similar:

> Any objection to evidence during a deposition shall be stated concisely and in a non-argumentative and non-suggestive manner.

INSTRUCTIONS NOT TO ANSWER: Fed. R. Civ. P. 30(c)(2)

R.I. Ct. R. 30(d)(1) is substantially similar:

> A person may instruct a deponent not to answer only when necessary to preserve a privilege, to enforce a limitation on evidence directed by the court, or to present a motion under paragraph (3).

DURATIONAL LIMIT: Fed. R. Civ. P. 30(d)(1)

Rhode Island has no comparable rule limiting the length of a deposition.

OBSTRUCTION SANCTIONS: Fed. R. Civ. P. 30(d)(2)

Rhode Island has no comparable rule establishing sanctions for frustrating the fair examination of a deponent.

SUSPENDING THE DEPOSITION: Fed. R. Civ. P. 30(d)(3)(A)

R.I. Ct. R. 30(d)(3) is conceptually similar:

> At any time during a deposition, on motion of a party or of the deponent and upon a showing that the examination is being conducted in bad faith or in such manner as unreasonably to annoy, embarrass, or oppress the deponent or party, the court in which the action is pending or the court in the county where the deposition is being taken may order the officer or examining attorney conducting the examination to cease forthwith from taking the deposition. . . . Upon demand of the objecting party or deponent, the taking of the deposition shall be

suspended for the time necessary to make a motion for an order or to obtain a ruling by telephone.

TRIAL ADMISSIBILITY: Fed. R. Civ. P. 32(b)

R.I. Ct. R. 32(b) is substantially similar:

> [O]bjection[s] may be made at the trial or hearing to receiving in evidence any deposition or part thereof for any reason which would require the exclusion of the evidence if the witness were then present and testifying.

OBJECTIONS TO EVIDENTIARY ERRORS: Fed. R. Civ. P. 32(d)(3)(A)

R.I. Ct. R. 32(e)(3)(A) is substantially similar:

> Objections to the competency of a witness or to the competency, relevancy, or the materiality of testimony are not waived by failure to make them before or during the taking of the deposition, unless the ground of the objection is one which might have been obviated or removed if presented at that time.

OBJECTIONS TO OTHER CORRECTABLE ERRORS: Fed. R. Civ. P. 32(d)(3)(B)(i-ii)

R.I. Ct. R. 32(e)(3)(B) is substantially similar:

> Errors and irregularities occurring at the oral examination in the manner of taking the deposition, in the form of the questions or answers, in the oath or affirmation, or in the conduct of parties and errors of any kind which might be obviated, removed, or cured if promptly presented, are waived unless seasonable objection thereto is made at the taking of the deposition.

The Rhode Island Supreme Court has held: "This Court has stated that where the Federal rule and our state rule are substantially similar, we will look to the Federal courts for guidance or interpretation of our own rule."[64]

SOUTH CAROLINA

TRIAL STANDARDS: Fed. R. Civ. P. 30(c)(1)

S.C. R. Civ. P. 30(c) is substantially similar:

> Examination and cross-examination of witnesses may proceed as permitted at the trial under the provisions of the South Carolina Rules of Evidence. . . .

CONTINUING TESTIMONY: Fed. R. Civ. P. 30(c)(2)

S.C. R. Civ. P. 30(c) is substantially similar:

> All objections made at time of the examination to the qualifications of the officer taking the deposition, or to the manner of taking it, or to the evidence presented, or to the conduct of any party, and any other objection to the proceedings, shall be noted by the officer upon the deposition. Evidence objected to shall be taken subject to the objections.

NONSUGGESTIVE OBJECTIONS: Fed. R. Civ. P. 30(c)(2)

S.C. R. Civ. P. (j)(4) is conceptually similar:

> Counsel shall not make objections or statements which might suggest an answer to a witness. Counsel's objections shall be stated concisely and in a non-argumentative and non-suggestive manner, stating the basis of the objection and nothing more.

This rule also prohibits explaining the ground of an objection.

---

64 *Heal v. Heal*, 762 A.2d 463, 466-67 (R.I. 2000).

INSTRUCTIONS NOT TO ANSWER: Fed. R. Civ. P. 30(c)(2)

S.C. Civ. R. P. 30(j)(3) is conceptually similar:

> Counsel shall not direct or request that a witness not answer a question, unless that counsel has objected to the question on the ground that the answer is protected by a privilege or a limitation on evidence directed by the court or unless that counsel intends to present a motion under Rule 30(d), SCRCP. In addition, counsel shall have an affirmative duty to inform a witness that, unless such an objection is made, the question must be answered. Counsel directing that a witness not answer a question on those grounds or allowing a witness to refuse to answer a question on those grounds shall move the court for a protective order under Rule 26(c), SCRCP, or 30(d), SCRCP, within five business days of the suspension or termination of the deposition. Failure to timely file such a motion will constitute waiver of the objection, and the deposition may be reconvened.

This rule establishes important requirements not present in the federal rule. First, defending counsel has an affirmative duty to inform the witness that he or she must answer every deposition question, not including the standard exceptions. And second, if defending counsel issues a valid instruction not to answer, they must move for an order with the court within five days to preserve the objection for trial.

DURATIONAL LIMIT: Fed. R. Civ. P. 30(d)(1)

South Carolina has <u>no comparable rule</u> limiting the length of a deposition.

OBSTRUCTION SANCTIONS: Fed. R. Civ. P. 30(d)(2)

S.C. R. Civ. P. 30(j)(9) is conceptually similar:

> Violation of this rule may subject the violator to sanctions under Rule 37, SCRCP.

This rule is similar to the federal rule, but it differs because, rather than generally sanctioning conduct that frustrates the fair examination of a deponent, the prohibited types of misconduct are explicitly listed in S.C. R. Civ. P. 30(j) and compiled at the end of this section.

SUSPENDING THE DEPOSITION: Fed. R. Civ. P. 30(d)(3)(A)

S.C. R. Civ. P. 30(d) is conceptually similar:

> At any time during the taking of the deposition, on motion of a party or the deponent and upon a showing that the examination is being conducted in bad faith or in such manner as unreasonably to annoy, embarrass, or oppress the deponent or party, the court in which the action is pending or the court in the place where the deposition is being taken may order the officer conducting the examination to cease forthwith from taking the deposition. . . . Upon demand of the objecting party or deponent, the taking of the deposition shall be suspended for the time necessary to make a motion for an order.

TRIAL ADMISSIBILITY: Fed. R. Civ. P. 32(b)

S.C. R. Civ. P. 32(b) is substantially similar:

> [O]bjection[s] may be made at the trial or hearing to receiving in evidence any deposition or part thereof for any reason which would require the exclusion of the evidence if the witness were then present and testifying.

OBJECTIONS TO EVIDENTIARY ERRORS: Fed. R. Civ. P. 32(d)(3)(A)

S.C. R. Civ. P. 32(d)(3)(A) is substantially similar:

> Objections to the competency of a witness or to the competency, relevancy, or materiality of testimony are not waived by failure to make them before or during the taking of the

deposition, unless the ground of the objection is one which might have been obviated or removed if presented at that time.

OBJECTIONS TO OTHER CORRECTABLE ERRORS: Fed. R. Civ. P. 32(d)(3)(B)(i-ii)

S.C. R. Civ. P. 32(d)(3)(B) is substantially similar:

> Errors and irregularities occurring at the oral examination in the manner of taking the deposition, in the form of the questions or answers, in the oath or affirmation, or in the conduct of parties, and errors of any kind which might be obviated, removed, or cured if promptly presented, are waived unless seasonable objection thereto is made at the taking of the deposition.

OTHER DIFFERENCES BETWEEN THE RULES

S.C. R. Civ. P. 30(j)(1)—Deponent's responsibilities:

> At the beginning of each deposition, deposing counsel shall instruct the witness to ask deposing counsel, rather than the witness' own counsel, for clarifications, definitions, or explanations of any words, questions or documents presented during the course of the deposition. The witness shall abide by these instructions.

S.C. R. Civ. P. 30(j)(2)—Preservation of unnecessary objections:

> All objections, except those which would be waived if not made at the deposition under Rule 32(d)(3), SCRCP, and those necessary to assert a privilege, to enforce a limitation on evidence directed by the Court, or to present a motion pursuant to Rule 30(d), SCRCP, shall be preserved.

S.C. R. Civ. P. 30(j)(5)—Attorney-client conferences:

> Counsel and a witness shall not engage in private, off-the-record conferences during depositions or during breaks or recesses regarding the substance of the testimony at the deposition, except for the purpose of deciding whether to assert a privilege or to make an objection or to move for a protective order.

This rule explicitly prohibits attorney-client conferences during the deposition, including during breaks when a question is not pending.

The Supreme Court of South Carolina has held: "Since our Rules of Procedure are based on the Federal Rules, where there is no South Carolina law, we look to the construction placed on the Federal Rules of Civil Procedure."[65]

SOUTH DAKOTA

TRIAL STANDARDS: Fed. R. Civ. P. 30(c)(1)

S.D. Codified Laws § 15-6-30(c) is substantially similar:

> Examination and cross-examination of witnesses may proceed as permitted at the trial as provided by law.

CONTINUING TESTIMONY: Fed. R. Civ. P. 30(c)(2)

S.D. Codified Laws § 15-6-30(c) is substantially similar:

> All objections made at time of the examination to the qualifications of the officer taking the deposition, or to the manner of taking it, or to the evidence presented, or to the conduct of any party, and any other objection to the proceedings, shall be noted by the officer upon the deposition. Evidence objected to shall be taken subject to the objections.

NONSUGGESTIVE OBJECTIONS: Fed. R. Civ. P. 30(c)(2)

S.D. Codified Laws § 15-6-30(d)(1) is virtually identical:

> Any objection during a deposition must be stated concisely and in a nonargumentative and nonsuggestive manner.

---

65 *Gardner v. Newsome Chevrolet-Buick, Inc.*, 404 S.E.2d 200, 201 (S.C. 1991).

INSTRUCTIONS NOT TO ANSWER: Fed. R. Civ. P. 30(c)(2)

S.D. Codified Laws § 15-6-30(d)(1) is virtually identical:

> A person may instruct a deponent not to answer only when necessary to preserve a privilege, to enforce a limitation directed by the court, or to present a motion under subdivision 15-6-30(d)(4).

DURATIONAL LIMIT: Fed. R. Civ. P. 30(d)(1)

S.D. Codified Laws § 15-6-30(d)(2) is virtually identical:

> [A] deposition is limited to one day of seven hours.

OBSTRUCTION SANCTIONS: Fed. R. Civ. P. 30(d)(2)

S.D. Codified Laws § 15-6-30(d)(3) is substantially similar:

> If the court finds that any impediment, delay, or other conduct has frustrated the fair examination of the deponent, it may impose upon the persons responsible an appropriate sanction, including the reasonable costs and attorney's fees incurred by any parties as a result thereof.

SUSPENDING THE DEPOSITION: Fed. R. Civ. P. 30(d)(3)(A)

S.D. Codified Laws § 15-6-30(d)(4) is conceptually similar:

> At any time during a deposition, on motion of a party or of the deponent and upon a showing that the examination is being conducted in bad faith or in such manner as unreasonably to annoy, embarrass, or oppress the deponent or party, the court in which the action is pending or the court in the circuit where the deposition is being taken may order the officer conducting the examination to cease forthwith from taking the deposition. . . . Upon demand of the objecting party or deponent, the taking of the deposition must be suspended for the time necessary to make a motion for an order.

TRIAL ADMISSIBILITY: Fed. R. Civ. P. 32(b)

S.D. Codified Laws § 15-6-32(b) is substantially similar:

> [O]bjection[s] may be made at the trial or hearing to receiving in evidence any deposition or part thereof for any reason which would require the exclusion of the evidence if the witness were then present and testifying.

OBJECTIONS TO EVIDENTIARY ERRORS: Fed. R. Civ. P. 32(d)(3)(A)

S.D. Codified Laws § 15-6-32(d)(3)(A) is substantially similar:

> Objections to the competency of a witness or to the competency, relevancy, or materiality of testimony are not waived by failure to make them before or during the taking of the deposition, unless the ground of the objection is one which might have been obviated or removed if presented at that time.

OBJECTIONS TO OTHER CORRECTABLE ERRORS: Fed. R. Civ. P. 32(d)(3)(B)(i-ii)

S.D. Codified Laws § 15-6-32(d)(3)(B) is substantially similar:

> Errors and irregularities occurring at the oral examination in the manner of taking the deposition, in the form of the questions or answers, in the oath or affirmation, or in the conduct of parties, and errors of any kind which might be obviated, removed, or cured if promptly presented, are waived unless seasonable objection thereto is made at the taking of the deposition.

The South Dakota Supreme Court has held: "South Dakota has generally adopted the Federal Rules of Civil Procedure. . . . Though federal interpretations of federal civil and appellate procedural rules are not binding on us in an interpretation of like rules in our State's courts, it is appropriate to 'turn to the federal court decisions for guidance in their application and interpretation.'"[66]

TENNESSEE

TRIAL STANDARDS: Fed. R. Civ. P. 30(c)(1)

Tenn. R. Civ. P. 30.03 is substantially similar:

> Examination and cross-examination of witnesses may proceed as permitted at the trial under the Tennessee Rules of Evidence.

CONTINUING TESTIMONY: Fed. R. Civ. P. 30(c)(2)

Tenn. R. Civ. P. 30.03 is substantially similar:

> All objections made at time of the examination . . . shall be noted by the officer upon the deposition. Evidence objected to shall be taken subject to the objections.

NONSUGGESTIVE OBJECTIONS: Fed. R. Civ. P. 30(c)(2)

Tenn. R. Civ. P. 30.03 is substantially similar:

> Any objection to evidence during a deposition shall be stated concisely and in a non-argumentative and non-suggestive manner.

INSTRUCTIONS NOT TO ANSWER: Fed. R. Civ. P. 30(c)(2)

Tenn. R. Civ. P. 30.03 is virtually identical:

> A deponent may be instructed not to answer only when necessary to preserve a privilege, to enforce a limitation on evidence directed by the court, or to present a motion to terminate or limit examination.

---

[66] *Sander v. Geib, Elston, Frost Prof'l Ass'n*, 506 N.W.2d 107, 122 (S.D. 1993) (internal citation omitted).

DURATIONAL LIMIT: Fed. R. Civ. P. 30(d)(1)

Tennessee has no comparable rule limiting the length of a deposition.

OBSTRUCTION SANCTIONS: Fed. R. Civ. P. 30(d)(2)

Tennessee has no comparable rule establishing sanctions for frustrating the fair examination of a deponent.

SUSPENDING THE DEPOSITION: Fed. R. Civ. P. 30(d)(3)(A)

Tenn. R. Civ. P. 30.04 is conceptually similar:

> At any time during the taking of the deposition, on motion of a party or of the deponent and upon a showing that the examination is being conducted in bad faith or in such manner as unreasonably to annoy, embarrass, or oppress the deponent or party, the court in which the action is pending may order the officer conducting the examination to cease forthwith from taking the deposition. . . . Upon demand of the objecting party or deponent, the taking of the deposition shall be suspended for the time necessary to make a motion for an order.

TRIAL ADMISSIBILITY: Fed. R. Civ. P. 32(b)

Tenn. R. Civ. P. 32.02 is substantially similar:

> [O]bjection[s] may be made at the trial or hearing to receiving in evidence any deposition or part thereof for any reason which would require the exclusion of the evidence if the witness were then present and testifying.

OBJECTIONS TO EVIDENTIARY ERRORS: Fed. R. Civ. P. 32(d)(3)(A)

Tenn. R. Civ. P. 32.04(3)(A) is substantially similar:

> Objections to the competency of a witness or to the competency, relevancy, or materiality of testimony are not waived by failure to make them before or during the taking of the deposition, unless the ground of the objection is one which might have been obviated or removed if presented at that time.

OBJECTIONS TO OTHER CORRECTABLE ERRORS: Fed. R. Civ. P. 32(d)(3)(B)(i-ii)

Tenn. R. Civ. P. 32.04(3)(B) is substantially similar:

> Errors and irregularities occurring at the oral examination in the manner of taking the deposition, in the form of the questions or answers, in the oath or affirmation, or in the conduct of parties, and errors of any kind which might be obviated, removed, or cured if promptly presented, are waived unless seasonable objection thereto is made at the taking of the deposition.

The Tennessee Supreme Court has held that "when interpreting our own rules of civil procedure, we consult and are guided by the interpretation that has been applied to comparable federal rules of procedure."[67]

TEXAS

TRIAL STANDARDS: Fed. R. Civ. P. 30(c)(1)

Tex. R. Civ. P. 199.5(d) is substantially similar:

> The oral deposition must be conducted in the same manner as if the testimony were being obtained in court during trial.

---

[67] *Turner v. Turner*, 473 S.W.3d 257, 268 (Tenn. 2015).

CONTINUING TESTIMONY: Fed. R. Civ. P. 30(c)(2)

Tex. R. Civ. P. 199.5(e) is conceptually similar:

> The officer taking the oral deposition will not rule on objections but must record them for ruling by the court. The officer taking the oral deposition must not fail to record testimony because an objection has been made.

NONSUGGESTIVE OBJECTIONS: Fed. R. Civ. P. 30(c)(2)

TRIAL ADMISSIBILITY: Fed. R. Civ. P. 32(b)

OBJECTIONS TO EVIDENTIARY ERRORS: Fed. R. Civ. P. 32(d)(3)(A)

OBJECTIONS TO OTHER CORRECTABLE ERRORS: Fed. R. Civ. P. 32(d)(3)(B)(i-ii)

Tex. R. Civ. P. 199.5(e) is conceptually similar:

> Objections to questions during the oral deposition are limited to "Objection, leading" and "Objection, form." Objections to testimony during the oral deposition are limited to "Objection, nonresponsive." These objections are waived if not stated as phrased during the oral deposition. All other objections need not be made or recorded during the oral deposition to be later raised with the court. The objecting party must give a clear and concise explanation of an objection if requested by the party taking the oral deposition, or the objection is waived.

This is conceptually similar to the federal rules, but it imposes stringent requirements governing which objections are proper at a deposition and the proper way to raise them. This rule implicitly preserves the right to object to the use of deposition testimony at trial that would be inadmissible if the witness were present and testifying. The committee note to Tex. R. Civ. P. 199.6 includes further guidance on what constitutes an objection to form:

> An objection to the form of a question includes objections that the question calls for speculation, calls for a narrative

answer, is vague, is confusing, or is ambiguious. Ordinarily, a witness must answer a question at a deposition subject to the objection. An objection may therefore be inadequate if a question incorporates such unfair assuptions or is worded so that any answer would necessarily be misleading. A witness should not be required to answer whether he has yet ceased conduct he denies ever doing, subject to an objection to form (i.e., that the question is confusing or assumes facts not in evidence) because any answer would necessarily be misleading on account of the way in which the question is put.

However, it is important to understand that Texas's definition of proper objections to form goes beyond what is considered a form objection based on federal case law.

INSTRUCTIONS NOT TO ANSWER: Fed. R. Civ. P. 30(c)(2)

Tex. R. Civ. P. 199.5(f) is substantially similar:

> An attorney may instruct a witness not to answer a question during an oral deposition only if necessary to preserve a privilege, comply with a court order or these rules, protect a witness from an abusive question or one for which any answer would be misleading, or secure a ruling pursuant to paragraph (g). The attorney instructing the witness not to answer must give a concise, nonargumentative, nonsuggestive explanation of the grounds for the instruction if requested by the party who asked the question.

However, this rule allows the defending attorney to instruct a witness not to answer a question if it is abusive, which the federal rule does not allow.

DURATIONAL LIMIT: Fed. R. Civ. P. 30(d)(1)

Tex. R. Civ. P. 199.5(c) is significantly different:

> No side may examine or cross-examine an individual witness for more than six hours.

This rule changes the presumptive limit of a deposition from seven hours to six hours.

OBSTRUCTION SANCTIONS: Fed. R. Civ. P. 30(d)(2)

Tex. R. Civ. P. 199.5(e) is conceptually similar:

> Argumentative or suggestive objections or explanations waive objection and may be grounds for terminating the oral deposition or assessing costs or other sanctions.

However, this rule explicitly states that speaking objections waive the objection for trial.

SUSPENDING THE DEPOSITION: Fed. R. Civ. P. 30(d)(3)(A)

Tex. R. Civ. P. 199.5(g) is conceptually similar:

> If the time limitations for the deposition have expired or the deposition is being conducted or defended in violation of these rules, a party or witness may suspend the oral deposition for the time necessary to obtain a ruling.

OTHER DIFFERENCES BETWEEN THE RULES

Tex. R. Civ. P. 199.5(d)—Attorney-client conferences:

> Private conferences between the witness and the witness's attorney during the actual taking of the deposition are improper except for the purpose of determining whether a privilege should be asserted. Private conferences may be held, however, during agreed recesses and adjournments. If the lawyers and witnesses do not comply with this rule, the court may allow in evidence at trial statements, objections, discussions, and other occurrences during the oral deposition that reflect upon the credibility of the witness or the testimony.

This rule explicitly prohibits attorney-client conferences during the deposition, unless they are during agreed-upon breaks.

Tex. R. Civ. P. 199.5(h)—Good-faith requirement:

> An attorney must not ask a question at an oral deposition solely to harass or mislead the witness, for any other improper purpose, or without a good faith legal basis at the time. An attorney must not object to a question at an oral deposition, instruct the witness not to answer a question, or suspend the deposition unless there is a good faith factual and legal basis for doing so at the time.

This rule establishes the general requirement of conducting depositions in good faith.

The Texas Supreme Court has held that "when interpreting our own rules of civil procedure, we consult and are guided by the interpretation that has been applied to comparable federal rules of procedure."[68]

UTAH

TRIAL STANDARDS: Fed. R. Civ. P. 30(c)(1)

Utah R. Civ. P. 30(c)(1) is substantially similar:

> Questioning of witnesses may proceed as permitted at the trial under the Utah Rules of Evidence.

CONTINUING TESTIMONY: Fed. R. Civ. P. 30(c)(2)

Utah R. Civ. P. 30(c)(2) is substantially similar:

> All objections shall be recorded, but the questioning shall proceed, and the testimony taken subject to the objections.

---

[68] *Sw. Ref. Co. v. Bernal*, 22 S.W.3d 425, 433 (Tex. 2000).

NONSUGGESTIVE OBJECTIONS: Fed. R. Civ. P. 30(c)(2)

Utah R. Civ. P. 30(c)(2) is virtually identical:

> Any objection shall be stated concisely and in a non-argumentative and non-suggestive manner.

INSTRUCTIONS NOT TO ANSWER: Fed. R. Civ. P. 30(c)(2)

Utah R. Civ. P. 30(c)(2) is virtually identical:

> A person may instruct a witness not to answer only to preserve a privilege, to enforce a limitation on evidence directed by the court, or to present a motion for a protective order under Rule 37.

DURATIONAL LIMIT: Fed. R. Civ. P. 30(d)(1)

Utah R. Civ. P. 30(d) is significantly different:

> During standard discovery, oral questioning of a nonparty shall not exceed four hours, and oral questioning of a party shall not exceed seven hours.

While the time limit for a party's deposition remains the same as in the federal rule, this rule sets a limit on nonparty depositions at four hours.

OBSTRUCTION SANCTIONS: Fed. R. Civ. P. 30(d)(2)

Utah has <u>no comparable rule</u> establishing sanctions for frustrating the fair examination of a deponent.

SUSPENDING THE DEPOSITION: Fed. R. Civ. P. 30(d)(3)(A)

Utah R. Civ. P. 30(c)(2) is conceptually similar:

> Upon demand of the objecting party or witness, the deposition shall be suspended for the time necessary to make a motion.

TRIAL ADMISSIBILITY: Fed. R. Civ. P. 32(b)

Utah R. Civ. P. 32(b) is substantially similar:

> [O]bjection[s] may be made at the trial or hearing to receiving in evidence any deposition or part thereof for any reason which would require the exclusion of the evidence if the witness were then present and testifying.

OBJECTIONS TO EVIDENTIARY ERRORS: Fed. R. Civ. P. 32(d)(3)(A)

Utah R. Civ. P. 32(c)(3)(A) is substantially similar:

> Objections to the competency of a witness or to the competency, relevancy, or materiality of testimony are not waived by failure to make them before or during the taking of the deposition, unless the ground of the objection is one which might have been obviated or removed if presented at that time.

OBJECTIONS TO OTHER CORRECTABLE ERRORS: Fed. R. Civ. P. 32(d)(3)(B)(i-ii)

Utah R. Civ. P. 32(c)(3)(B) is substantially similar:

> Errors and irregularities occurring at the oral examination in the manner of taking the deposition, in the form of the questions or answers, in the oath or affirmation, or in the conduct of parties, and errors of any kind which might be obviated, removed, or cured if promptly presented are waived unless seasonable objection thereto is made at the taking of the deposition.

The Utah Supreme Court has held: "We may also rely on interpretations of similar federal rules by federal courts to assist our own interpretation."[69]

---

[69] *Robinson v. Taylor*, 356 P.3d 1230, 1234 (Utah 2015).

VERMONT

TRIAL STANDARDS: Fed. R. Civ. P. 30(c)(1)

Vt. R. Civ. P. 30(c) is substantially similar:

> Examination and cross-examination of witnesses may proceed as permitted at the trial under the provisions of the Vermont Rules of Evidence.

CONTINUING TESTIMONY: Fed. R. Civ. P. 30(c)(2)

Vt. R. Civ. P. 30(c) is substantially similar:

> All objections made at the time of the examination to the qualifications of the officer taking the deposition, or to the manner of taking it, or to the evidence presented, or to the conduct of any party, and any other objection to the proceedings, shall be noted by the officer upon the deposition. Evidence objected to shall be taken subject to the objections.

NONSUGGESTIVE OBJECTIONS: Fed. R. Civ. P. 30(c)(2)

Vt. R. Civ. P. 30(d)(1) is virtually identical:

> Any objection to evidence during a deposition shall be stated concisely and in a nonargumentative and nonsuggestive manner.

INSTRUCTIONS NOT TO ANSWER: Fed. R. Civ. P. 30(c)(2)

Vt. R. Civ. P. 30(d)(1) is virtually identical:

> A party may instruct a deponent not to answer only when necessary to preserve a privilege, to enforce a limitation on evidence directed by the court, or to present a motion under paragraph (3).

DURATIONAL LIMIT: Fed. R. Civ. P. 30(d)(1)

Vermont has no comparable rule establishing a presumptive time limit.

OBSTRUCTION SANCTIONS: Fed. R. Civ. P. 30(d)(2)

Vt. R. Civ. P. 30(d)(2) is substantially similar:

> If the court finds that conduct contrary to paragraph (1) of this subdivision, or other conduct, has impeded or delayed the examination and has prevented a fair examination of the deponent, the court may extend the time for taking the deposition pursuant to paragraph (b)(3) of this rule, and may impose upon the persons responsible an appropriate sanction, including the reasonable costs and attorney's fees incurred by any parties as a result thereof.

SUSPENDING THE DEPOSITION: Fed. R. Civ. P. 30(d)(3)(A)

Vt. R. Civ. P. 30(d)(3) is conceptually similar:

> At any time during a deposition, on motion of a party or of the deponent and upon a showing that the examination is being conducted in bad faith or in such manner as unreasonably to annoy, embarrass, or oppress the deponent or party, any superior judge may order the officer conducting the examination to cease forthwith from taking the deposition. . . . Upon demand of the objecting party or deponent, the taking of the deposition shall be suspended for the time necessary to make a motion for an order.

TRIAL ADMISSIBILITY: Fed. R. Civ. P. 32(b)

Vt. R. Civ. P. 32(b) is substantially similar:

> [O]bjection[s] may be made at the trial or hearing to receiving in evidence any deposition or part thereof for any reason which would require the exclusion of the evidence if the witness were then present and testifying.

OBJECTIONS TO EVIDENTIARY ERRORS: Fed. R. Civ. P. 32(d)(3)(A)

Vt. R. Civ. P. 32(d)(3)(A) is substantially similar:

> Objections to the competency of a witness or to the competency, relevancy, or materiality of testimony are not waived by failure to make them before or during the taking of the deposition, unless the ground of the objection is one which might have been obviated or removed if presented at that time.

OBJECTIONS TO OTHER CORRECTABLE ERRORS: Fed. R. Civ. P. 32(d)(3)(B)(i-ii)

Vt. R. Civ. P. 32(d)(3)(B) is substantially similar:

> Errors and irregularities occurring at the oral examination in the manner of taking the deposition, in the form of the questions or answers, in the oath or affirmation, or in the conduct of parties, and errors of any kind which might be obviated, removed, or cured if promptly presented, are waived unless seasonable objection thereto is made at the taking of the deposition.

The Vermont Supreme Court has held that its "interpretation of Vermont Rules of Civil Procedure is often guided by federal precedent on identical federal rules."[70]

VIRGINIA

TRIAL STANDARDS: Fed. R. Civ. P. 30(c)(1)

Va. Sup. Ct. R. 4:5(c)(1) is substantially similar:

> Examination and cross-examination of witnesses may proceed as permitted at the trial.

---

70   *Follo v. Florindo*, 970 A.2d 1230, 1237 (Vt. 2009).

CONTINUING TESTIMONY: Fed. R. Civ. P. 30(c)(2)

Va. Sup. Ct. R. 4:5(c)(2) is virtually identical:

> An objection at the time of the examination . . . must be noted on the record, but the examination still proceeds; the testimony is taken subject to any objections.

NONSUGGESTIVE OBJECTIONS: Fed. R. Civ. P. 30(c)(2)

Va. Sup. Ct. R. 4:5(c)(2) is virtually identical:

> Any objection must be stated concisely in a nonargumentative and nonsuggestive manner.

INSTRUCTIONS NOT TO ANSWER: Fed. R. Civ. P. 30(c)(2)

Va. Sup. Ct. R. 4:5(c)(2) is virtually identical:

> A person may instruct a deponent not to answer only when necessary to preserve a privilege or protection for attorney work-product pursuant to Rule 4:1(b)(3), to enforce a limitation ordered by the court, or to present a motion under subsection (d).

DURATIONAL LIMIT: Fed. R. Civ. P. 30(d)(1)

Virginia has <u>no comparable rule</u> establishing a presumptive time limit.

OBSTRUCTION SANCTIONS: Fed. R. Civ. P. 30(d)(2)

Virginia has <u>no comparable rule</u> establishing sanctions for frustrating the fair examination of a deponent.

SUSPENDING THE DEPOSITION: Fed. R. Civ. P. 30(d)(3)(A)

Va. Sup. Ct. R. 4:5(d) is conceptually similar:

> At any time during the taking of the deposition, on motion of a party or of the deponent and upon a showing that the examination is being conducted in bad faith or in such manner as unreasonably to annoy, embarrass, or oppress the deponent or party, the court in which the action is pending or the court in the county or city where the deposition is being taken may order the officer conducting the examination to cease forthwith from taking the deposition. . . . Upon demand of the objecting party or deponent, the taking of the deposition shall be suspended for the time necessary to make a motion for an order.

TRIAL ADMISSIBILITY: Fed. R. Civ. P. 32(b)

Va. Sup. Ct. R. 4:7(b) is substantially similar:

> [O]bjection[s] may be made at the trial or hearing to receiving in evidence any deposition or part thereof for any reason which would require the exclusion of the evidence if the witness were then present and testifying.

OBJECTIONS TO EVIDENTIARY ERRORS: Fed. R. Civ. P. 32(d)(3)(A)

Va. Sup. Ct. R. 4:7(d)(3)(A) is substantially similar:

> Objections to the competency of a witness or to the competency, relevancy, or materiality of testimony are not waived by failure to make them before or during the taking of the deposition, unless the ground of the objection is one which might have been obviated or removed if presented at that time.

OBJECTIONS TO OTHER CORRECTABLE ERRORS: Fed. R. Civ. P. 32(d)(3)(B)(i-ii)

Va. Sup. Ct. R. 4:7(d)(3)(B) is substantially similar:

> Errors and irregularities occurring at the oral examination in the manner of taking the deposition, in the form of the questions or answers, in the oath or affirmation, or in the conduct of parties, and errors of any kind which might be obviated, removed, or cured if promptly presented, are waived unless seasonable objection thereto is made at the taking of the deposition.

The Supreme Court of Virginia has not yet provided a general rule allowing for the use of federal case law to interpret the state's rules of civil procedure. When interpretive issues involving civil procedure have arisen, however, the court has applied federal case law about specific rules, including Fed. R. Civ. P. 37,[71] to construe the state's corresponding rules of civil procedure.

WASHINGTON

TRIAL STANDARDS: Fed. R. Civ. P. 30(c)(1)

Wash. Super. Ct. Civ. R. 30(c) is substantially similar:

> Examination and cross examination of witnesses may proceed as permitted at the trial under the provisions of the Washington Rules of Evidence (ER).

In addition to the codified requirements, Wash. Super. Ct. R. 30(h)(6) applies a standard of courtroom conduct to depositions:

> All counsel and parties shall conduct themselves in depositions with the same courtesy and respect for the rules that are required in the courtroom during trial.

---

71 *Brown v. Black*, 534 S.E.2d 727, 729-30 (Va. 2000).

CONTINUING TESTIMONY: Fed. R. Civ. P. 30(c)(2)

Wash. Super. Ct. Civ. R. 30(c) is substantially similar:

> All objections made at the time of the examination ... shall be noted by the officer upon the deposition. Evidence objected to shall be taken subject to the objections.

NONSUGGESTIVE OBJECTIONS: Fed. R. Civ. P. 30(c)(2)

Wash. Super. Ct. Civ. R. 30(h)(2) is substantially similar:

> Only objections which are not reserved for time of trial by these rules or which are based on privileges or raised to questions seeking information beyond the scope of discovery may be made during the course of the deposition. All objections shall be concise and must not suggest or coach answers from the deponent. Argumentative interruptions by counsel shall not be permitted.

This rule also explicitly prohibits making deposition objections that are preserved for trial or not allowed in Wash. Super. Ct. Civ. R. 30(h)(1-3).

INSTRUCTIONS NOT TO ANSWER: Fed. R. Civ. P. 30(c)(2)

Wash. Super. Ct. Civ. R. 30(h)(3) is substantially similar:

> Instructions to the deponent not to answer questions are improper, except when based upon privilege or pursuant to rule 30(d). When a privilege is claimed the deponent shall nevertheless answer questions related to the existence, extent, or waiver of the privilege, such as the date of communication, identity of the declarant, and in whose presence the statement was made.

Relatedly, Wash. Super. Ct. Civ. R. 30(h)(4) requires the deponent to testify productively:

> Witnesses shall be instructed to answer all questions directly and without evasion to the extent of their testimonial knowledge, unless properly instructed by counsel not to answer.

DURATIONAL LIMIT: Fed. R. Civ. P. 30(d)(1)

Washington has no comparable rule establishing a presumptive time limit.

OBSTRUCTION SANCTIONS: Fed. R. Civ. P. 30(d)(2)

Washington has no comparable rule establishing sanctions for frustrating the fair examination of a deponent.

SUSPENDING THE DEPOSITION: Fed. R. Civ. P. 30(d)(3)(A)

Wash. Super. Ct. Civ. R. 30(d) is conceptually similar:

> At any time during the taking of the deposition, on motion of a party or of the deponent and upon a showing that the examination is being conducted in bad faith or in such manner as unreasonably to annoy, embarrass, or oppress the deponent or party, the court in which the action is pending or the court in the county where the deposition is being taken may order the officer conducting the examination to cease forthwith from taking the deposition. . . . Upon demand of the objecting party or deponent, the taking of the deposition shall be suspended for the time necessary to make a motion for an order.

TRIAL ADMISSIBILITY: Fed. R. Civ. P. 32(b)

Wash. Super. Ct. Civ. R. 32(b) is substantially similar:

> [O]bjection[s] may be made at the trial or hearing to receiving in evidence any deposition or part thereof for any reason which would require the exclusion of the evidence if the witness were then present and testifying.

OBJECTIONS TO EVIDENTIARY ERRORS: Fed. R. Civ. P. 32(d)(3)(A)

Wash. Super. Ct. Civ. R. 32(d)(3)(A) is substantially similar:

> Objections to the competency of a witness or to the competency, relevancy, or materiality of testimony are not waived by failure to make them before or during the taking of the deposition, unless the ground of the objection is one which might have been obviated or removed if presented at that time.

OBJECTIONS TO OTHER CORRECTABLE ERRORS: Fed. R. Civ. P. 32(d)(3)(B)(i-ii)

Wash. Super. Ct. Civ. R. 32(d)(3)(B) is substantially similar:

> Errors and irregularities occurring at the oral examination in the manner of taking the deposition, in the form of the questions or answers, in the oath or affirmation, or in the conduct of parties, and errors of any kind which might be obviated, removed, or cured if promptly presented, are waived unless seasonable objection thereto is made at the taking of the deposition.

OTHER DIFFERENCES BETWEEN THE RULES

Wash. Super. Ct. Civ. R. 30(h)(1)—Good-faith examination:

> Examining counsel will refrain from asking questions he or she knows to be beyond the legitimate scope of discovery, and from undue repetition.

Wash. Super. Ct. Civ. R. 30(h)(5)—Attorney-client conferences:

> Except where agreed to, attorneys shall not privately confer with deponents during the deposition between a question and an answer except for the purpose of determining the existence of privilege. Conferences with attorneys during normal recesses and at adjournment are permissible unless prohibited by the court.

The Washington State Supreme Court has held that, "[w]here a state rule parallels a federal rule, analysis of the federal rule may be looked to for guidance, though such analysis will be followed only if the reasoning is found to be persuasive."[72]

WEST VIRGINIA

TRIAL STANDARDS: Fed. R. Civ. P. 30(c)(1)

W.Va. R. Civ. P. 30(c) is substantially similar:

> Examination and cross-examination of witnesses may proceed as permitted at the trial under the provisions of the West Virginia Rules of Evidence.

CONTINUING TESTIMONY: Fed. R. Civ. P. 30(c)(2)

West Virginia has no comparable rule requiring that all objections are placed on the record, and that the deposition proceeds subject to any objection.

NONSUGGESTIVE OBJECTIONS: Fed. R. Civ. P. 30(c)(2)

W.Va. R. Civ. P. 30(d)(1) is virtually identical:

> Any objection to evidence during a deposition shall be stated concisely and in a non-argumentative and non-suggestive manner.

INSTRUCTIONS NOT TO ANSWER: Fed. R. Civ. P. 30(c)(2)

W.Va. R. Civ. P. 30(d)(1) is virtually identical:

> A party may instruct a deponent not to answer only when necessary to preserve a privilege, to enforce a limitation on evidence directed by the court, or to present a motion under paragraph (3).

---

[72] *Beal for Martinez v. City of Seattle*, 954 P.2d 237, 241 (Wash. 1998).

DURATIONAL LIMIT: Fed. R. Civ. P. 30(d)(1)

West Virginia has no comparable rule establishing a presumptive time limit.

OBSTRUCTION SANCTIONS: Fed. R. Civ. P. 30(d)(2)

W.Va. R. Civ. P. 30(d)(2) is substantially similar:

> If the court finds such an impediment, delay, or other conduct that has frustrated the fair examination of the deponent, it may impose upon the persons responsible an appropriate sanction, including the reasonable costs and attorney's fees incurred by any parties as a result thereof.

SUSPENDING THE DEPOSITION: Fed. R. Civ. P. 30(d)(3)(A)

W.Va. R. Civ. P. 30(d)(3) is conceptually similar:

> At any time during the taking of the deposition, on motion of a party or of the deponent and upon a showing that the examination is being conducted in bad faith or in such manner as unreasonably to annoy, embarrass, or oppress the deponent or party, the court in which the action is pending or the circuit court of the county where the deposition is being taken may order the officer conducting the examination to cease forthwith from taking the deposition. . . . Upon demand of the objecting party or deponent the taking of the deposition shall be suspended for the time necessary to make a motion for an order.

TRIAL ADMISSIBILITY: Fed. R. Civ. P. 32(b)

W.Va. R. Civ. P. 32(b) is substantially similar:

> [O]bjection[s] may be made at the trial or hearing to receiving in evidence any deposition or part thereof for any reason which would require the exclusion of the evidence if the witness were then present and testifying.

OBJECTIONS TO EVIDENTIARY ERRORS: Fed. R. Civ. P. 32(d)(3)(A)

W.Va. R. Civ. P. 32(d)(3)(A) is substantially similar:

> Objections to the competency of a witness or to the competency, relevancy, or materiality of testimony are not waived by failure to make them before or during the taking of the deposition, unless the ground of the objection is one which might have been obviated or removed if presented at that time.

OBJECTIONS TO OTHER CORRECTABLE ERRORS: Fed. R. Civ. P. 32(d)(3)(B)(i-ii)

W.Va. R. Civ. P. 32(d)(3)(B) is substantially similar:

> Errors and irregularities occurring at the oral examination in the manner of taking the deposition, in the form of the questions or answers, in the oath or affirmation, or in the conduct of parties, and errors of any kind which might be obviated, removed, or cured if promptly presented, are waived unless seasonable objection thereto is made at the taking of the deposition.

The West Virginia Supreme Court of Appeals has held: "Because the West Virginia Rules of Civil Procedure are patterned after the Federal Rules of Civil Procedure, we often refer to interpretations of the Federal Rules when discussing our own rules."[73]

---

[73] *Keplinger v. Virginia Elec. & Power Co.*, 537 S.E.2d 632, 641 (W. Va. 2000).

WISCONSIN

TRIAL STANDARDS: Fed. R. Civ. P. 30(c)(1)

W.S.A. § 804.05(4)(a) is substantially similar:

> Examination and cross-examination of deponents may proceed as permitted at the trial.

CONTINUING TESTIMONY: Fed. R. Civ. P. 30(c)(2)

W.S.A. § 804.05(4)(b) is conceptually similar:

> All objections made at time of the examination . . . shall be noted by the officer upon the deposition. . . . In the absence of a ruling by the court, the evidence objected to shall be taken subject to the objections.

NONSUGGESTIVE OBJECTIONS: Fed. R. Civ. P. 30(c)(2)

Wisconsin has <u>no comparable rule</u> requiring deposition objections to be concise, nonargumentative, or nonsuggestive.

INSTRUCTIONS NOT TO ANSWER: Fed. R. Civ. P. 30(c)(2)

W.S.A. § 804.05(4)(b) is conceptually similar:

> Upon request of any party, where the witness has refused to answer, and with the consent of the court, the court may rule by telephone on any objection. The court's ruling shall be recorded in the same manner as the testimony of the deponent. In the absence of a ruling by the court, the evidence objected to shall be taken subject to the objections.

This rule permits any party to contact the court—with its consent—to immediately rule on an objection at a deposition, which is not provided in the federal rule. However, it does not explicitly prohibit instructions not to answer (subject to the three normal exceptions).

DURATIONAL LIMIT: Fed. R. Civ. P. 30(d)(1)

W.S.A. § 804.045 is substantially similar:

> A party shall be limited ... to a reasonable number of depositions, not to exceed 10 depositions, none of which may exceed 7 hours in duration.

———

OBSTRUCTION SANCTIONS: Fed. R. Civ. P. 30(d)(2)

Wisconsin has no comparable rule establishing sanctions for frustrating the fair examination of a deponent.

———

SUSPENDING THE DEPOSITION: Fed. R. Civ. P. 30(d)(3)(A)

W.S.A. § 804.05(5) is conceptually similar:

> At any time during the taking of the deposition, on motion of a party or of the deponent and upon a showing that the examination is being conducted in bad faith or in such manner as unreasonably to annoy, embarrass, or oppress the deponent or party, the court in which the action is pending may order the officer conducting the examination to cease forthwith from taking the deposition. ...

However, this rule does not explicitly grant any party the right to suspend the deposition to move for such an order.

———

TRIAL ADMISSIBILITY: Fed. R. Civ. P. 32(b)

W.S.A. § 804.07(2) is substantially similar:

> [O]bjection[s] may be made at the trial or hearing to receiving in evidence any deposition or part thereof for any reason which would require the exclusion of the evidence if the witness were then present and testifying.

———

OBJECTIONS TO EVIDENTIARY ERRORS: Fed. R. Civ. P. 32(d)(3)(A)

W.S.A. § 804.07(3)(c)(1) is substantially similar:

> Objections to the competency of a witness or to the competency, relevancy, or materiality of testimony are not waived by failure to make them before or during the taking of the deposition, unless the ground of the objection is one which might have been obviated or removed if presented at that time.

OBJECTIONS TO OTHER CORRECTABLE ERRORS: Fed. R. Civ. P. 32(d)(3)(B)(i-ii)

W.S.A. § 804.07(3)(c)(2) is substantially similar:

> Errors and irregularities occurring at the oral examination in the manner of taking the deposition, in the form of the questions or answers, in the oath or affirmation, or in the conduct of parties, and errors of any kind which might be obviated, removed, or cured if promptly presented, are waived unless seasonable objection thereto is made at the taking of the deposition.

The Wisconsin Supreme Court has instructed the bench and bar as follows: "When 'a state rule mirrors the federal rule, we consider federal cases interpreting the rule to be persuasive authority.'"[74]

WYOMING

TRIAL STANDARDS: Fed. R. Civ. P. 30(c)(1)

Wyo. R. Civ. P. 30(c)(1) is substantially similar:

> The examination and cross-examination of a deponent proceed as they would at trial under the Wyoming Rules of Evidence....

---

74   *Luckett v. Bodner*, 769 N.W.2d 504, 511 (Wis. 2009).

CONTINUING TESTIMONY: Fed. R. Civ. P. 30(c)(2)

Wyo. R. Civ. P. 30(c)(2) is virtually identical:

> An objection at the time of the examination . . . must be noted on the record, but the examination still proceeds; the testimony is taken subject to any objection.

NONSUGGESTIVE OBJECTIONS: Fed. R. Civ. P. 30(c)(2)

Wyo. R. Civ. P. 30(c)(2) is virtually identical:

> An objection must be stated concisely in a nonargumentative and nonsuggestive manner.

INSTRUCTIONS NOT TO ANSWER: Fed. R. Civ. P. 30(c)(2)

Wyo. R. Civ. P. 30(c)(2) is virtually identical:

> A person may instruct a deponent not to answer only when necessary to preserve a privilege, to enforce a limitation ordered by the court, or to present a motion under Rule 30(d)(3).

DURATIONAL LIMIT: Fed. R. Civ. P. 30(d)(1)

Wyo. R. Civ. P. 30(d)(1) is virtually identical:

> [A] deposition is limited to one day of seven hours.

OBSTRUCTION SANCTIONS: Fed. R. Civ. P. 30(d)(2)

Wyo. R. Civ. P. 30(d)(2) is virtually identical:

> The court may impose an appropriate sanction—including the reasonable expenses and attorney's fees incurred by any party—on a person who impedes, delays, or frustrates the fair examination of the deponent.

SUSPENDING THE DEPOSITION: Fed. R. Civ. P. 30(d)(3)(A)

Wyo. R. Civ. P. 30(d)(3)(A) is virtually identical:

> At any time during a deposition, the deponent or a party may move to terminate or limit it on the ground that it is being conducted in bad faith or in a manner that unreasonably annoys, embarrasses, or oppresses the deponent or party. . . . If the objecting deponent or party so demands, the deposition must be suspended for the time necessary to obtain an order.

TRIAL ADMISSIBILITY: Fed. R. Civ. P. 32(b)

Wyo. R. Civ. P. 32(b) is virtually identical:

> [A]n objection may be made at a hearing or trial to the admission of any deposition testimony that would be inadmissible if the witness were present and testifying.

OBJECTIONS TO EVIDENTIARY ERRORS: Fed. R. Civ. P. 32(d)(3)(A)

Wyo. R. Civ. P. 32(d)(3)(A) is virtually identical:

> An objection to a deponent's competence—or to the competence, relevance, or materiality of testimony—is not waived by a failure to make the objection before or during the deposition, unless the ground for it might have been corrected at that time.

OBJECTIONS TO OTHER CORRECTABLE ERRORS: Fed. R. Civ. P. 32(d)(3)(B)(i-ii)

Wyo. R. Civ. P. 32(d)(3)(B) is virtually identical:

> An objection to an error or irregularity at an oral examination is waived if: (i) it relates to the manner of taking the deposition, the form of a question or answer, the oath or affirmation, a party's conduct, or other matters that might have been

corrected at that time; and (ii) it is not timely made during the deposition.

The Wyoming Supreme Court has held: "We consider federal authority interpreting procedural rules highly persuasive when our rules are sufficiently similar or identical."[75]

---

75   *CSC Grp. Holdings, LLC v. Automation & Elecs., Inc.*, 638 P.3d 302, 308 (Wyo. 2016).

ABOUT THE AUTHOR

Mark Kosieradzki is a trial lawyer from Minneapolis. His 40-year career has spanned a vast array of cases throughout the United States. Mark's landmark civil rights case on behalf of an incarcerated woman resulted in the application of Section 1983 protections to detainees. His work on sexual abuse was featured in a CNN series on rape in nursing homes. The *Minneapolis Star Tribune* has described him as "one of the nation's most feared elder abuse litigators."

Mark is recognized in the "Best Lawyers in America." He is certified by the National Board of Trial Advocacy and the Minnesota State Bar Association as Civil Trial Specialist. He is a past president of the Minnesota Association for Justice and the Minnesota Chapter of the American Board of Trial Advocates. He is a member of AAJ's National College of Advocacy Board of Trustees and is one of the founding faculty of the NCA Deposition Colleges.

Mark is recognized as one of the country's leading authorities on discovery strategy, jurisprudence, and its implementation. He is the author of *30(b)(6): Deposing Corporations, Organizations & the Government* (Trial Guides), as well as the chapter "Accelerated Discovery: Cutting Through Obstructions" in *Anatomy of a Personal Injury Lawsuit*, 4th edition (AAJ Press/Trial Guides) and the DVD *Deposing the Corporate Representative* (AAJ Press).

From his roots as the oldest son of Polish immigrants in a small town in central Iowa, to founding the Kosieradzki Smith Law Firm, Mark has been a fierce advocate for those who do not have a voice. He has joined trial teams throughout the United States in a wide variety of wrongful death and catastrophic injury cases, including malpractice, bad faith, construction injuries, nursing home abuse, interstate trucking accidents, and products liability.

When Mark turned 50, he had a midlife crisis and started playing the blues harmonica.

INDEX

A

abusive behavior, 33, 36

admissibility, 10, 39, 59, 61–62, 138, 154, 178, 202, 237, 258

admission, 39, 143, 154, 159, 162, 172, 198, 201, 210, 240, 248, 262, 271, 307

adverse party, 15–16, 24, 46–47, 152–53

Alabama, 164–166

Alaska, 166–169

Arizona, 169–173

Arkansas, 173–176

asked and answered, 70, 73, 89–90, 222

attorney-client conferences, 1, 103, 106, 109–13, 228, 250, 278–79, 287, 299

attorney-client privilege, 63, 72, 79, 81–82, 105–6, 109, 113

attorney fees, 70, 86, 89, 117, 123–24, 146, 150, 152, 156–60, 162, 168, 186, 195, 198, 207, 213, 219, 228, 231, 239, 245, 262, 268, 280, 292, 301, 306

B

bad faith, 42, 61, 77, 84, 119–20, 128–30, 150, 162, 165, 168, 171, 174, 177, 180, 183, 186, 189, 192, 195, 198, 201, 204, 207, 210, 213, 216, 219, 223, 225, 229, 231, 234, 237, 239, 242, 245, 248, 251, 254, 256, 259, 262, 265, 268, 270, 273, 277, 280, 283, 292, 295, 298, 301, 304, 307, 310

beyond the scope, 61, 73, 91, 95–96, 98–99, 297

C

California, 176–179

changes in testimony, 109, 111

coaching, 49, 62–63, 65–66, 73, 107, 113, 221–22

Colorado, 179–181

311

communications, 78–80, 82, 140–41, 250, 297

privileged, 81–82

comparable rule, 163–65, 174, 176–77, 180, 183, 186, 189, 191–92, 197, 200, 204, 207, 210, 212, 215–16, 222–23, 225, 228, 233–37, 242, 246–51, 254, 256–57, 259, 262, 264, 270–71, 273, 276, 283, 289, 292, 294, 298, 300–301, 303–4

competence, 39, 41, 43–45, 59, 154, 162, 165, 169, 172, 175, 178, 181, 184, 187, 190, 192, 196, 199, 202, 205, 208, 211, 214, 217, 220, 223, 226, 229, 232, 235, 240, 243, 245–46, 252, 255, 258, 260, 263, 265, 268, 271, 274, 277, 281, 284, 290, 293, 295, 299, 302, 305, 307

conduct of parties and errors, 175, 190, 205, 214, 230, 238, 255, 266, 274

conferences, 82, 104, 106–8, 110–13, 135, 143–45, 299

Connecticut, 182–185

court orders, 7, 15, 21–23, 25, 83, 87, 125–26, 135, 137–39, 142–44, 147, 151, 154, 157, 186, 286

D

defect, evidentiary, 59

Delaware, 185–188

deposition misconduct, 1, 32–33, 117–19, 129, 171, 216, 257

deposition objections, requiring, 164, 176, 204, 233, 236, 247, 256, 259, 303

deposition obstruction, 1, 3, 7, 9, 11, 15, 17, 19, 21, 23, 25, 30–31, 33, 35, 39, 41, 43, 45, 47, 49, 51, 53, 55, 61, 63, 65, 67, 69, 71, 73, 77, 79, 81, 83, 85, 87, 89, 91, 95, 99, 103, 105, 107, 109, 111, 113, 117–19, 121, 123, 125, 127, 133, 135, 137, 139, 141, 143, 145, 149, 151, 153, 155, 157, 159, 161, 163, 165, 167, 169, 171, 173, 175, 177, 179, 181, 183, 185, 187, 189, 191, 193, 201, 207, 211, 213, 215, 217, 219, 221, 223, 225, 227, 229, 231, 233, 235, 237, 241, 243, 257, 259, 261, 263, 269, 271, 273, 275, 277, 281, 283, 285, 287, 289, 291, 293, 295, 297, 299, 301, 309

designation, 95, 99, 122, 137, 148, 156

disclosures, 7, 63, 67, 79, 84, 120, 123–24, 134–40, 142–45, 155–56, 177, 225, 256

compelling, 67, 122, 155

incomplete, 122, 156

discovery, 2, 7–11, 15–16, 22, 24, 61–62, 67, 83–84, 117, 120, 122–24, 127–29, 131–32, 138–39, 141–45, 155–57, 159, 177, 201, 222, 243, 257, 297, 299

E

errata sheet changes, 112

errors, 40, 45–47, 154–55, 163, 166, 169, 175, 178, 181–82, 184, 187, 190, 193, 196, 199, 202, 205, 208, 211, 214, 217, 220, 223, 226, 230, 232, 235, 238, 240, 243, 246, 252, 255, 258, 260, 263, 266, 269, 271, 274, 278, 281, 284, 290, 293, 296, 299, 302, 305, 307

correctable, 40, 50, 59, 65, 163, 166, 172–73, 175, 178, 181, 184, 187, 190, 193, 196, 202, 205, 208, 211, 214, 217, 220, 226, 230, 232, 235, 238, 240, 243, 246, 249, 252, 255, 258, 260, 263, 271, 274, 278, 281, 284–85, 290, 293, 296, 299, 302, 307

errors and irregularities, 166, 169, 175, 178, 181, 184, 187, 190, 193, 196, 202, 205, 214, 220, 226, 230, 232, 235, 238, 243, 246, 255, 258, 260, 266, 269, 271, 274, 278, 281, 284, 290, 296, 299, 302

evidentiary errors, 162, 165, 169, 172, 175, 178, 181, 184, 187, 190, 192, 196, 202, 205, 208, 211, 214, 217, 220, 226, 229, 232, 235, 237, 240, 243, 245, 248, 252, 255, 258, 260, 263, 265, 271, 274, 277, 281, 284–85, 290, 293, 295, 299, 302, 305, 307

expenses, 7, 19–20, 23, 30, 84, 123–25, 129–30, 138, 141–42, 147, 152, 156, 158, 257

reasonable, 70, 86, 117, 123–25, 128, 146, 150, 152, 156–60, 162, 198, 207, 228, 239, 245, 262, 306

F

failure to attend, 126–27, 152, 159

fair examination, 70–71, 86, 106, 117–19, 122, 129, 150, 162, 165, 168, 171, 174, 177, 180, 183, 186, 189, 192, 195, 198, 204, 207, 210, 213, 216, 219, 222, 225, 228, 231, 234, 236, 239, 242, 245, 248, 251, 254, 257, 259, 262, 264, 267, 270, 273, 277, 280, 283, 289, 292, 294, 298, 301, 304, 306

Florida, 188–191

form objections, 45, 47, 52–53, 67, 286

foundation, 43–45, 52, 54, 77, 178, 253

G

Georgia, 191–193

H

harassment, 41, 84–87, 89–90

Hawaii, 194–196

hearsay objections, 61–62

I

Idaho, 197–199

if you know, 66–67, 73

Illinois, 199–203

impeachment, 134, 137, 152, 154

impediment, 117, 168, 174, 186, 195, 213, 219, 231, 280, 301

improper speaking objection, 65

Indiana, 203–206

instruction not to answer, 66–67, 77–79, 83–89, 98, 110, 177, 179, 216, 225, 276

instructions not to answer, 66–67, 86, 88, 90–91, 95, 97–98, 100, 118, 162, 164, 167, 170, 174, 176–77, 179, 182, 186, 188–89, 191, 194, 197, 200, 203, 207, 209, 212, 215, 218, 222, 225, 228, 231, 234, 236, 239, 241, 244, 247, 250, 253, 257, 259, 261, 264, 267, 270, 273, 276, 280, 282, 286, 289, 291, 294, 297, 300, 303, 306

interrogatories, 138, 140, 143, 156, 159, 246

Iowa, 206–209

irregularities, 24, 40, 45, 154–55, 163, 166, 169, 175, 178, 181–82, 184, 187, 190, 193, 196, 199, 202, 205, 208, 211, 214, 217, 220, 223, 226, 230, 232, 235, 238, 240, 243, 246, 252, 255, 258, 260, 263, 266, 269, 271, 274, 278, 281, 284, 290, 296, 299, 302, 307

K

Kansas, 209–211

Kentucky, 212–214

L

lack of understanding, 68–69, 73

length of depositions, 21–22, 138, 250

limitation, 21, 50, 77, 91, 96–97, 138–39, 145, 149, 153, 162, 167, 174, 179, 182, 186, 188, 194, 197, 207, 209, 212, 218, 225, 227–28, 231, 239, 241, 244, 250, 253, 261, 264, 267, 270, 273, 276, 278, 280, 282, 289, 291, 294, 300, 306

location of depositions, 16

Louisiana, 215–218

M

Maine, 218–220

Maryland, 221–224

Massachusetts, 224–227

Michigan, 227–230

Minnesota, 230–233

misconduct, 33, 41, 66, 91, 119, 122–23, 129, 277

Mississippi, 233–235

Missouri, 235–238

Montana, 238–241

motion, 16, 21, 24, 42, 50, 53, 61, 66–67, 77, 83–84, 87, 89, 91–92, 110–11, 117, 119–24, 126–27, 129, 138–39, 142, 146, 149–50, 153, 155–59, 162, 165, 167–68, 170, 174–76, 179–80, 182–83, 186–87, 189, 192, 194–95, 197, 201–4, 207, 209–10, 212–13,

216–19, 222, 225–26, 228–29, 231–32, 234, 237, 239, 241, 244, 251, 253–54, 256–57, 259–62, 264–65, 267–68, 270–71, 273–74, 276–78, 280, 282–83, 289, 291–92, 294–95, 298, 300–301, 304, 306

N

Nebraska, 241–243

Nevada, 244–246

New Hampshire, 246–249

New Jersey, 249–252

New Mexico, 252–255

New York, 256–258

nonparty, 11, 20, 25, 122, 126, 128, 155, 289

nonsuggestive objections, 162, 164, 167, 170, 173, 176, 179, 182, 185, 188, 191, 194, 197, 200, 204, 206, 209, 212, 215, 218, 221, 224, 227, 231, 233, 236, 239, 241, 244, 247, 250, 253, 256, 259, 261, 264, 267, 270, 273, 275, 279, 282, 285, 289, 291, 294, 297, 300, 306

North Carolina, 258–261

North Dakota, 261–263

O

object, 39–41, 50–51, 55, 68, 71–72, 86–88, 250, 285, 288

objecting deponent, 150, 162, 171, 198, 210, 240, 242, 262, 307

objecting party, 60, 165, 168, 172, 174, 180, 187, 192, 195, 201, 204, 207, 213, 216, 219, 225, 228, 232, 234, 237, 251, 254, 260, 265, 268, 273, 277, 280, 283, 285, 289, 292, 295, 298, 301

objections

excessive, 60, 70–71, 73

hearsay, 61–62

making, 51, 185

relevance, 60, 90

suggestive, 51, 54, 287

objection to competence, 43, 45, 59, 154

objection to form, 42, 51–52

obstruction, 2, 31, 75, 90, 129, 132, 309

obstruction sanctions, 162, 165, 168, 171, 174, 177, 180, 183, 186, 189, 192, 195, 198, 201, 204, 207, 210, 213, 216, 219, 222, 225, 228, 231, 234, 236, 239, 242, 245, 248, 251, 254, 257, 259, 262, 264, 267, 270, 273, 276, 280, 283, 287, 289, 292, 294, 298, 301, 306

off-the-record conference, 109, 278

Ohio, 263–266

Oklahoma, 266–269

Oregon, 269–272

P

Pennsylvania, 272

preservation, 63, 144, 248–49, 278

pretrial disclosures, 137

private conferences, 104, 106, 287

privilege, 2, 50, 63, 66, 72, 77–84, 91–92, 104–6, 109–10, 113, 141, 144, 149, 162, 167, 170, 174, 177, 179, 182, 186, 188, 194, 197, 207, 209, 212, 218, 225, 227–28, 231, 239, 241, 244, 247, 250, 253, 261, 264, 267, 270, 273, 276, 278, 280, 282, 286–87, 289, 291, 294, 297, 299–300, 306

prohibited speaking objections, 66–67

proper objections, 50, 286

protective order, 2, 16–17, 41, 83–85, 87–88, 92, 124, 127, 138, 142, 153, 156–57, 159, 176–77, 248, 256–57, 267, 276, 278, 289

R

Rambo litigation, 71–73

recesses, 105–9, 113, 185, 278, 287

recording, 22–24, 34, 140, 147–48, 150–51, 233

relevance, 39, 41, 43, 59–61, 73, 87–88, 154, 162, 165, 169, 172, 175, 178, 181, 184, 187, 190, 192, 196, 199, 205, 211, 214, 217, 220, 223, 226, 229, 232, 235, 240, 243, 245, 252, 255, 260, 263, 265, 268, 271, 274, 277, 281, 284, 290, 293, 295, 299, 302, 305, 307

remote depositions, 21, 25

request, 83–84, 92, 107, 109, 119, 139, 143, 146–47, 150, 159, 182, 221, 276, 303

response, 3, 51–52, 82, 99, 110, 122, 124, 143, 145–46, 156, 159, 236

Rhode Island, 272–275

S

sanctions, 3, 42, 64, 67, 70, 86, 91, 117–19, 123, 125–30, 146, 149–50, 155, 157–60, 162, 168, 171, 174, 186, 189, 195, 198, 201, 207, 213, 216, 219, 228, 231, 239, 245, 262, 267, 276, 287, 292, 301, 306

establishing, 165, 177, 180, 183, 192, 204, 210, 222, 225, 234, 236, 242, 248, 251, 254, 257, 259, 264, 270, 273, 283, 289, 294, 298, 304

scope, 2, 7–10, 50, 61, 73, 83–84, 91, 95–100, 133, 138–39, 142, 150, 297, 299

seasonable objection, 166, 169, 175, 181, 184, 187, 193, 196, 202, 214, 220, 226, 230, 235, 238, 243, 246, 255, 260, 269, 271, 274, 278, 281, 284, 290, 293, 296, 299, 302, 305

South Carolina, 275–279

South Dakota, 279–282

speaking objections, 64, 66, 72–73, 91, 118, 200, 287

suspending the deposition, 41, 84, 162, 165, 168, 171, 174, 177, 180, 183, 186, 189, 192, 195, 198, 201, 204, 207, 210, 213, 216, 219, 223, 225, 228, 231, 234, 237, 239, 242, 245, 248, 251, 254, 256, 259, 262, 265, 268, 270, 273, 277, 280, 283, 287, 289, 292, 295, 298, 301, 304, 307

T

Tennessee, 282–284

Texas, 284–288

trial admissibility, 162, 165, 168, 172, 175, 178, 180, 183, 187, 190, 192, 195, 198, 202, 205, 208, 210, 213, 217, 219, 223, 226, 229, 232, 234, 237, 240, 242, 248, 251, 254, 257, 260, 262, 268, 271, 274, 277, 281, 283, 285, 290, 292, 295, 298, 301, 304, 307

trial standards, 161, 164, 166, 169, 173, 176, 179, 182, 185, 188, 191, 194, 197, 199, 203, 206, 209, 212, 215, 218, 221, 224, 227, 230, 233, 235, 238, 241, 244, 246, 249, 252, 256, 258, 261, 263, 266, 269, 272, 275, 279, 282, 284, 288, 291, 293, 296, 300, 305

U

unacceptable excuses, 127, 135, 159

Utah, 288–290

V

vagueness, 67–68, 73, 286

Vermont, 291–293

Virginia, 293–296

W

waiver, 82, 154, 248–49, 276, 297

Washington, 296–300

West Virginia, 300–302

Wisconsin, 303–305

witness coaching, 54, 62–64, 103

prohibited, 63, 69

Wyoming, 305–308

Z

zealous advocacy, 29–30, 36

INDEX OF CASES

A

Abu Dhabi Commercial Bank v. Morgan Stanley & Co., 53

Aeroflex Wichita, Inc. v. Filardo, 211

Afram Export Corp. v. Metallurgiki Halyps, SA, 19

AG Equip. Co. v. AIG Life Ins. Co., 64

Albuquerque Redi-Mix, Inc. v. Scottsdale Ins. Co., 255

Alexander v. F.B.I, 70

Ambler v. Archer, 193

Am. Directory Serv. Agency, Inc. v. Beam, 60, 71

Am. Gen. Life Ins. Co. v. Billard, 24

Anderson v. Dobson, 24

Applied Telematics Inc. v. Sprint Corp., 51–52, 64, 68, 71

Arctic Cat v. Injection Research Specialists, Inc., 119

Armsey v. Medshares Mgmt. Servs., 19

Associated Med. Networks, Ltd. v. Lewis, 206

Auscape Int'l v. Nat'l Geographic Soc'y, 51

B

Bahamas Agric. Indus. Ltd. v. Riley Stoker Corp., 40

Baker v. Standard Indus., Inc., 19, 272

Barnhill v. Iowa Dist. Ct. for Polk Cnty., 208

Batts v. Cnty. of Santa Clara, 95–96

Bd. of Trs. of Leland Stanford Junior Univ. v. Tyco Int'l. Ltd., 106

Beach Mart, Inc. v. L & L Wings, Inc., 126

Beal for Martinez v. City of Seattle, 300

Beckman Indus. Inc. v. Int'l Ins. Co., 17

Bicknell v. CBT Factors Corp., 193

Black Horse Lane Assoc., L.P. v. Dow Chem. Corp., 119

BNSF Railway Co. v. San Joaquin Valley Railroad Co., 71, 123

Boswell v. Cnty of Sherburne, 54

Bourn v. Tomlinson Interest, Inc., 235

Boyd v. Univ. of Md. Med. Sys., 78

Bracey v. Delta Tech. Coll., 106

Branyan v. Koninklijke Luchtvaart Maatschappij, 19

Brody v. Ruby, 209

Brown v. Lange, 169

C

Cabello v. Fernandez-Larios, 39, 41

Cadent Ltd. v. 3M Unitek Corp., 17–19

Canal Barge Co. v. Commonwealth Edison Co., 22

Carpenter v. Forest Meadows Owners Ass'n, 24

Cates v. LTV Aerospace Corp., 20

Cede & Co v. Technicolor, Inc., 188

Chacon v. Sperry Corp., 199

Chambers v. NASCO, Inc., 117, 128

Chassen v. Fid. Nat'l Title Ins. Co., 106

Cincinnati Ins. Co. v. Serrano, 39, 61, 66–68

City of Fort Smith v. Carter, 176

Clay v. Consol Penn. Coal Co., 32, 123

Collins v. Anthem Health Plans, Inc., 184

Cont'l Ill. Nat'l Bank & Trust Co. of Chi. v. Caton, 16

Cordero v. City of New York, 90

Cordova v. United States, 64, 107–8, 111

Cox v. Burke, 77

Coyote Springs Inv. v. Eighth Jud. Dist. Ct. of State ex rel. Cnty. of Clark, 107

Craig v. St. Anthony's Med. Ctr., 71, 106

Crest Infiniti, II, LP v. Swinton, 269

Cronin v. Strayer, 227

CSC Grp. Holdings, LLC v. Automation & Elecs., Inc., 308

Cullen v. Nissan N. Am., Inc., 65, 107

D

D'Agostini v. City of Roseville, 230

Damaj v. Farmers Ins. Co., Inc., 9–10, 51–52

Dennis v. Se. Kansas Gas Co., 211

Detoy v. City and Cnty. of S.F., 78, 96–97

Deville v. Givaudan Fragrances Corp., 64

Diebold, Inc. v. Cont'l Cas. Co., 108–9, 111–12

Dravo Corp. v. Liberty Mut. Ins. Co., 99

Duckworth v. Deane, 224

Duncan v. Husted, 24

E

Ecker v. Wis. Cent. Ltd., 108–9, 112

Edwards v. Young, 16, 173

EEOC v. Bok Fin. Corp., 88–89

Eggleston v. Chi. Journeymen Plumber's Local Union, 101, 104

E.I. DuPont de Nemours & Co. v. Kolon Indus., Inc., 18–19

Elyria-Lorain Broad. Co. v. Lorain Journal Co., 46

Ethox Chem., LLC v. Coca-Cola Co., 53

Executive Mgmt., Ltd. v. Ticor Title Ins. Co., 246

F

Farquhar v. Shelden, 18

Farr Man Coffee, Inc. v. Chester, 62

Feeley v. City of Billings, Mont., 41

Felix v. Ganley Chevrolet, Inc., 266

Few v. Yellowpages.com, 107

Fisher v. Goord, 106

Fletcher v. Honeywell Int'l, Inc., 53

Follo v. Florindo, 293

Fort Worth Emps.' Ret. Fund v. J.P. Morgan Chase & Co., 51

Freeman v. Lincoln Beach Motel, 252

G

Gall v. St. Elizabeth Md. Ctr., 9

Gardner v. Newsome Chevrolet-Buick, Inc., 279

Garrigan v. Bowen, 181

Gateway Co. v. DiNoia, 184

Gavrity v. City of N.Y., 80, 106

Gernstein v. Lake, 243

Giddens v. Kansas City So. Ry. Co., 238

Ginardi v. Frontier Gas Servs., LLC, 107

Index of Cases

Gleneagle Ship Mgmt. Co. v. Leondakos, 191

GMAC Bank v. HTFC Corp., 41, 91, 119

Goins v. Puleo, 261

H

Hall v. Clifton Precision, 1, 8–9, 60, 62, 64–65, 68–71, 77, 82, 103–4, 106–9, 112–13, 117, 123

Harrington v. Polk Cnty. Fed. Sav. & Loan Ass'n of Des Moines, 208

Henderson v. B & B Precast & Pipe, LLC, 53, 62, 185

Herchenroeder v. Johns Hopkins Univ. Applied Physics Lab., 10

Heriaud v. Ryder Transp. Servs., 64

Hernandez v. Hendrix Produce, Inc., 120

Hickman v. Taylor, 7–8

Highland Realty, Inc. v. Indianapolis Airport Auth., 206

Hill v. Forward Air Sols., Inc., 16

Hofer v. Mack Trucks, Inc., 10

Horton v. Maersk Line Ltd., 32

I

In re Amezaga, 106

In re Anonymous Member, 106

In re Bayview Crematory, 249

In re Domestic Air Transp. Antitrust Litig., 107

In re Golden, 33

In re Moncier, 30

In re Outsidewall Tire Litig., 16, 19

In re St. Jude Med. Inc., 51–52, 82, 104, 123

In re Stratosphere Corp. Sec. Litig., 50, 60, 71, 107–8, 123

Int'l Union of Elec., Radio & Mach. Workers AFL-CIO v. Westinghouse Elec. Corp., 78

J

Jackson v. Russell, 206

Jadwin v. Abraham, 64, 123

Johnson v. Nationwide Mut. Ins. Co., 61–62

Jordan v. Medley, 45

K

Kawamata Farms, Inc. v. United Agric. Prods., 196

Keller v. Edwards, 16

Keplinger v. Virginia Elec. & Power Co., 302

King v. Pratt & Whitney, 96–97, 99, 107

Kirschner v. Broadhead, 41, 46

Kramer v. Boeing Co., 10

L

Larson v. Unlimited Bus. Exch. of N. Dakota, Inc., 263

Leist v. Union Oil Co. of Cal., 17, 20

LM Ins. Corp. v. ACEO, Inc., 106

Luangisa v. Interface Operations, 91

Luckett v. Bodner, 305

M

Mac's Car City, Inc. v. Am. Nat'l Bank, 184

Madison v. Travelers Ins. Co., 218

Maranville v. Utah Valley Univ., 24

Marlboro Prods. Corp. v. North Am. Philips Corp., 24

Mashal v. City of Chicago, 203

McDonough Const. Co. v. McLendon Elec. Co., 193

McDonough v. Keniston, 64–65

McKinley Infuser Inc. v. Zdeb, 107

Meridien BIAO Bank Tanzania Ltd, 18, 119

Meyer Corp. v. Alfay Designs, Inc., 51–52

Mill-Run Tours Inc. v. Khashoggi, 18–19

Mitsui & Co. (U.S.A.), Inc. v. P.R. Water Res. Auth., 126

Montez v. Tonkawa Vill. Apartments, 211

Morales v. Zondo, Inc., 70, 104, 106

Murnan v. Joseph J. Hock, Inc., 224

Murray v. Nationwide Better Health, 107

N

Nat'l City Mortgage Co. v. Tidwell, 193

Nat'l Hockey League v. Metro. Hockey Club, Inc., 125, 127

New England Carpenters Health Benefits Fund v. First DataBank, Inc., 126

Newton v. Hornblower, Inc., 211

Ngai v. Old Navy, 63

NGM Ins. Co. v. Walker Const. & Dev., LLC, 62

Nutterville v. McLam, 45

O

Oberlin v. Marlin Am. Corp., 46

O'Connell v. Cowan, 214

Odone v. Croda Int'l PLC, 71, 107–9, 111

Okoumou v. Horizon, 106

Ott v. Stipe Law Firm, 24

P

Index of Cases

Pain Ctr. of SE Ind. v. Origin Healthcare Sols. LLC, 107

Paparelli v. Prudential Ins. Co., 97

Pearman v. Schlaak, 214

Pelarinos v. Henderson, 185

Pengilly, James W., 35

Peronist v. United States, 106

Perrymond v. Lockheed Martin Corp., 106

Perry v. Com., ex rel. Kessinger, 214

Perry v. Leeke, 103, 214

Philip Morris Inc. v. Angeletti, 224

Phillips v. Gen. Motors Corp., 17

Pia v. Supernova Media Inc., 107, 111

Pioneer Drive LLC v. Nissan Diesel America, Inc., 23–24, 126

Plaisted v. Geisinger Med. Ctr., 84

Planning Bd. of Howard Cnty. v. Mortimer, 224

Potashnick v. Port City Constr. Co., 108, 111

Pratt & Whitney, 96

Preyer v. U.S. Lines, Inc., 78

P.R.S. Int'l, Inc. v. Shred Pax Corp., 203

Q

Quantachrome Corp v. Micromeritics Instrument Corp., 51

R

Rainey v. Am. Forest and Paper Ass'n, Inc., 99

Ralston Purina Co v. McFarland, 78

Rapoca Energy Co., L.P. v. AMCI Export Corp., 18

Redwood v. Dobson, 9, 30–31, 84–85, 123

Resolution Trust Corp. v. Worldwide Ins. Mgmt. Corp., 19

Richter v. Union Pac. R.R. Co., 238

Rivas v. Greyhound Lines, Inc., 97

Roadway Express, Inc. v. Piper, 129

Roberts v. Homelite Div. of Textron, Inc., 24

Robinson v. Taylor, 290

Rojas v. X Motorsport, Inc., 32, 123

Ross v. Kansas City Power & Light Co., 32

S

Sander v. Geib, Elston, Frost Prof'l Ass'n, 282

323

Sciarretta v. Lincoln Nat'l Life Ins. Co., 117, 120, 128–29

Scruggs v. Int'l Paper Co., 121

Sec. Nat'l Bank of Sioux City, IA v. Day, 53

Sec. Nat'l Bank of Sioux City, Iowa v. Abbott Laboratories, 30, 53, 62, 66

Sequoia Prop. & Equip. Ltd. P'ship v. United States, 62

Shcherbakovskiy v. Da Capo Al Fine, Ltd., 125

Shuffle Master, Inc. v. Progressive Games, Inc., 120–21

Sicurelli v. Jeneric/Pentron, Inc., 119

S. La. Ethanol, LLC v. Fireman's Fund Ins. Co., 106

Smith v. Wilcox Cnty. Bd. of Educ., 166

Soft Water Utilities, Inc. v. Le Fevre, 206

Specht v. Google, Inc., 64, 72–73

Starlight Int'l, Inc. v. Herlihy, 18, 119

State ex rel. Zidell v. Jones, 272

Stein v. Tri-City Healthcare Dist., 16

Sw. Ref. Co. v. Bernal, 288

T

T.A. Schifsky & Sons, Inc. v. Bahr Const., LLC, 233

Taylor v. Baker, 7–8, 272, 290

Ternes v. Galichia, 211

Tingley Sys. v. CSC Consulting, Inc., 112

Tisdale v. Rawson, 220

Tomingas v. Douglas Aircraft Co., 19

Turner v. Glock, 51

Turner v. Prudential Ins. Co., 16–20, 51, 62, 284

U

United States v. Jones, 81, 272

United States v. One 1999 Forty Seven Foot Fountain Motor Vessel, 125

United States v. Philip Morris Inc., 104, 224

Upjohn Co. v. United States, 79

U.S. Fid. & Guar. Co. v. Rodgers, 241

V

Valencia v. City of Santa Fe, 51

Vander Veer v. Toyota Motor Distributors, Inc., 272

Van Stelton v. Van Stelton, 87

Vargas v. Florida Crystals Corp., 53

VirtualAgility, Inc. v. Salesforce.com, Inc., 20

Vnuk v. Berwick Hosp. Co., 63, 106

W

Watson v. Best Fin. Servs. Inc., 214

Wells Dairy Inc. v. Am. Indus. Refrigeration, Inc., 208

White v. Halstead Indus., 18

Wilson v. Kautex, A Textron Co., 21

Z

Zottola v. Anesthesia Consultants of Savannah, 32, 41, 115, 128